NEXT STEPS IN
RAILWAY MODELLING

Chris Ellis

MIDLAND

An imprint of
Ian Allan Publishing

CONTENTS

First published 2004
Reprinted 2007

ISBN (10) 1 85780 171 7
ISBN (13) 978 1 85780 171 2

© Chris Ellis 2004

Published by Midland Publishing,
an imprint of Ian Allan Publishing Ltd.

Printed in England by Ian Allan Printing Ltd,
Hersham, Surrey KT12 4RG.

Code: 0711/A

Visit the Ian Allan Publishing website at
www.ianallanpublishing.com

Front cover and back cover, top: **Inspiration for the aspiring 'Next Steps' modeller from the camera of Brian Monaghan. A selection of layouts that shows what the individual modeller can achieve over a period of time.** *Ian Allan Library*

Back cover, lower left: **Simple scenery (chapter 6) can be made to look very effective.**

Back cover, lower right: **A Weston, Cleveland & Portishead Railway four-wheel coach in 4mm scale.**

Title page: **(top left) British N gauge — a pick-up goods train, late 1970s' style, on a layout built by the author; (top right) Yarmouth Docks branch compact layout in 00 gauge, built by Andrew Knights; (bottom left) industrial narrow gauge in 1:32 scale built by German enthusiasts; (bottom right) an excellent depiction of a modern scrap metal yard and traffic on a German HO demonstration layout by Roco.**

GLOSSARY

This useful glossary was originally compiled by Cyril Freezer for *First Steps in Railway Modelling*, the companion volume to this book. It is repeated here, but I have added some further entries to cover subjects featured in this book, or terms you may encounter if you follow some of the modelling ideas suggested.

AC Alternating current. Electric current which changes polarity in a regular cycle. It is the normal mains supply.

Advance uncoupling A system of automatic uncoupling where the vehicles are pushed over an actuating mechanism which uncouples them, leaving the vehicles uncoupled whilst being pushed. Also called delayed uncoupling.

Auto-coupler A device for automatically coupling locomotives and rolling stock when pushed together. Frequently the vehicles can also be uncoupled, normally at a ramp or magnet situated in the track.

Baseboard The substructure on which a model railway is built.

Baseboard unit One part of a sectional layout. Also sometimes called a module.

Bracket signal A semaphore signal array with two or more arms indicating different routes ahead. Found at junctions and station approaches where there is more than one platform or running road. Often termed junction signal.

Bridge rail This form of flat-based rail was formerly used on the broad gauge GWR. The Broad Gauge Society has had sections drawn for 4mm and 7mm scales.

Bridge rectifier An arrangement of four diodes which converts both cycles of an AC input to DC. Additional smoothing devices are required for pure DC but the unsmoothed output is adequate for most model railway purposes.

Broad gauge Any railway with a gauge wider than 4ft 8½in. Often regarded solely as applying to Brunel's defunct 7ft gauge, it also applies to contemporary Irish, Iberian, Russian, Indian and some Australian railways.

Bullhead rail A pattern of rail used mainly in Great Britain until 1950. It has a narrow base and is secured to the sleeper with chairs. It is still in use, particularly on the London Underground system. On model railways it is mainly found on accurate steam age models.

Caboose American equivalent to a brake van in Britain.

Car A term much used in America and elsewhere for what would be called a wagon or a coach in Britain. For example, a box car in the USA would be the same as a box van in Britain.

Cassette A specialised form of fiddle yard. The trains run on to a length of track, usually made from inverted aluminium angle. Complete trains can be juggled in this fashion.

Catenary The complete arrangement of contact and support wires of an electrified railway is a catenary. This term is often loosely applied to the entire overhead.

Below: **As described in Chapter 3, it is possible to fit American-made magnetic couplers of the Kadee type to British 4mm scale models, allowing both closer coupling and 'hands off' uncoupling over a magnet set in the track. This is the Hornby 'J94' and a Hornby coal wagon so fitted.**

Picture Credits:
All photographs are from the author's collection unless otherwise specified.

Acknowledgements
Special thanks for contributing track plan drawings to this book go to Jack Trollope and David Thomas. For other drawings thanks are due to Richard Gardner and Paul A. Lunn. For ideas, assistance and photographs I would like to thank Julian Andrews, Giles Barnabe, Dave Carson, Greg Dodsworth, Steve Grantham, Keith Harcourt, George Lowen, Andrew Knights, Arthur North, Stuart Robinson, Graham Weller and Alan Wright.

Centre third A system of current collection using a central third rail. Formerly used by ready-to-run systems and now virtually obsolete, though the Märklin HO system uses a modern 'stud contact' version.

Combination coach American coach combining passenger, luggage and sometimes mail compartments, similar to a brake end coach in Britain.

Controller A device that modifies a 12-Volt DC supply to control the speed and direction of a locomotive.

Crossing 1. A track formation that crosses one track over another without any connection, as at a double junction. Frequently termed a diamond crossing. 2. In strict railway parlance, the part of a turnout where the rails cross.

Culvert A small bridge or large drain carrying a stream under a railway.

Cutting A large trench with sloping walls and railway tracks at the bottom.

DC Direct current. Electric current of constant polarity as supplied by batteries or from AC supplies via a rectifier.

Diesel era A common term for the post-steam age.

Digital command control (DCC) A system of model railway control where a constant voltage is applied to the rails. Each locomotive or railcar is fitted with a decoder which interprets a command sent over the rails. The control unit incorporates advanced electronics and requires a microprocessor. It permits independent operation of two or more trains in the same section of track. It also eliminates most wiring which is a great benefit on very large layouts. It also has its value on very simple systems. Against this the cost of the central unit can be very high and modules not only add to the cost of each locomotive, but they need to be fitted. The US-based NMRA (qv) has established a set of standards and recent British command control systems conform to these rules. However, for a medium-sized British layout, the hard-wired system is more cost-effective. See also Chapter 9.

Diode An electronic device that will pass DC current only in one direction. It will produce a pulsating DC output from AC by suppressing one half of each cycle.

Distant signal A warning signal, normally ¼ mile in front of a home signal, giving the driver time to slow down and stop.

Doodlebug American term for a single-unit diesel railcar once much used on branch lines.

Embankment A bank of soil to carry a railway line (or other track) above the natural ground level.

Engineer American term for an engine driver.

Epoch As in Britain, German railway modellers and manufacturers exploit the nostalgic value of the steam age. Whereas in Britain the various eras are given descriptive names, the Germans broke their timescale into epochs, possibly because they were reluctant to give a name to the very innovative 1930s. Unfortunately, not only does the epoch system require a crib sheet, but, being based sensibly on the obvious design breaks, when applied to other systems, ie the Swiss, the dates had to be changed. With hindsight the decade system, which is slowly gaining currency, is better.

Exhibition circuit When a model railway is invited to more than one exhibition within a year it has entered the exhibition circuit. Its owner is then liable to find his spare time spoken for and needs to collect a small band of helpers to man the layout and to help move and erect it. In extreme cases, the layout may be operated only at exhibitions, being too large to assemble fully in its home base. This is very advanced railway modelling.

Fiddle yard A series of offstage storage tracks used to hold trains so they can emerge in turn on the layout proper, ideally to a schedule. It is permissible to rearrange the train formation in a fiddle yard.

Fine scale A contradiction in terms, since the scale is not affected. Originally applied to a more accurate system of track and wheels for O gauge, it has come to mean models that are built to more exacting standards of detail and accuracy than current commercial products. It usually means what the speaker intends it to mean, neither more nor less.

Flange The projection on a railway wheel which keeps it on the track.

Flat-bottom rail As the name implies, this section rail has a wide flat base. It was formerly called Vignoles rail. This is the standard rail section in use on all modern systems. The rail has a wide base and, originally, was spiked directly to the sleeper. With increasing train loadings, baseplates were introduced to spread the load, and all but lightly laid track now has the rail secured either by bolts and clips or patent clips.

Frog The part of a turnout where the inner rails cross. In strict railway parlance, this is a crossing.

Gantry signal A lightweight bridge structure crossing several tracks carrying many signal posts or colour light heads. Only found at large stations or over quadruple tracks in confined sites. Often used on a model a) to fit in three or more signals in the usually confined space on the model, and b) to create the illusion that the station is an important one.

Gauge The distance between the inner faces of the rails.

Grade crossing American term for a level crossing (see below).

Gradient The slope of a railway. It can be expressed as a percentage (%), as per mile (0/00) or, more commonly in Britain, as a ratio (1 in xxx). The ratio is easier to use in railway modelling; a 1 in 40 grade means a rise of one unit every 40 units of measurement (inches, feet, millimetres, centimetres or metres). The important point to remember is that the higher the ratio, the shallower the grade, whereas the higher the percentage, the steeper the grade.

Home signal The semaphore signal controlling entry into a block section.

Below: **The modern modeller has a huge choice of structure kits, accessories and scenic items available to create realistic settings. Everything in this German HO layout scene — sawmill, crane, paving, lorry, figures and logs — comes as an over-the-counter item from a model shop.**

Left: **Despite the many kits and RTR models available today, some enthusiasts still prefer scratch-building. This American 'backwoods' narrow gauge breakdown crane set in G scale was built in wood by the late Derek Gigg for his Central Lines layout.**

Interurban   An American term used to describe light railway systems (almost invariably electrified) which link nearby towns (inter-urban = between towns). In town centres the lines usually run along streets, but in the country they are either beside the highway or strike across country.

Kleinlok   Literally 'small locomotive'. Applied to a type of very small four-wheel diesel shunting locomotive in Germany that is used for yard and station shunting and may also be seen in industrial use. Popular in model form because of its small size. Also used in Switzerland and Austria.

Level crossing   A road crossing on the level. Formerly closed by gates, but today lifting barriers are preferred.

Light railway   Legally a railway authorised under the Light Railway Act by means of an Order issued by the Department of Transport rather than an enabling Act. Such lines were frequently built to less exacting standards and, according to the individual Order, could omit certain features required on normal railways (eg raised platforms, complete fencing, etc). Most preserved railways operate under a Light Railway Order, but are otherwise indistinguishable from a 'proper' railway.

Livery   The paint scheme for a locomotive or coach.

Lokführer   German term for an engine driver.

Modern Image   A term introduced in the 1960s to describe the then new diesel-hauled and (occasionally) electrified trains on British Rail. The object was to distinguish between current practice and the historic steam-hauled system. With the rapid development of new train designs and the simplification of track layouts, it is now necessary to distinguish between current practice and 'Historic Modern Image'.

Multiple aspect   Modern colour light signals have three or four aspects, ie arrangements of lights. Green indicates line ahead clear; red indicates line ahead blocked (ie occupied by another train); a single yellow light indicates that the signal ahead is showing red; two yellow lights (double yellow) indicates that the signal ahead is yellow.

Narrow gauge   Any prototype railway with a gauge less than 4ft 8½in is 'narrow' gauge. Such railways fall into two groups: relatively short feeder systems, usually associated with mineral traffic (eg the Ffestiniog Railway), and major systems which are either situated in mountainous regions (eg the several Swiss metre-gauge systems) or, in the case of 3ft 6in, metre or 3ft gauge, the de facto standard gauge for certain countries (eg New Zealand's 3ft 6in systems). Narrow gauge modelling is now well established.

NEM   (Les Normes Européenes de Modelisme) An international committee (MOROP) of European model railway manufacturers was set up in 1952 to establish common standards of scale, compatibility, couplers, etc. It took some years before it made a real impact, but virtually all European models now conform. NEM standard codes you may see referred to include NEM 362 covering the standard close-coupling mount for HO models, and NEM 311 covering the HO wheel profile, but there are, of course, many more. Recent British models by Bachmann and Hornby have the NEM standard coupler mount.

NMRA   National Model Railway Association. An American organisation that, among other things, sets standards for fundamental features of model railways. Its wheel standards for 16.5mm gauge are slowly gaining international acceptance.

Occupation bridge   A small underbridge maintaining access between parts of an estate or farm bisected by a railway embankment or cutting.

Occupation crossing   A level crossing provided to maintain access between parts of an estate or farm bisected by a railway. It is more correctly an uncontrolled crossing, since no warning of a train's approach is given to users.

Overbridge   A bridge carrying a road or canal over a railway.

Overhead supply   Most prototype electrified railways have an overhead feed, the rails forming the return. Models of modern electrified railways should be so equipped, but in most instances the overhead is only a cosmetic feature. Some ready-to-run models are fitted with a changeover switch permitting the model to collect from the overhead wire.

Point   1. A track formation where two tracks are linked to one that allows trains to be diverted to one of two tracks. Also known as a turnout. 2. In strict railway parlance, the tapered rails of a point. Generally used in the plural.

Portable layout   A model railway which can be easily moved from place to place. Increasingly applied to layouts that are normally stored in a dismantled form and erected only for operating sessions. See transportable layout.

Pre-group   In 1923 the many independent companies that formed Britain's railway system were compulsorily amalgamated into four groups. Any model set prior to this date is pre-group(ing). The term is going out of use as historical railway modelling becomes more diverse.

Private owner   A wagon or van owned by a company or trading partnership for exclusive use by the owner.

Prototype   The full-size original on which a model is based.

Rangierer   German term for the 'shunter' — the man who couples and uncouples coaches and wagons.

Rangierlok   German for shunting locomotive.

Rapid transit   An urban railway which is characterised by a very frequent service of trains but which has a low overall speed since frequent station stops are made. The London Underground is the best-known British rapid transit system.

Rectifier   An electronic device which converts AC current to DC.

Reefer   American term, short for refrigerator car. 'Billboard Reefer' was a term for the reefers (also box cars) that were painted in colourful advertising livery in the USA up to the early 1930s. They were disallowed after 1937.

Relay   An electro-magnet switch which is employed to change circuits.

RP (Recommended Practice) The NMRA has since its early days as a modellers' organisation in the USA put out specifications which it suggests manufacturers follow in the interests of standardisation and compatibility. These now run to a great many, but those you might see in print will include RP25 for the wheel profile used by all makers on the American market (and now spreading to Europe).

RTR Abbreviation for 'ready to run' — in connection with commercially produced locomotives and rolling stock, for use 'straight from the box'.

Scale The ratio between sizes on the prototype and model, expressed either as a ratio (1:76, 1/76 or 1 to 76) or linear equivalent (4mm to 1 foot).

Short Line Small local line in America/ Canada (actually defined by revenue level) serving industrial and commercial customers. Some also offered a passenger service in the past.

Signal box A structure housing a lever frame controlling points and signals on a section of track. Early systems were wholly mechanical and controlled only a limited area. Modern electro-mechanical installations control large sections of a railway; the signalmen rely on illuminated panels and monitors to track the position of trains.

Spur Term most often used in America for what might be called a 'siding' in Britain, ie a track ending in a buffer stop. In America a siding usually refers to a doubled-ended loop. This might be short and used for serving a lineside facility, but might also be long enough to hold a complete train off the main line (hence the term side-tracked).

Staging yard (or staging tracks) American term for the area on a layout where trains can be held or made up, sometimes forming part of the visible layout, but they may also be offstage, equivalent to the British fiddle yard.

Steam age A useful portmanteau term used to knit together all model railways set in a period prior to dieselisation.

Strassenbahn German term for street tramways.

Streetcar (or Trolley) American term for street tramcar.

Stud contact A system of current collection where the feed is through a series of studs along the centre line of the track. Locomotives are fitted with a long skate. Used by Märklin for its non-standard HO system and by many garden railway workers in O and 1 gauges.

Right: 'Dream Layouts', like the old Midland gauge O layout at Derby Museum, superb as they are, need huge resources to make and operate and are beyond the attainment level of most of us. They do, however, provide a lot of inspiration and ideas B. Monaghan

Switch, Switcher and Switching Much-used terms in American railroading. Switching is the equivalent to 'shunting' in Britain, and a switcher or switch engine is the term for a 'shunting locomotive'. To switch is to shunt, but the term switch is also sometimes used in place of a point or turnout. A switch-man or brakeman is the equivalent to the 'shunter' in Britain, doing the uncoupling and changing the direction of the points etc.

Three-rail A system of electrical supply where the rails form the return and a third rail forms the feed. It is now obsolete with models, but is still used on the electrified lines of the former Southern Region and on London Underground and other rapid transit systems. Models based on these systems usually use two-rail supply with cosmetic third (and fourth) rails.

Tie (or Cross-tie) The American term for what is called a 'sleeper' in Britain. In the USA/Canada 'sleeper' is short for 'sleeping car'.

Track 1. An assembly of two rails set at a fixed gauge held in fixings to a series of wooden cross beams termed sleepers 2. A loose description of a series of tracks forming a layout.

Train turntable A form of fiddle yard where the entire yard turns around a central pivot. It is mainly used on exhibition-orientated layouts since, in the home, there is rarely room to swing the table.

Tramway Originally used to describe early mineral horse-worked systems, the term is now always applied to electric street-level rail systems.

Tramway overhead Electric trams collect current from a single contact wire. A few small electrified railways and interurban lines also use a single wire. It allows considerable economy, but is suitable only for low-speed operation.

Transformer A device to change the line voltage of an electric current. It will work only with AC supplies.

Transportable layout A model railway that is normally erected, but, being built on several baseboard units, can be dismantled and taken to another site, generally a public exhibition.

Traverser A mechanical arrangement whereby a track, or series of tracks, can be moved sideways to line up with other fixed tracks. On the prototype it is generally used in repair works, and in Continental Europe, in modern electric or diesel locomotive depots. Commercial versions are available. In British modelling it is usually used for fiddle yards.

Truck American term frequently encountered for what is called a bogie in Britain.

Turnout A track formation where two tracks are linked to one. More commonly termed point.

Two aspect A colour light signal with just two lights: red/green or red/yellow. It is a straight replacement of a semaphore signal.

Two-rail The common system of current collection on model railways, where the rails are insulated one from another and the current is fed to each rail. All wheels must be insulated.

Underbridge A railway bridge spanning a road or waterway.

CHAPTER 1

MODEL RAILWAYS TODAY

THE CHANGING SCENE

In the 21st century the model railway hobby has never been so exciting as it is now. This may sound contradictory if you accept the fact that the old way into the hobby has almost disappeared. Many people long in the hobby started at school age (or even before), usually with a single train set, and then stayed with the hobby through school days and often into adulthood. In those earlier decades there was much to stimulate interest. There were real trains everywhere, lots of goods yards and most young people actually travelled on trains, with railway enthusiasm and train spotting being a major hobby in its own right. Much of this stimulated entry into railway modelling, too, and model railway shows of 20-30 years ago were well attended by keen youngsters.

The 1980s changed all that, for we entered the age of alternative pastimes in abundance, including computers, computer games, more television, and all sorts of short-lived but well-publicised crazes. At the same time real railways were being rationalised and cut back, so we arrived at a situation where young people saw fewer trains and no more goods yards bursting with activity (at least in Britain, and to a lesser extent elsewhere), and seldom rode on a train either. The new attractions of computers etc took over, train set sales declined, and the lack of young people

taking an interest in model railways became distinctly noticeable.

HOW IT IS TODAY

So how does the model railway hobby still continue to survive today? Well, the number of shops (in Britain, and to an extent elsewhere) still catering for the model railway hobby has certainly declined, but those that remain are mostly bigger and better, and mail order specialists are keen and efficient, some catering for special interests such as American or other overseas railways with extensive stock to match.

Most modellers are of mature years these days, though there are recent encouraging signs of a return of younger enthusiasts. This may be linked to the fact that the model railway hobby itself has embraced the computer age in a big way — see the section later in this book. However, the mature modellers tend to have reasonable spending power, discernment and staying power, and many of them, like the author, started with train sets as schoolboys many years ago. But another big group of mature modellers are what may be called 'returnees', in that they have schoolboy memories of train sets, their interest lapsed in teen or university years, but they have rediscovered the hobby recently, like what they see, and have become 'born again' enthusiasts.

All these enthusiasts have one thing

in common in that they appreciate the wonderful scope of the hobby, most notably as a pleasing escape from the pressure of modern life, and a way of relaxing and exercising the imagination in a way few other pastimes allow.

It also remains a fact that a very old saying, 'work on a model railway layout is never finished' is as true today as it ever was. You could stay with the model railway hobby for the rest of your life and never run out of projects to do or ideas to follow up. If you get bored or frustrated with model railways it probably means you aren't going about the hobby the right way! With luck this book will help you take the right approach.

One advantage is that the model railway hobby is a pastime not bound by any compulsory rules, or the need for licences, tests, or time restrictions. You can approach it exactly as you like, for as long as you like (or have time for), without limit of age or ability, and without spending a lot of money. For the hobby is also budget-friendly in that whatever the level of your spending money you'll find what you need to keep going.

Some people do get intense and serious about their model railway, while others are light-hearted and flippant. Again there are no rules about this. But I, and many others, favour the middle way which takes a relaxed and not too intense approach, but takes due note of the need for accuracy and a good standard of modelling.

We don't, of course, all have the same level of skill and knowledge. Some are brilliant at scratch-building from raw materials, and sophisticated electrical work. Others might have difficulty in assembling a simple kit or understanding a wiring diagram. But the model railway hobby today is very forgiving and you can work in it at any level, usually improving your personal modelling skill the longer you stay at it. One last observation here is that the hobby will exercise, and teach, lots of skills, for you have to do a bit of everything in most layout projects, including track laying, wiring, ballasting, scenic settings, structures, the trains themselves and the operations. Then for accuracy everything must be

Left: **The scope is wide for today's modeller. You can even model the earliest days of railways with this Norris locomotive and coaches from the Bachmann HO range.**

researched, models must be made or acquired, imagination and thought will be needed in some measure too, for the hobby is both creative and educative.

TODAY'S CHOICES

The conventional way to enter and follow the hobby in Britain, as in other countries, has been to model the national railways in miniature. This is still the way forward for most modellers and it is logical enough for we are mostly inspired to model what we see or know about. All the leading countries with big model railway markets have their own major manufacturers serving their respective markets, together with many smaller firms providing accessories of all sorts.

The leading firms serving the hobby are the starting point for most enthusiasts who begin with a train set or locomotives and stock of choice. And most ranges cover both the modern or recent periods and past eras too. Many of the firms are well-known names, such as Hornby and Bachmann (UK), Fleischmann and Märklin (Germany), Roco (Austria) and Athearn, Bachmann and Atlas (USA), but there are many more covering various popular scales and gauges.

OVERSEAS RAILWAYS

There has been quite a movement in the past 20-25 years, however, away from solely modelling home railways, particularly among British enthusiasts. Go to almost any model railway show in Britain today and you'll see among the British layouts, further layouts covering American, German and French railways, and other countries too. The spread is widening all the time, even including China now since Bachmann makes a good range of Chinese HO models. There are societies or special interest groups in Britain (and some other countries) covering German, French, Italian, Austrian, Belgian, Japanese, American/Canadian, Australian, New Zealand, Scandinavian and yet other rail systems. Current addresses appear from time to time in model railway magazines.

Initially this interest in overseas railways came about because most of the overseas models available — even

Right: **Some exotic interests are catered for by overseas makers, such as Swiss Om (metre gauge O scale) by Roco. Stock, locomotives and track are available for this.**

Above: **American HO is increasingly popular as a modelling subject today due to its high quality, modest price and good running qualities. This locomotive is the Athearn EMD SW7 switcher.**

40 years ago — were better detailed and had superior performance compared with British models at the time. Also with overseas models popular small scales of HO, N and TT have always had the correct scale/gauge relationships, which the British equivalent of OO, N and 3mm scale lacked, the gauge being inaccurate in each case.

Those who appreciated the superior performance and correct scale/gauge ratio were tempted into modelling the overseas scene to take advantage of these virtues. It must be said, however, that many British models (mainly in OO) produced very recently have caught up with overseas standards at least as far as detailing and performance go, even if the track gauge is still under true scale.

Other trends of recent years have accelerated interest in Britain for overseas railways. Very much an influence has been the growth in overseas holidays — so British enthusiasts have been to, say, Switzerland and USA, seen the railway systems in action, and bought the models. Keen British distributors have helped too, and there are now a good

Left: **The difference between OO gauge (16.5mm — upper locomotive and track) and EM gauge (18.2mm) is well shown by these two Hornby Class 29 models, the nearer one being re-wheeled for EM.**

few mail order model shops who carry overseas models, some concentrating on them almost exclusively. At the same time the British railway system has been rationalised, sectorised and privatised in recent years, removing much of the interesting activity that used to inspire model projects. But elsewhere rail systems are busier, much more like they were in Britain in the old days, so modelling the overseas scene can greatly increase the operational scope on a layout, and even if you experience failures like broken wheels or defective motors, spares and repairs are easy to find. In expenditure terms and time needed to build a layout, you are likely to get the best results from OO or HO, and that is a fact that cannot be disputed.

Next in popularity is N, which is 1:148 scale in Britain and 1:160 scale elsewhere. Again availability is wide, ranges are quite big, and there is the advantage of compactness, so it is a popular scale for those who have only a tiny space available for a layout or for those wanting to depict a big scene in the space you might otherwise use for a OO or HO layout.

While most modern N scale locomotives work well, the ease of use is not so good, especially if you want the sort of shunting you can do in OO or HO. To do this you need magnetic couplers or 'delay' couplers (like the German Profi type) but only American outline stock takes these easily — and some of it comes with magnetic

couplers ready fitted. For all others you have to do work on the couplers if you do not like the hefty standard N gauge coupler supplied on RTR.

SCALES AND GAUGES

If you bought this book you will not be a complete beginner to the model railway hobby, so you will be familiar with the popular gauges already. They are also outlined in some detail in the companion book *First Steps in Railway Modelling* by C. J. Freezer.

However, some comment is useful, for choice of gauge and scale can influence your financial outlay and time.

First of all, over 80% of all modellers prefer HO (1:87 scale/3.5mm to 1ft), or its near British equivalent OO (1:76 scale/4mm to 1ft). They both use the same 16.5mm track gauge. Almost all model railway retailers sell models and accessories for this scale, and just as 35mm film has long proved the optimum film size used by most photographers, so HO or OO is the most favoured model railway size. It wins on availability, scope of ranges, kits and accessories, ease of use, compactness and technical perfection. It is as near to 'instant' railway modelling as you can get, and in general prices are more modest than in other scales and gauges. There is good secondhand availability as well.

Virtually all modern HO and OO locomotives and stock work well. More on this is in Chapter 3.

The smaller scales (ie, Z and TT) and the larger ones (O, S, 1) have their enthusiasts and they are delightful to work in. But you need more space for O, S and 1, usually face higher costs and fewer sources of supply, and you need more time to make models and build layouts as a general rule.

Those of more advanced years may prefer larger scales for this very reason, for the small scales of N, Z and TT can certainly be hard on the eyes, even when it comes to placing a model locomotive on the track, let alone operating it!

Left: **British 2mm scale is truly 'fine scale', not to be confused with the much coarser standards of British N gauge. Clive Road Sidings is a neat Inglenook-style layout about 3ft long built by Mark Fielder to very high standards.**

FINE SCALE

Another very worthy cause is what is generally called 'fine scale' where you can have very precise dimensions of scale and gauge. Examples are P4/S4 and EM, 'purer' forms of OO with the correct track gauge of 18.83mm (P4/S4) or 18.2mm (EM).

There is also now Scale Seven (a 'purer' O gauge working), P87 (finer HO standards) and 2mm scale — and yet others.

Upper left: **G scale (1:22.5), started by LGB but also now made by other firms, offers huge scope for those who prefer very large-scale modelling. This is the LGB Porter 0-4-0ST extensively altered, detailed, and repainted by the late Derek Gigg.**

Left: **Endless scope is available in the model railway hobby to convert, alter, and adapt models to other types or appearances. The cheap Modelpower 'Hustler' diesel switcher in HO has here been converted to a diesel loco for On16.5 narrow gauge by adding a new wood and cardboard cab after sawing off the original. The model is still to be painted and fitted with magnetic couplers.**

These yield superb results when you see layouts at shows, but they demand care, skill experience, and much more time than mere 'off the shelf' models in HO, OO or N etc..

NARROW GAUGE

Finally there is an ever-growing enthusiasm for narrow gauge. G is well known (the large 1:22.5 scale models made by LGB, Bachmann and others) and is easy to work in if you have the space and money.

But those scales utilising 16.5mm gauge (such as On16.5 and Oe, or Sm and Sn3½) have the same advantages as already outlined for OO and HO. Most of the same mechanisms and chassis are used for a start, and for the less skilled modeller this sort of narrow gauge (or smaller scales using 9mm track — HOe, OO9 — or 12mm track, which allows HOm or OOn3) will be easiest for most modellers wishing to follow the narrow gauge path.

FROM OO TO EM (OR EVEN P4/S4)

Most modellers of British outline stay with OO gauge, but it is not too difficult to convert some OO models to run on EM gauge (18.2mm) or even P4/S4 (18.83mm) which is exactly to scale. Firms such as Ultrascale and Alan Gibson, and the EM Society (members only), have conversion wheelsets for rolling stock and some locomotives. Other firms, such as C&L and SMP make flexible EM and P4/S4 track. A few small traders also offer conversion and point making services, and all these specialist suppliers tend to be at the larger model shows in Britain if you want to see what is currently on offer. Some examples of what can be done are shown here. The old Lima Class 73 is shown having its wheels changed from OO to EM, with an EM wheel gauge checking for accuracy. The finished model stands on SMP EM track. The 'J94' has its wheels eased out to EM gauge and the Hornby wagons have Ultrascale EM wheelsets in place of the Hornby wheels.

CHAPTER 2

GETTING THE BEST PERFORMANCE

Below: **It is most important to keep locomotive wheels clean and the easy way to do it is with a cotton bud lightly dampened with white spirit.**

Centre: **Really recalcitrant grime can be removed from wheel treads by gently scraping with a small screwdriver. Note the foam packing from the locomotive box used as a handy maintenance cradle for the upturned locomotive.**

Bottom: **Always read the instruction sheet. This example from Hornby shows the carbon brush replacement for its diesel locomotives with the 'pancake' motor.**

SIMPLE LOCOMOTIVE MAINTENANCE

On a real railway system, considerable effort is spent on servicing the locomotive fleet. Apart from routine servicing and cleaning, often overnight so that a locomotive can be at work again on the morrow, there are periodic major overhauls where the locomotive is taken apart, completely cleaned and reworked, and re-assembled, to emerge once more in sparkling fresh paint to take its place in the roster.

All this has its equivalent in miniature, for model locomotives also need servicing and cleaning if you are to get the best from them and ensure a long working life.

In fact, today's models sold in ready-to-run form are nearly all remarkably fine designs and the crudity sometimes seen years ago in 'train set' type models is completely replaced by a high standard of finish and mechanical reliability at whatever price level you buy. What has advanced considerably in recent years is motor design. Today there are several types of motor used in model locomotives which vary in appearance. Some models produced in recent years have 'throw away' can motors which are simply unplugged and replaced when the carton brushes are worn down. A new motor must be bought as a spare part and instructions for fitting are given in the instruction leaflet with the locomotive.

It is possible to keep a model locomotive in service for many years if it is looked after properly, and there are cases of models which have run many hundreds of real miles over a period of years and still manage to look as good as new. Clearly if you purchase a favourite locomotive model you want it to run well and run whenever you put it on the track. As with a real railway, any locomotive which does not perform properly is a waste of resources.

The starting point for ensuring good running is, in fact, cleanliness of the track and the locomotive. Dirt is the

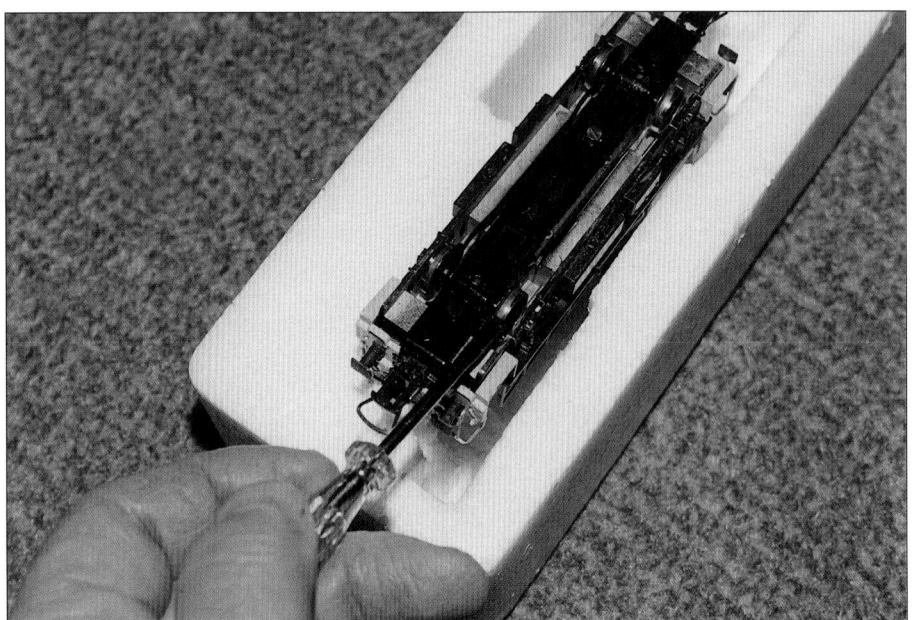

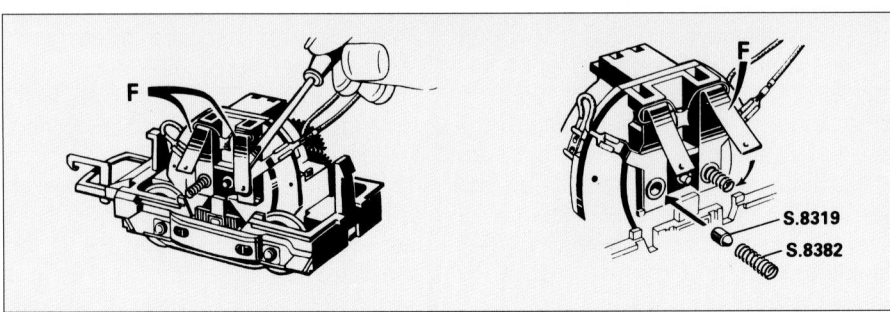

curse of miniature railways, in particular the 12V DC 2-rail variety. After a good period of time a patina of dirt and oil forms on the running surface of rails and this makes a partial insulation barrier reducing the amount of current getting through to be picked up by the wheels. If you experience sluggish running by a locomotive check that the rail surfaces of the layout are cleaned before automatically assuming that the locomotive is faulty. An essential purchase is a track cleaner block (such as that made by Peco) which is then used before every running session lightly rubbed over the rail surfaces. More on this on page 13.

From the track and its connections we pass on to the model locomotives, for it is cleanliness here that makes all the difference to performance. It is a well-known fact that most of the problems which arise with model locomotives are not due to mechanical or electrical faults but are caused entirely by dirt! Several famous firms have found that a very large proportion of the models returned to them as 'faulty' prove to be suffering only from an excess of dirt, and after cleaning are as good as new!

Consider what happens. All layouts are affected by dust and other domestic debris such as fluff from carpets and hair from pets and humans. The layout itself may have loose particles of ballast or flock powder. These may not be loose when the layout is built, but they break off later. There is light oil on the locomotive gears when new, and the layer of grease and carbon builds up on rail surfaces, caused by oil from the locomotive and the 'arcing' between wheel and track due to the electrical pick-up.

These conditions lead in no time to dust, fluff and hair getting picked up and wrapped round axles and gears, all of which will eventually jam the axles and drive.

A similar problem arises with the pick-ups on 2-rail models. Many of these models have either sprung wire or sprung metal brushes bearing on the backs of the wheel rims. The current is picked up by the tyre and flange from the track, and carried to the motor by the contact brushes. Clearly if fluff and dirt build up between the wheel backs and the brushes, the pick-up eventually isolates itself and the locomotive no longer runs.

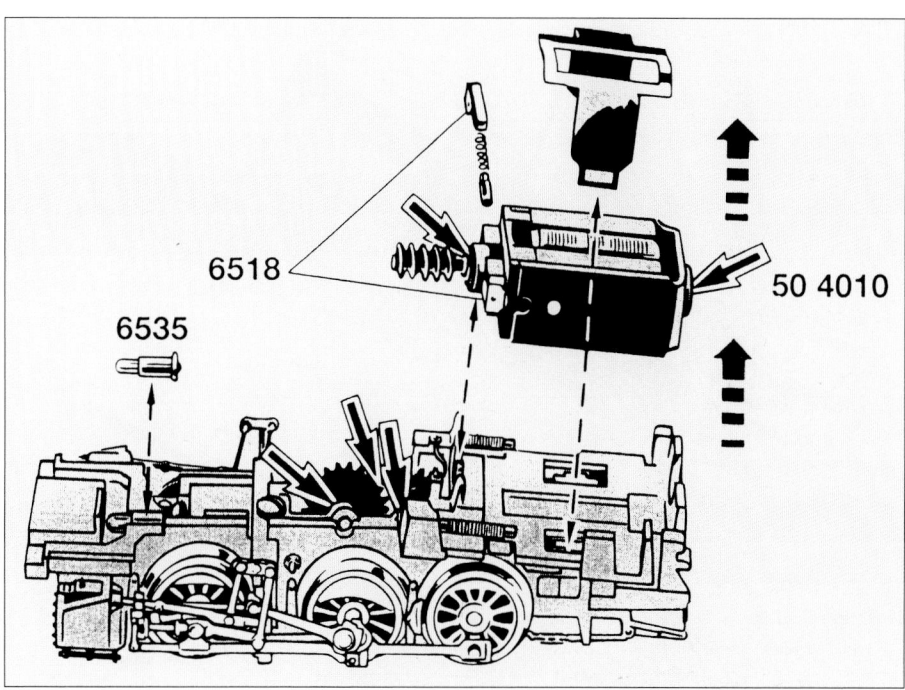

Above: **Modern models by leading manufacturers are generally designed for easy maintenance and are well covered by instruction sheets. This example from the Fleischmann HO Prussian 'T3' 0-6-0T instructions shows lamp replacement, motor removal, brush replacement and lubrication points — arrowed.**

Finally there can be a build-up of greasy grime on the tyres of the locomotive wheels, just as on the rail surface, and once again an insulating effect is caused.

The cure for all these problems is regular cleaning. It is a good idea at least once a month to set an hour or so aside for routine cleaning. You will need tweezers or some sort of probe (such as a small screwdriver or a needle), fine emery paper, tissues, a cotton bud, and plain old rags such as a piece from an old shirt. This is actually preferable to a cotton bud, because a cotton bud can leave fibres behind and cause more trouble. But much here depends on the size of your models and the surfaces you are cleaning.

When you up-end the locomotive, it is useful to have a 'cradle' to hold it in. In many cases you can use the foam packing in which many models are now supplied, but another idea is to cut out a suitable recess in a block of sponge rubber in which the top half of the locomotive will fit so that the chassis is exposed upwards. Now check all the pick-ups and use the tweezers or needle to clean any fluff or dirt from the pick-up ends. Then check all visible moving parts, such as axle bearings, side motion bearings and any exposed gear wheels, and gently remove any hair or fluff. You can carry out this inspection as often as you like, in fact, and if a locomotive starts to run in an erratic way (or fails to run at all), carry

out this inspection and cleaning first — it may be the only problem!

Next look at the wheels. If the track has been kept clean you may see no significant dirt there, but if dirt has built up on the tread it may be carefully scraped off with the small screwdriver. Don't scrape too hard — the key word is 'gently' — as it is important not to scratch the tread. If the black grime proves to be recalcitrant, put a little white spirit on to a cotton bud or piece of rag, and rub this gently round the wheel tread. Ensure any loosened grime is then wiped away with a clean cotton bud or piece of rag.

A problem that does crop up concerns traction tyres. A number of models still have these and they can cause trouble. For a start, buy a supply of spare tyres. Your stockist should have them (or can get them to order). Where a traction tyre is heavily worn or very grimy it is best replaced. A cotton bud with white spirit can also be effective, but be careful here because white spirit affects some of the rubbers or plastic and can cause them to perish. If in doubt, replace! Even better is to choose models that don't have traction tyres whenever you can. Don't run a model without its traction tyres;

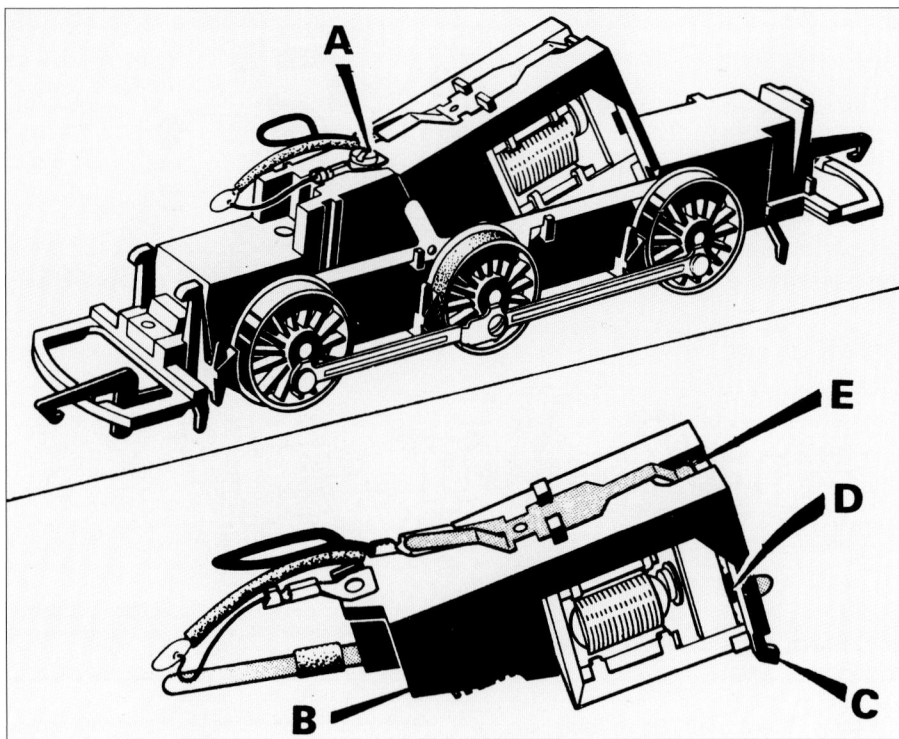

The body must be removed, of course, to give access to the motor. Even this must be done with care. If there is an instruction sheet check to see if there is any special procedure for body removal. Sometimes buffers or handrails must be unclipped first, for example, and often there is a screw to remove. Some models these days have no instruction sheet, so special care must be taken. Keep all loose parts safely until the body is replaced. One thing for certain is that if you find yourself having to exert undue force to remove the body, stop and look again, because you are probably doing something wrong. Generally speaking, the body comes off easily if you follow the instructions.

Getting back to the chassis, there remains lubrication. Special light oil is available from Peco, Fleischmann and other firms, intended specially for oiling locomotives. The Peco tube of oil has a thin applicator, but if you use other oils you can make an applicator from a length of wire.

On a 'pancake' motor oiling is needed on the motor spindle. Light oiling is also needed on axle bearings, coupling rod bearings and gear chains, and any other moving parts.

Make a final check of the motor and chassis before assembling the body back in position. It is a good idea to run the 'naked' chassis without the body in place as part of the final check. Even re-assembling the body to the chassis needs care. Often there are lugs or tabs requiring the body to be spread slightly. If you do not ensure all the locating lugs are engaged you may end up with a distorted or stressed body that is not correctly levelled or aligned. It is worth remarking here that if any small details break on the locomotive body, ensure they are glued back quickly before they are lost.

AVOIDING PROBLEMS

Modern locomotive models from leading makers are today surprisingly good in engineering terms. This is

the locomotive will certainly run, but as the tyre fits inside a groove, the locomotive will often 'limp' if the tyre is missing.

Maintenance can also be carried out on the motor and drive in some cases. But there is much variation here. Many recent models have motors that are entirely sealed except for access to the carbon brushes. There is little you can do to these motors, nor would need to do other than change the carbon brushes when required.

Most typical is the 'pancake' type Ringfield motor found in some Fleischmann, Lima and Hornby models. If any fault develops in this sort of motor it is usually merely replaced in its entirety. This is what would happen if, for example, teeth were broken or missing from the plastic gear drive wheel. So if cleaning and brush replacement does not cure any running problems you would need to see your dealer or send the model back to the service department of the maker. Brush replacement is possible, as shown in the model instructions.

particularly true of diesel locomotive types made in the USA, China or Japan. The Americans long ago worked out the ideal mechanical design for getting optimum performance with minimum maintenance. In recent years European firms have been switching over to the same idea.

It was probably Athearn in the 1960s which came up with the idea. Here we have a heavy die-cast chassis and frame with a centrally mounted motor driving a shaft to each power truck (bogie) where power is transferred to the wheels through gear trains. On one or both drive shafts is a flywheel. There are no traction tyres.

What you get is a very smooth running performance, generally down to 'creep' speed, and with no danger at all of stalling on dead frogs or bad rail joins as notoriously happened on British locomotive models of yester-year. Many of these USA-style models have sealed motors and seem to be maintenance free. I've had some Atlas and Kato HO and N locomotives for over ten or twelve years at the time of writing which still run perfectly with no attention from me except, perhaps, for a wheel clean once a year. Some models like those by Athearn (and Roco of Austria who now use similar drives) need minimal oiling at the usual points, but no more.

All of which suggests you can often avoid frustration by wise choice of motive power to start with. Some of these American models seem to press on regardless over very dirty track too!

CLEAN TRACK

But clean track goes hand in hand with clean, well-maintained locomotives in any case. Lots has been written on this subject, but I suspect problems have arisen from use of the poor performing British outline locomotives of the past,

some of which are still around. Clean track obviously helped these lamer locomotives to run better. If you have American or German (or even recent British) flywheel drive locomotives you may wonder what all the fuss is about since they all seem to run well whatever the state of the track.

However, that is no excuse for not keeping the track clean, or at least the top surface and all 'live' contacts such as at power feeds or point mechanisms. People often ask me (at shows) how I keep the track so clean and I have to confess that all I use — and have ever used — is the simple track rubber made by Peco and others and sold at modest prices in all model shops. I run the rubber over the track before every operating session, and again at 'coffee break' time in a long session — or at lunchtime if I have the layout at a day-long show. This applies in all gauges in which I work — N, HO, OO, EM, S, O and 1 — with no exception or extra measures needed.

You can get track cleaning vehicles — firms like Fleischmann and Roco make

Above: **The modern type of diesel (or electric) locomotive chassis that gives perfect stall-free slow running for HO, shown on a Life-Like Proto 2000 EMD SW9 switcher. Note the metal chassis, centrally-mounted can motor, twin brass flywheels and geared drive to each axle.**

them — which are HO or N vans with an abrasive pad under the chassis. You run them in a train and in theory they clean the track. They seem to be effective but can do no better than the simple track rubber as far as I can see.

The other much publicised item is the electronic track cleaning module, of which Relco is the best known. A lot of people swear by them and use them on layouts. I suspect that on a very large layout where access to all the rail surfaces may be difficult, there is merit and value in these units. But I've never found them necessary in any of the small layouts I've built in the past forty years.

One last observation here is that access to the track for cleaning purposes is obviously necessary, so tunnels need removable roofs and there must be access for the hand pushing the track rubber! Bear this in mind when planning your scenic work. Clearly, too, all track cleaning must be done with care, taking a good look at the stretch of track before you begin to note any signals, telegraph poles or other items close to the track. Clumsy hand movements here could knock them over.

Left: **Recent British 00 gauge models have caught up with American technology. The Hornby Class 50, superbly detailed, has a chassis and drive similar to that on the Life-Like model shown above, with an admirable performance to match the American diesel locomotives in every way.**

CHAPTER 3

COUPLINGS

Fundamental to effective (and efficient) layout operation is a foolproof way of coupling and uncoupling that does not involve immense complexity but gives a pleasing degree of realism.

Couplers (and coupling methods) have always required a degree of compromise on miniature railways, necessarily so because there are no miniature men to carry out the coupling and uncoupling done by hand (or shunter's pole) in real life. Also, real couplers reduced to true scale are very small indeed and a good degree of skill and good workmanship is necessary to make scale couplers work satisfactorily.

SCALE COUPLERS

However, scale couplers make a good starting point. In the larger scales and gauges, scale couplers (or some slightly oversized versions of these) depicting 3-link, Instanter and screw couplers are quite commonly used and fitted. We are talking here of S, O and 1 gauge models where kits and ready-to-run models are commonly supplied with scale couplers or provision for fitting them. Exceptions are the Czech ETS and Märklin gauge 1 ranges where conventional auto-couplers are fitted, but even so,

Above: **Scale three-link coupler fitted on a cattle wagon from a Slater's 0 gauge kit, showing the bar (plastic rod in this case) between the buffers to prevent buffer-locking.**

provision is made for scale couplers to replace them, if desired, and Märklin offers scale couplers in its accessory range.

Quite a few modellers working in 4mm scale (OO, EM or S4) also choose the scale couplers for aesthetic or 'authentic' reasons, and all the following comments apply whatever scale you use.

First of all, the scale coupler wins in looks, of course, for it is just like the real thing. But in any scale (and particularly in 4mm) they are fiddly things to hook up or unhook. You need a miniature version of the shunter's pole, steady hands, a light touch, a good eye and good light. Some modellers tape a miniature torch to the side of their (home-made) shunter's pole to solve the light problem. Any wavering or mis-hooking can cause derailing of the wagon (or wagons) and, of course, the human hand hovering above the models does not aid the illusion of realism!

Once a train is coupled up, haulage rarely causes problems unless you make jerky progress and cause the buffers to hit each other. Pushing the rolling stock, however, is where the problems arise. Most model railway curves are sharper than the gentle radius used in real life, the 'heft' of real loaded wagons (and the springing) is rarely reproduced, and buffers are not always sprung as in real life. Pushing wagons or coaches in these circumstances can lead to the buffers of one wagon striking and 'locking' behind a facing buffer and in no time at all the wagon is derailed, usually bringing all the adjacent wagons with it! It is true that there are some layouts where this rarely happens (due to gentle curves, sprung buffers, perfect running, etc) but these are the exception rather than the rule.

One measure you can take to prevent buffer locking is to solder or glue a wire or plastic rod bar between the two buffers; this is quite successful, and certainly works well

on my British O gauge models. Some extreme dexterity is called for, however, in lifting the coupler links over the buffer bar when coupling up.

AUTO-COUPLERS

It was all the problems noted above that caused model railway manufacturers to adopt some form of auto-coupler from the earliest days. Tight curves and rigid buffers on model railways are best overcome by keeping the buffers of adjacent vehicles apart from each other, and auto-couplers give either shanks or loops big enough to do this. The bonus is some form of hook, loop or claw that joins automatically when pushed against another coupler so that the human hand is not needed to make the connection.

TENSION-LOCK

Many auto-couplers have been used over the years, but the most common type, found on most British-outline 4mm scale models, is the so-called 'tension-lock', which itself has been developed in even smaller and more compact forms in recent years. In general, though, large and small versions of this coupler will work with each other. Most new models today have the smaller, less conspicuous version of the tension-lock.

Hornby (then Triang) introduced this design for its TT-3 range in the 1950s, then enlarged it for 4mm scale. This coupler was itself developed from a 'home-made' coupler idea by the pioneer modeller A. R. Walkley in the 1920s.

Advantages of the tension-lock coupler are cheapness (it comes with the model and is cheap as an accessory too), ease of use with a sprung uncoupling ramp (also readily available and cheap), and the fact that if you are happy with it, then you can stop worrying about the subject.

The main limitation of this coupler is the fact it has no 'delay' facilities. You cannot uncouple, then push a wagon further along a siding, for if you do this it couples again automatically. Hence it is necessary to have an uncoupler ramp in any position where a wagon is required to be left, which is awkward.

There are two extra aids here. First, you can use transparent plastic strips pinned between the rails and bowed to make a 'home-made' ramp which is less visible than the rather intrusive

wooden cocktail stick that can be inserted from the side to lift the claws apart.

In Z scale the main supplier is Märklin with its Miniclub range. It has a claw-type coupler, and all the comments above apply equally to this.

OTHER AUTO-COUPLERS

Another 4mm scale auto-coupler you may encounter is the Simplex. This is a very neat horizontally operating device that gives quite close coupling and was used back in the 1950s and 1960s by Hornby-Dublo and Trix. It is still made by Peco, but you would need to fit it to your model fleet in place of other types, which would not always be easy. It has its own dedicated type of uncoupler ramp, different again from others.

Once very common was the American design called the 'horn-hook', or sometimes the 'A2Z', which roughly resembles an automatic knuckle coupler. This, again, is cheap and cheerful, engages horizontally, and is found still on many American HO models though much less so that a few years ago. As with the N gauge Arnold coupler this has a springy uncoupler ramp which unless set up very precisely

black plastic uncoupler ramp. Next, from a lolly stick you can make an uncoupler device to lift the hooks from trackside and separate the vehicles anywhere on the layout.

The tension-lock coupler is mainly fitted on British 4mm scale models, but similar versions are found on Fleischmann HO models and some German O gauge models.

N AND Z GAUGE

Universally fitted on almost all N gauge models is the claw type, usually called the Arnold type after the company that first developed it in the 1960s. Given the small scale of N, this claw-type coupler is quite efficient, certainly when it comes to coupling — you just push adjacent vehicles together and it works every time.

For uncoupling, however, a ramp is required. Some European firms offer electrically operated ramps in their ranges, and Peco in Britain has a hand-operated ramp. In theory these ramps lift the claw coupler high enough to

enable the uncoupled vehicles to be drawn apart, but personal experience suggests you need to have the ramp very precisely set up for it is only too easy for the ramps to lift not only the couplers but the vehicles as well, causing an unwelcome derailment! However, quite an effective uncoupler pole can be made from an ordinary

Right: **A cheap, cheerful and quite effective way of uncoupling the standard type of N gauge coupler is to use a wooden cocktail stick which can push the couplers up, gently, from below.**

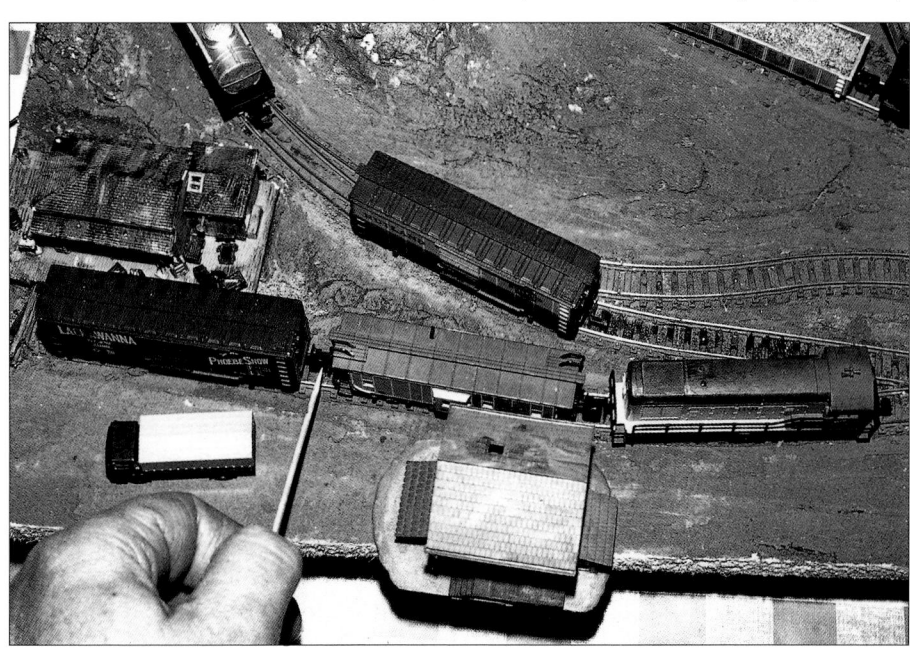

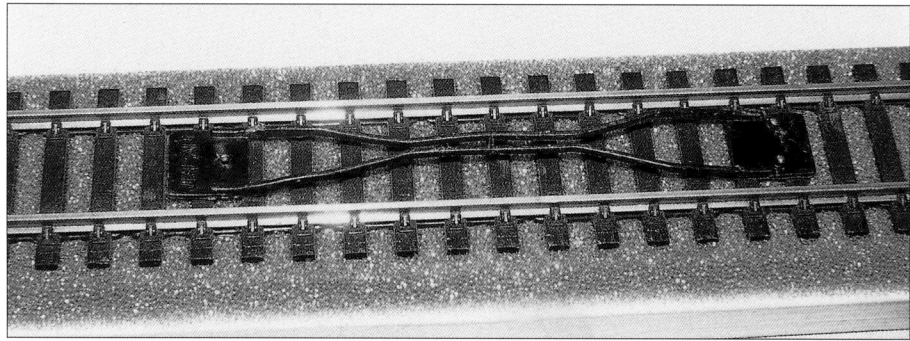

Top: **Much used on American HO RTR models is the 'horn hook', shown fitted here on two different makes of freight car. Magnetic couplers are fast replacing these, however, even on cheap RTR models.**

Above: **The special uncoupler ramp (made in the USA) needed for 'horn hook' couplers. It needs careful setting up, however, to ensure the freight cars are not lifted and derailed.**

can result in derailing the entire train. A favourite way of uncoupling these by hand is to slice a lolly stick diagonally to give a pointed tip and insert this vertically between the couplers and twist it to separate them. But a light touch is needed to avoid derailing the stock in the process.

A coupler which is a sort of hybrid between the Simplex and the horn-hook may also be found on old Lima and Rivarossi O gauge models, while the horn-hook type was also once included with some British plastic wagon kits.

DELAYED UNCOUPLING

What gives added realism to model railway operation is the ability to uncouple wagons (or an entire train) and shunt it around, all without the need to touch it in the process. It is pleasing to you as the operator of your own layout, but it intrigues and impresses others who watch it, particularly those who don't know how

it is done. Doubters are often sceptical about this statement, but once they've tried it they rarely want to go back to more primitive and toy-like methods.

Several ways have been evolved. Two British systems worth mentioning are the Alex Jackson coupler and the Sprat & Winkle. The Alex Jackson system is favoured by those working in fine scale 4mm, but is used in 7mm scale as well. The late Alex Jackson evolved this magnetic coupler system in the 1950s and it uses fine wire spring couplers activated by magnets hidden in the track. You will see this system in use on fine scale layouts at shows, and it always impresses onlookers. The bad news for less skilled modellers is that it needs perfect running, gentle radius curves and scale gauge (EM or P4/S4) track rather than OO gauge. And you have to make it all yourself, set up to very fine tolerances to work correctly, though a few 'kits of parts' or frets using the principle have been offered by small traders.

The second British magnetic system is the Sprat & Winkle which uses a vertical dropper and inconspicuous loop, which is all nicely disguised to generally resemble the British style of 3-link couplers. Again it is impressive and effective in use, but it all has to be assembled and precisely set up to work

well, and might not be suitable for those without the necessary skills for fine assembly work. It is available for 4mm and 7mm scale from the more specialised hobby shops in Britain.

Various other magnetic coupler systems are available from small British companies, mostly produced as frets for home assembly. Again very precise assembly and setting up is needed for these to work properly. If you don't do that you face disappointment. Makes available cover between them, N, 3mm, 4mm and 7mm scales.

KADEE AND OTHERS

Magnetic uncoupler systems all work in the same general way in that the vehicle to be uncoupled is stopped over a magnet in the track. Using the 'like poles/unlike poles' principle of magnetics, the facing couplers spring apart over the magnet. Provided that couplers are shaped so that they do not re-connect as soon as they are moved away from the magnet it is possible to push a vehicle, once uncoupled, down the length of a siding to position it at, say, a loading bank, or inside a covered goods shed. Whole trains can be similarly handled. For example, your station pilot can push a full coach set into a terminus platform and draw away to leave the coaches in place all with no manual assistance from operators.

Magnetic systems in effect allow 'hands off' operation with a vast improvement in realism. The big name in magnetic uncoupling is Kadee in the USA, whose inventors, Keith and Dale (ie Kadee) Edwards perfected the system in its present form in the early 1960s. It is almost universally used in the Americas and in other countries (eg Australia) where railways have a lot of American influence. But today it is increasingly used in Europe too. The Kadee design of coupler, in many variations to suit all requirements, is available to suit all scales and gauges from Z up to G. Since the original Kadee patents expired a few years ago several other firms have offered similar (and compatible) designs, mainly for HO and N, and names in the business now include McHenry, Bachmann EZmate and Accumate.

The Kadee-type magnetic coupler, of course, depicts the buckeye coupler universally used in the Americas and elsewhere, and not unknown in Europe, where it is used, for example, on

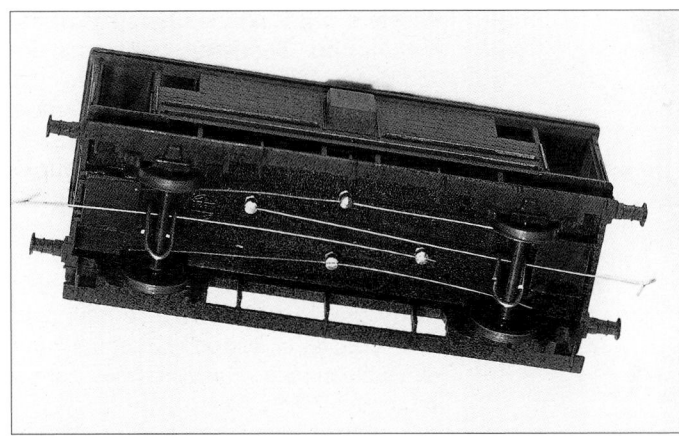

Above: The very inconspicuous Alex Jackson coupler fitted on a P4/S4 brake van. It works magnetically.

Above: The Sprat & Winkle magnetic coupler fitted to a Ratio GWR four-wheel coach by Julian Andrews on his Weston, Clevedon & Portishead layout.

Left: The O gauge version of the Kadee magnetic coupler fitted to an Atlas 'bobber' caboose which is also having extra detail added.

Above: The highly detailed Micro-Trains N scale freight stock (American prototype) comes with the Micro-Trains version of the magnetic coupler already fitted.

modern British coaching stock. The 'standard' designs of model buckeye are strictly speaking slightly overscale, but a recent development is the production of dead scale size couplers (eg, Kadee No 58) which nonetheless still work with earlier types.

The Kadee range is extensive. There are not only couplers to suit all requirements and fittings (though the Kadee No 5 is most commonly used on American HO models) but there are magnets and electro-magnets of several types for different needs, coupler height gauges, lubricants,

Upper right: Two key items from the Kadee HO magnetic coupler range: the No 321 uncoupler magnet that fits between the rails and the coupler height gauge for checking the accurate coupler setting.

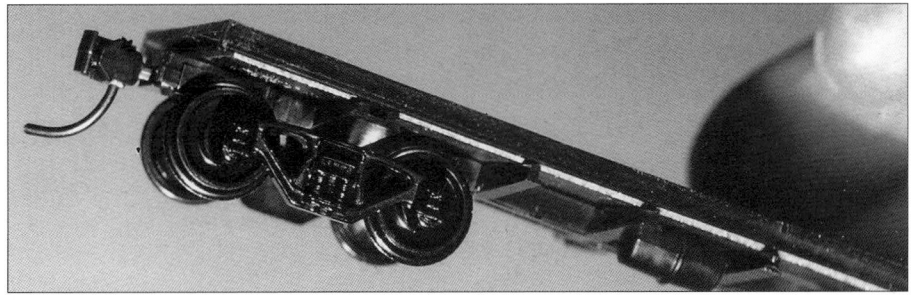

Right: Close-up view of the Kadee magnetic coupler in its draft box fitted to the underframe of a freight car.

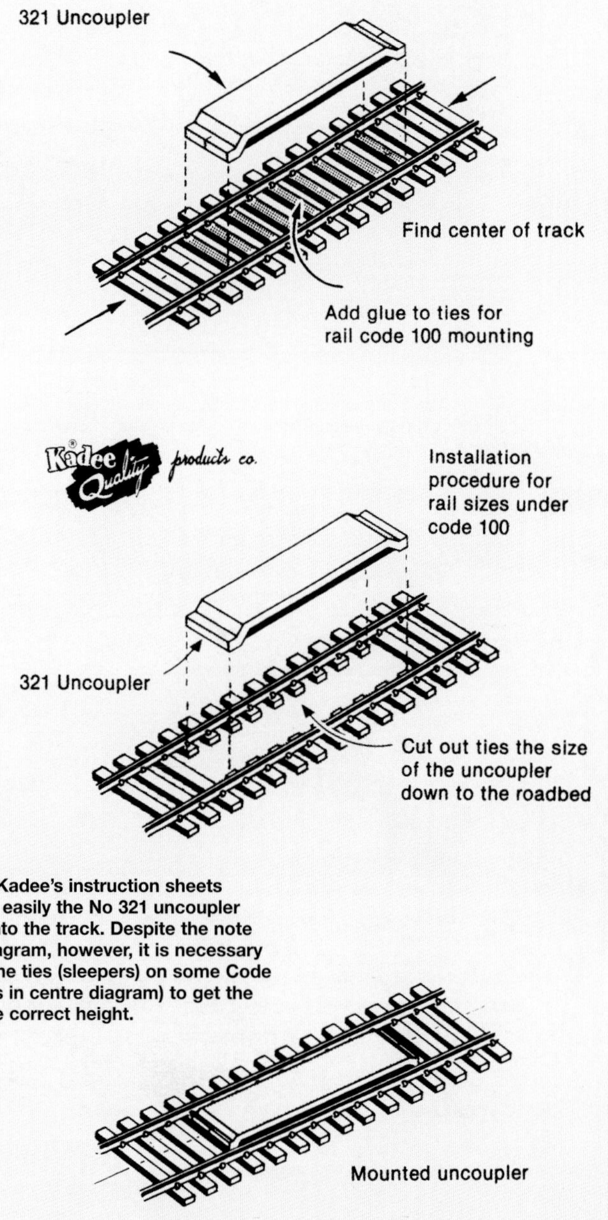

321 Uncoupler

Find center of track

Add glue to ties for
rail code 100 mounting

Kadee Quality products co.

Installation
procedure for
rail sizes under
code 100

321 Uncoupler

Cut out ties the size
of the uncoupler
down to the roadbed

Extract from Kadee's instruction sheets
showing how easily the No 321 uncoupler
magnet fits into the track. Despite the note
on the top diagram, however, it is necessary
to cut away the ties (sleepers) on some Code
100 tracks (as in centre diagram) to get the
magnet to the correct height.

Mounted uncoupler

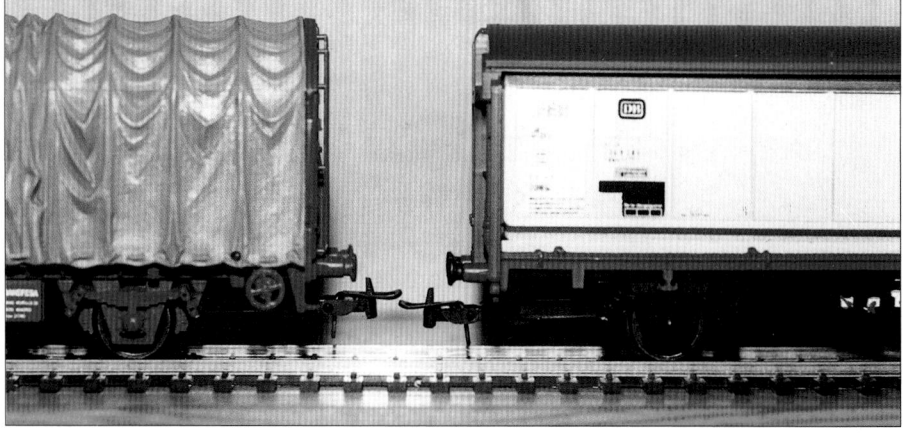

washers, pliers and spares of all sorts.
For N and Z scales, an associate
company Micro-Trains provides the
equivalent items under this name rather
than Kadee which handles scales larger
than N.

At the time of writing the American
style of magnetic coupler is fast
becoming more common on the
American market than the simpler old
horn-hook type. Virtually all new
American, O, S, N and HO models and
kit built models today come with a
magnetic coupler as standard and even
European firms producing American
ranges, such as Roco and Trix, are
doing the same. If you start modelling
the American scene today, therefore,
you are virtually certain to use magnetic
coupling from the start. For those still
using the old horn-hook coupler it is
easy enough to convert. Of course, the
magnetic coupler sets cost money, but
it is a relatively modest sum and more
than outweighed by the extra operating
pleasure magnetics will give.

EUROPEAN COUPLERS

Models produced in HO or OO for the
European market for many years past
have had auto-couplers as a matter of
course: tension-lock for British, for
example, and a standardised hook
and loop for European. These lack the
all-important 'delay' facility that
characterises magnetic couplers, and
in Europe the leading manufacturers
Märklin, Roco and Fleischmann all
produce new coupler types that are
not magnetic, but do offer the 'delay'
facility. Märklin and Roco call theirs a
'close coupler' and both feature
truncated hook and loop
combinations. Fleischmann calls its
the Profi, and it disengages or
engages vertically. Over either a
manual or electrically operated
uncoupling ramp the coupler will
separate and stay apart while the
vehicle is shunted along a loop or
siding. In other words, the ramp
substitutes for the track magnet in the
magnetic system. These European
systems are neat and operate well and
have found great favour. However, the
coupler cost is usually rather higher

Left: **The standard 'hook and loop' coupler found
on most RTR Continental Europe HO models. As
this view shows, the coupler heights of different
makes do not always match exactly. Some
adjustment is advisable, and if magnetic couplers
replace them, exact standard height is essential.**

than the magnetic option, and the ramp is more costly than a magnetic and needs wiring in or else requires a large hand for the manual version to operate.

Some progress has been made with a Fleischmann Profi delayed-action coupler in N, but at the time of writing, the use and fitting of it are far from widespread.

STANDARDISED MOUNTS AND CLOSE COUPLING

Collectively the main European model train manufacturers in HO have made huge efforts to improve operation and appearances by concentrating on the complex problem over the past 15-20 years. In the old days every maker had a different way of fitting couplers, and there were even slight variations of common coupler designs. Therefore cross-operating between makes was difficult, as was the fitting of alternative coupler types. Also the heftier couplers of those days gave hugely over-scale distances between adjacent coupled vehicles.

The long-defunct German firm of Röwa tackled the problem in the 1960s by designing a small standardised coupler socket into which a smaller version of the European type auto-coupler would fit. Röwa was taken over by Roco, which perfected development. A very clever close coupling device was designed whereby the coupler socket was fitted to a sprung arm which travelled in an arc-shaped slot in the vehicle's underframe. The smaller coupler gave buffer-to-buffer (or almost buffer-to-buffer) contact, a huge increase in realism. When the train reached a curve, of course, pressure would be put on the coupler shanks as the vehicles moved into the curve. With rigid couplers derailment would follow, but the close-coupler system allows

Upper right: **These three views of Märklin coaches with close couplers fitted in the NEM 362 coupler boxes show how the system works. On the straight (centre view) the coaches are held close together, but moving around sharp curves, the coupler boxes move in chevron-shaped slots that force the coaches apart. Back on the straight they close up again.**

Lower right: **On some makes of European HO rolling stock the NEM 362 coupler mount may droop or be set too low. Here is a way to overcome that — a No 56 office staple drilled into the wagon floor will hold the box at the correct height. This Piko wagon is fitted with the Kadee No 18 magnetic coupler.**

the coupler arm to move along the arc to maintain correct coupler distance and tension. When the train gets back on to straight track the springs pull the vehicles back to buffer-to-buffer appearance.

The European body that advises the trade on standards took up this system under the designation NEM 362 and it is found today on virtually all European models except some very old ones that might remain in production. There are some variations in fit of the close-coupler system, mainly when lack of space in, say, a short chassis allows only a truncated version, but in general it works superbly. The NEM 362 coupler boxes all have to be at a standard working height and here the old problem arises where a wagon has them set too low. In some cases this is because the coupler arm is drooping. A way to overcome this is to make a 'stirrup' from a wire staple glued into the underside of the chassis to hold the drooping coupler up. The alternative is to discard the model, or better still check for correct coupler mount height before buying.

Roco makes a useful pack of close-coupler converter fittings so that old

models without close coupling can be altered to modern style.

'SWALLOW TAIL' SHANK
With the development of the European close-coupler system came a standardised coupler shank that enables any make or type of coupler to be slotted into the NEM 362 coupler box. Known as the 'swallow tail' from its shape, it gives good flexibility. For example, couplers can be changed on vehicles depending on the system used on layouts. Your layout may have magnetic couplers, but a friend's layout may use Profi couplers. By changing

Above: **It is not all plain sailing — the nicely detailed Bachmann UK 'Blue Riband' PO wagons have NEM 362 coupler boxes fitted, but they are set too high so magnetic couplers will not operate, as is evident from this view of the wagon against the Kadee coupler height gauge.**

the couplers a locomotive might be used on either layout.

All types of couplers are made with the 'swallow tail' fitting. Kadee produced a European version of its magnetic coupler (Nos 17, 18, 19, 20 — with short, standard, long, extra long shank lengths respectively) so that magnetic coupling is equally feasible on European models. With typical flexibility a coach fixed set might use standard hook and loop couplers as supplied through the set except for the ends of the outer vehicles which have, say, Kadee or Profi couplers fitted to match the system used on the layout.

BRITISH CLOSE COUPLING
In British OO gauge, the makers ignored these European developments for years and all stuck with their own styles of tension-lock and ways of fitting them. Developments are happening as this book is written, however, and both Hornby and Bachmann UK are making new rolling stock (and some locomotives) with the NEM 362-type coupler box and versions of the close-coupling system. For example, the Hornby 'Super Detail' Pullmans are so fitted. On these latest models, therefore, couplers can be changed to suit your preference, though it will be years before all British outline models are like this.

For retrospective fitting of close coupling to British rolling stock, mainly coaches, the Keen company does a good conversion kit which has similar characteristics to the European system and is well worth considering.

#20 is 11.68mm (.460 Inches)
#19 is 10.16mm (.400 Inches)
#18 is 8.63mm (.340 Inches)
#17 is 7.11mm (.280 Inches)

.390"
9.9mm

.279"
7.1mm

.3347"
8.5mm

0.8mm (.031")

Pull off

Above: **The Kadee European Coupler instruction sheet includes this diagram which gives correct heights and settings (in the NEM 362 mount) for the No 17, 18, 19 and 20 couplers. Shank lengths given are dimension A.**

Below: **Kadee No 18 magnetic couplers fitted to Roco German HO models. Here the Class 290 locomotive has just uncoupled 'hands off' from the open wagon over the No 321 magnet, and is pulling away. The magnet is between the rails immediately below the couplers which are displaced left and right by the magnetic effect.**

MAGNETIC OPERATION FOR BRITISH MODELS

Some clever modellers have converted British tension-lock couplers for magnetic operation, and Peco did a magnetic conversion kit for the Arnold-type N gauge coupler. But in general it was hard going. However, experiments with the Kadee European coupler enabled me to use magnetic coupling with British OO (or EM) models without too many problems. The method works best with Bachmann, old Mainline, or Replica rolling stock, all of which have the same design roots.

Quite by luck, and certainly not by design, the screw mount for the tension-lock coupler (the sort with the spring in it) provides the correct operating height for the Kadee coupler. If you use the most common coupler, the No 18, you also get a perfect coupling distance between wagons, just closer than the distance given by the tension-locks themselves. You need a Minidrill to drill out a securing hole in the coupler shank, quickly done by holding the swallow tails in pliers in the left hand, and using your right hand to direct the Minidrill right through the No 18 engraved on the shank — a perfect aiming mark. (Obviously use the opposite hand if you are left-handed.) A 1.5mm drill is required. It takes only seconds to drill each hole and you can drill out a batch of coupler shanks at a time. Then unscrew the tension-lock coupler and screw the Kadee No 18 into its place. You get the correct operating height and don't even need a height gauge for this — it's right every

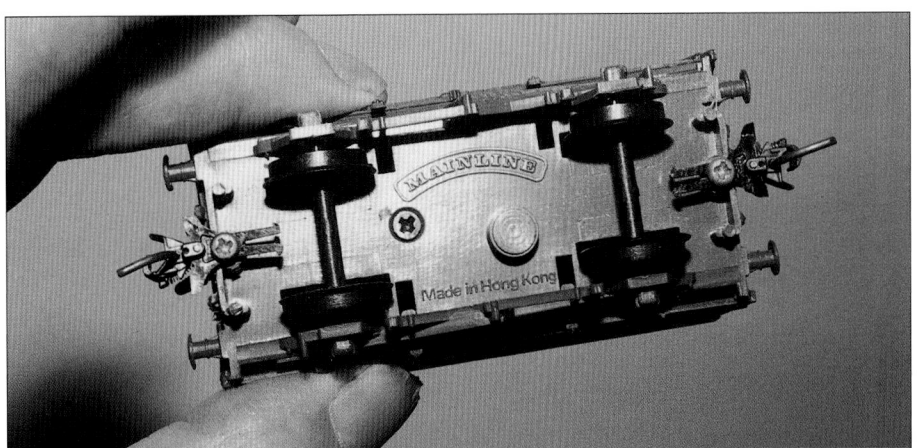

Top right: **Adapting the Kadee No 18 coupler for British 4mm scale wagons. Here a hole has been drilled through the No 18 engraved on the coupler shank.**

Middle right: **The Kadee No 18 couplers attached to a Mainline (or early Bachmann) wagon by the screws used to attach the original tension-lock couplers, and using the same screw holes.**

Lower right: **On old Airfix, Dapol and some Hornby wagons which have a different type of tension-lock coupler mount, this can be removed and a Kadee No 16 coupler can be screwed or glued direct to the wagon floor, as on this Airfix wagon (the No 16 is actually from the American coupler range).**

Right: **This diagram shows the modification to the Kadee No 18 coupler as in the top right photograph. The 'swallow tail' standard European coupler shank can also be seen here.**

Far right: **Another alternative for some Hornby wagons, such as the Lowmac, is to attach the Kadee No 18 coupler by cutting its shank short and using contact adhesive to glue it in place.**

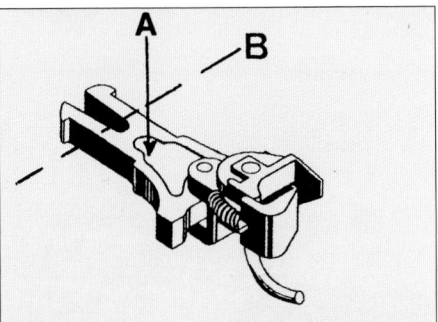

Modification needed for the Kadee No 18 coupler. (A) Drill (1.5mm diameter) through the '18' engraved here on the shank. (B) Cut off shanks where space is restricted behind mounting, as on some locomotives. Same procedure applied if modifying No 19 or No 20 couplers

Left: '**State of the art**', as far as British 4mm models go, for shunting with magnetic uncoupling is the Bachmann Class 08. It has the NEM 362 coupler draft boxes set at the correct height, as shown in this underside view where Kadee No 18 or 19 couplers can be fitted directly in place.

time. With long or short wheelbase stock there is sufficient spring in the coupler head to get round the tightest radius Setrack curves, and small radius Setrack or Hornby points with no problems at all. I carried out extensive tests and found no hiccups in the system.

Some coaches are harder. The early Mainline coaches, plus some of the Replica coaches (such as its scale length BG) have the tension-lock coupler fitted to the bogies by screw, and on these you can fix the No 18 Kadee coupler in the same way. Easy again. But later coaches, such as most of Bachmann's, have a 'production economy' whereby the coupler is moulded integral with the bogie. You can saw this off, but you do not often get a convenient fixing position. For example, having fitted the Kadee coupler to a Hornby Bulleid Pacific you might fancy a set of Bachmann Bulleid coaches for it to pull. But saw off the fixed coupler from the Bulleid bogie and you just have an empty void above with no easy way of fitting the Kadee. So you don't win every time, but there are enough 'easy' fitting models for the inconvenient ones to be avoided.

Some of the new Bachmann 'Blue Riband' models offer problems because they have the NEM 362 coupler box but it is set at the wrong height. I found that by chance the Kadee No 17 or 18 magnetic couplers can be glued below the coupler box (with impact adhesive) on the ordinary wagons to overcome this discrepancy.

YOU NEED SLOW RUNNING
A key necessity with good magnetic coupler operation and shunting is a slow, reliable running locomotive and this is where some limitations may creep in. In a letter to the American magazine *Railroad Model Craftsman*, the design director for Life-Like's Proto 2000 series says they aim to achieve a steady low speed of three scale miles per hour which is what they consider absolutely essential for efficient switching/shunting in HO. In my experience, Bachmann USA gets even slower than this with its GE 44- or 70-ton switchers, as do Atlas and Kato with their HO diesel switcher models. Finding any British 4mm model that matches this is difficult. I tested all the small shunting engines that I could lay hands on to find out which would run at slow, steady speed without faltering, stalling on dead frogs, or failing to

respond to the controls. Essential is the steady speed with magnetic coupling, since if the locomotive judders or hesitates the chances are that the couplers will re-engage and spoil the shunting move. Rubber traction tyres have a bad effect here. Likewise stalling on a dead frog (all too common with earlier British model locomotives) defeats any effort at realistic shunting/switching. With British 4mm models I found that such recent types as the Hornby J94 and Terrier, and the Bachmann Class 08 are satisfactory for slow, smooth shunting but few others are. Virtually all American HO small locomotives, where flywheel drive and metal chassis are common, work well for realistic switching, as do the more recent European locomotives, but some of these are let down by rubber traction tyres as previously noted. If you want smooth, slow running for shunting, therefore, try to avoid models with rubber traction tyres.

SMALLER SCALES
All the above comments apply to N and Z scales, except that there are more limitations of availability. All American modern N scale flywheel-fitted diesel locomotives, for example, have

Below: **Bachmann BR Class 08 shunter** (repainted, weathered and with driver added) is here shown with Kadee No 18 couplers fitted, close-coupled with an older Bachmann wagon also converted to Kadee No 18 couplers as shown on page 21.

Upper right: **On this old Lima N gauge CCT the standard N gauge coupler has been cut away and a standard Micro-Trains 1016 magnetic coupler has been glued in its place. Not all conversions are this easy, however.**

Below left: **The easiest German N gauge locomotive to convert to magnetic couplers is the Roco Class 290, here with the Micro-Trains 1015 glued below the buffer beams.**

Below right: **To convert most British or Continental N scale wagons to magnetic coupling it is first necessary to cut away the old Arnold-type coupler mount completely, then glue a Micro-Trains 1015 or 1016 coupler in its place.**

Bottom: **A Roco DB Class 290 N gauge model hauling two Fleischmann wagons, all fitted with Micro-Trains magnetic couplers.**

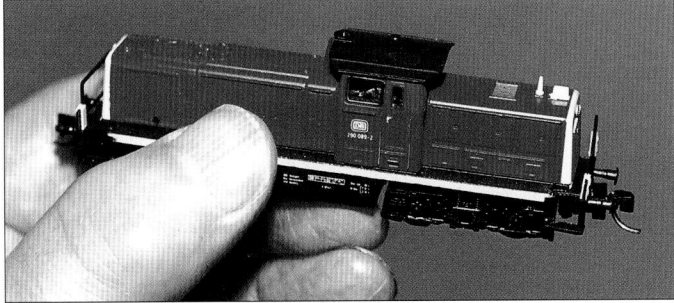

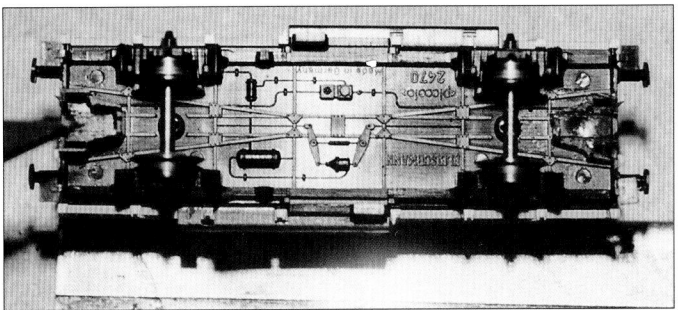

excellent performance, often as good as their HO equivalents, and in combination with Micro-Trains (and similar) magnetic couplers you can switch/shunt as smoothly and pleasingly as with HO. With British and European outline models though it is a bleaker story. All British models come with the Arnold-type claw coupler so that magnetics have to be fitted if you want to shunt. However, having done that task, few, if any, British outline locomotives have a sufficiently smooth performance to run slow enough for shunting successfully.

It is almost the same with European models. A few vehicles are fitted with the Profi coupler (or have the close-

coupler mount for it) but most come with the Arnold coupler. Hence you need to convert everything to take the Profi coupler or Micro-Trains magnetic if you want to shunt or do 'hands off' uncoupling. This in turn is not always feasible — some locomotives and stock have insufficient space to take the coupler — and many locomotives have traction tyres which give them occasional judders and these can spoil operations.

I have converted a number of German and British N models to take magnetic couplers. This took a lot of cutting and adjustment in the main, but because of the less-than-perfect performance of the locomotives,

shunting operations are more frustrating than with American models. It is not surprising therefore that most British and Continental N gauge layouts are more or less restricted to running through the scenery. Some are happy with that, but if you hanker after shunting and train make-up etc, you may be disappointed. In my experience only American N allows full unrestricted operation in all aspects.

American Z models also come with Micro-Trains magnetic couplers, and the few locomotives available work well so that full operation, including switching, is possible as with American HO and N. However, the German Z models have a large claw coupler, and fitting the Micro-Trains magnetic coupler in its place is not easy, and does not work well in any case as the coupler height is lower than the American norm. Hence German Z is best restricted to running trains round layouts rather than full operations.

AXLE ATTRACTION AND FREE RUNNING

Two problems encountered with European models fitted for magnetic operation are axle attraction and free running. American stock has trucks (bogies) which provide enough friction to stay stationary when uncoupled. Most have non-magnetic axles too. With some (not all) European stock the metal axle or wheels are attracted by the uncoupling magnet and roll back over it, often recoupling to the locomotive in the process. In addition, most wagons have pin-point bearings on the axles which makes them very free running so again they can roll back or away from their intended position. These frustrations can be overcome by fitting non-magnetic (or plastic) wheels and by 'damping' the axles by inserting foam plastic between the axle and

underframe. This usually solves the axle attraction and the free running problem both at the same time.

CURVES

When using uncoupling magnets and planning spurs or sidings, it is necessary to use straight track where the magnet is placed, and also at the point where you need to couple up. This is because the coupler faces need to 'kiss' each other straight on to couple. If displaced to one side by the curvature of the track, one coupler will miss the other. Having said that, coupling can often be done on gently curved track where the vehicles or locomotives are short and the displacement of adjacent couplers is about the same, so that they still touch when pushed together.

One last point to mention is that uncoupling of magnetic couplers can be done when away from magnets, or in the fiddle yard for example by using devices sold in model shops that either feature magnets to open the couplers when held over them, or allow you to twist the couplers apart from above. If you can't get these devices, a very small Phillips screwdriver or a wooden

cocktail stick with its end filed flat makes a good substitute.

IN CONCLUSION

Couplers and the process of coupling and uncoupling are often taken for granted by modellers, and the subject is rarely emphasised in books or magazine articles. But if you are concerned with realistic and satisfying operation it is very much a subject of prime concern.

However, as successful coupling and uncoupling is dependent on slow and reliable running it affects your choice of locomotives too, at least as far as your shunting or switching engines are concerned. A good looking or favourite locomotive that won't run well enough for shunting smoothly is a liability, an embarrassment and a waste of money! Better therefore to keep perfect operation in the forefront of your mind and take time to think out your needs. In model railway operation it is not always obvious that there is a link between coupling and performance, just as there is between track laying and power supply. This applies to whatever type of coupler and uncoupler you choose.

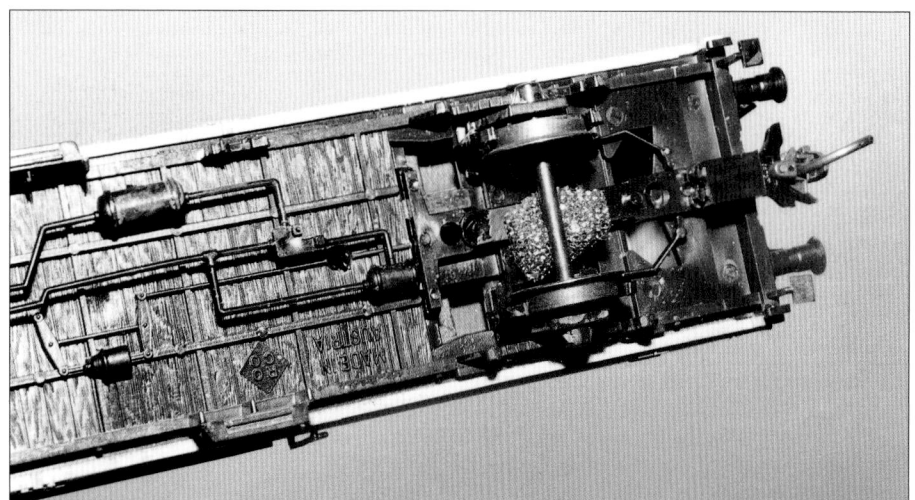

Left: **The method of 'damping down' free-running European models by a wedge of foam plastic between the axle and the underframe. Note also the Kadee No 18 coupler fitted in the NEM 362 coupler mount, and the slot of the close-coupling mechanism.**

Lower left: **Various hand uncoupling aids. Far left: a wood 'lifter' for tension-lock uncoupling. Bottom to top: 'shunting pole' with hook for scale three-link couplers; Accumate 'twister' for separating magnetic couplers; portable 'straddle magnet' (made in the USA) for uncoupling magnetics anywhere away from magnets in the track; plastic coffee stirrer; lolly stick cut to a point.**

Lower right: **A hand uncoupling aid in use. In this case the lolly stick cut to a point is used vertically, inserted and twisted, to separate freight cars fitted with horn-hook couplers.**

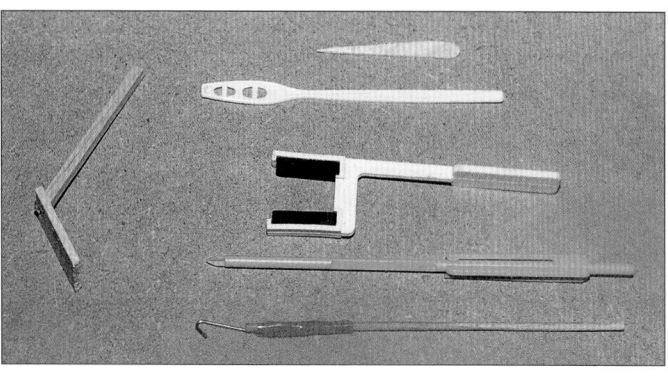

CHAPTER 4

COMPACT LAYOUT PLANNING

Unless you are a 'collector' pure and simple, who only buys models to store or display, the main objective for most of us in the model railway hobby is to build and operate a realistic layout. Seeing fine layouts at shows or reading about them in magazines captures our imagination. Beginners want to build a layout of their own and those who already have a layout are tempted to build something better.

Layout planning or building, however, has problems of its own. First of all, if you read a selection of model magazines you'll find tempting or attractive layout ideas in every issue. Sometimes just as you settle on one pleasing plan, you pick up another magazine and see an even better idea. It is possible to become so dazzled and confused, you end up doing nothing at all!

Most of us run into another problem at this stage and that is lack of space for the layout idea we really like. That's another reason a lot of modellers give for not getting started at all.

But I've encountered other factors that most of us experience. In no particular order these are:

1. Over-ambition. You have room, maybe, for a very big layout. These look great when you see them at model shows, but most layouts of this sort are team or club efforts utilising the skills and resources of several modellers. Big layouts need complex wiring, complex operating and a lot of detailed planning.
2. Time. This spins off from the above. The bigger the layout the longer it takes to build and get something running. Your enthusiasm may well run out before the first train runs.
3. Skill — or lack of it. Big layouts need lots of expertise to be successful — which is why they are usually team efforts.
4. Money. The bigger your project the more it will cost. If your budget is tight it's better to think small, and get something running you can afford.
5. Knowledge. You need to know the

subject area reasonably well to make a success of any given project.

You can gain the knowledge, or plug gaps in it, by checking out the appropriate references (see Chapter 10 for more on this). Knowledge is closely related to your personal enthusiasm, of course. Most hobbyists have some sort of keen railway interest when they start. You may be a devoted fan of the Great Western Railway, to take a simple example. You have some books on aspects of the GWR, you build up a familiarity with the subject, and not surprisingly you gravitate to modelling the GWR as well, so you look for a GWR-style layout as a project. My childhood was spent in Southern Railway territory so I've always had an enthusiasm for the SR and LBSCR, etc.

But I also model American, French and German railways and I got into these areas by visiting the countries concerned, seeing the railways in action, and quickly studying the subject areas and buying the models. Quite a lot of modellers will tell similar tales.

The object of these comments is to suggest it is best to focus on your own knowledge and interests before you buy the models.

Quite frequently I get letters from novice modellers saying something like: 'I have just bought a nice model of an American locomotive called an "F7". Can you tell me all about it, and how American railways operate?' This is a tall order that can't be answered in a short reply, other than to suggest you research it yourself first!

KEEPING IT COMPACT

For all the above reasons I have deliberately used the word 'compact' in this section of the book and avoided suggesting you model huge layouts, unless, of course, you join a club and get involved in one of their team efforts.

The modern home usually has small rooms, many of us have little space in which to set up layouts — quite literally on the kitchen table in my case! — and there are so many other demands on modern living that smallish layouts which do not involve too much time, space or money in the building will suit most people best.

How 'compact' is 'compact'? Well it can be as small as you want to make it. As it happens, the two most recent layouts I have built as these words are written are extremely simple, one with only one turnout (point), and they are no

Right: **This simple but effective 00 gauge layout built by the author, only 4ft by 1ft in size, featured two levels and a dummy wagon lift between upper and lower levels, based on the small yards in East London in the steam age. The LNER open-cab 'J55' on the upper level is converted from the Hornby 'J52'.**

Left: Keeping it simple is good advice for a first scenic layout. Here is a typical GWR halt, easy to reproduce effectively in miniature. The classic 'pagoda roof' shelter is available in kit form, with the embankment behind and the footpath easy to depict scenically.

Lower left: Even simpler would be this very basic halt, just long enough for a single diesel railcar or a push-pull train auto-trailer. Again a simple kit is available (Wills in 4mm scale) of a similar type, but it would not be difficult to build from scratch either, using this photograph as a guide.

building a good, large layout, but there must be an equal number of enthusiasts who embark on a layout project — buying the track, points and stock is the easy bit — and sooner or later run into some of the problems that most of us encounter at some time in our involvement with the hobby.

As you proceed, you can run into any number of snags, discovering, amongst other things, that even laying flexible track is not as easy as it looks; ballasting can be a lot messier than you thought; nobody warned you how much wiring might be needed to make a really complex station layout work; and your scenic efforts don't quite match the fineness of the detail you see in published articles.

Some people don't even get far enough to discover their limitations at scenic modelling, for they give up, baffled by the complexity of it all, long before track laying is finished. Either they leave the layout part finished, or they dismantle it while they think again... and they go back to reading about other layouts and thinking that they'll have another go some day!

It seems likely that a lot of potential enthusiasts who would like to get started, fail to make much progress for some or all of the reasons listed above. Either they have a go and get discouraged by the complication, or else they make no progress because it all seems so forbidding. 'Start with something simple' is a frequent exhortation to beginners, but it might also apply to modellers who may consider themselves to be some way on from being a novice. But how 'simple' is 'simple'?

At its simplest, a layout could be a metre or so of plain track, fully ballasted and developed scenically on each side; a slightly more complicated version might have a siding added, but the operating limitations of any scheme like this are severe. You can't do much more than run a locomotive and rolling

more than 4ft long in HO or OO scale. Yet they give great — though simple — operating pleasure because the context of each is right. Both are drawn and illustrated here — one a two-siding segment depicting lines serving industry, the other an inner-city freight yard, 'Small Street' or 'Kleinhof' — but each is a pleasant and relaxing layout to use for gently running and shunting at the end of a busy day, so for me they meet the criterion of making the model railway hobby a nice diversion from the cares of everyday life.

Most small layouts are rather bigger than these two 'tiddlers', however, and some suggestions for slightly more ambitious schemes, again based on real life originals, are given here. You can follow these as they are presented, or develop your own variations. One simple tip for making

your own layout look different from somebody else's published plan is to flip it to a mirror image. I've done this a few times and nobody seems to notice it is essentially a copy of a well-known scheme.

A FEW SMALL IDEAS
There is a lot to be said, as I've suggested above, for not being too ambitious for a first serious project. Keeping it simple makes for success in track laying, operating and even scenic development, especially if you do not profess to be an expert, but would like a prototypically correct layout. With this in mind, let's look at one way of getting started.

Clearly, everybody has individual levels of previous experience and modelling skill, and many modellers who think big have no great problems in

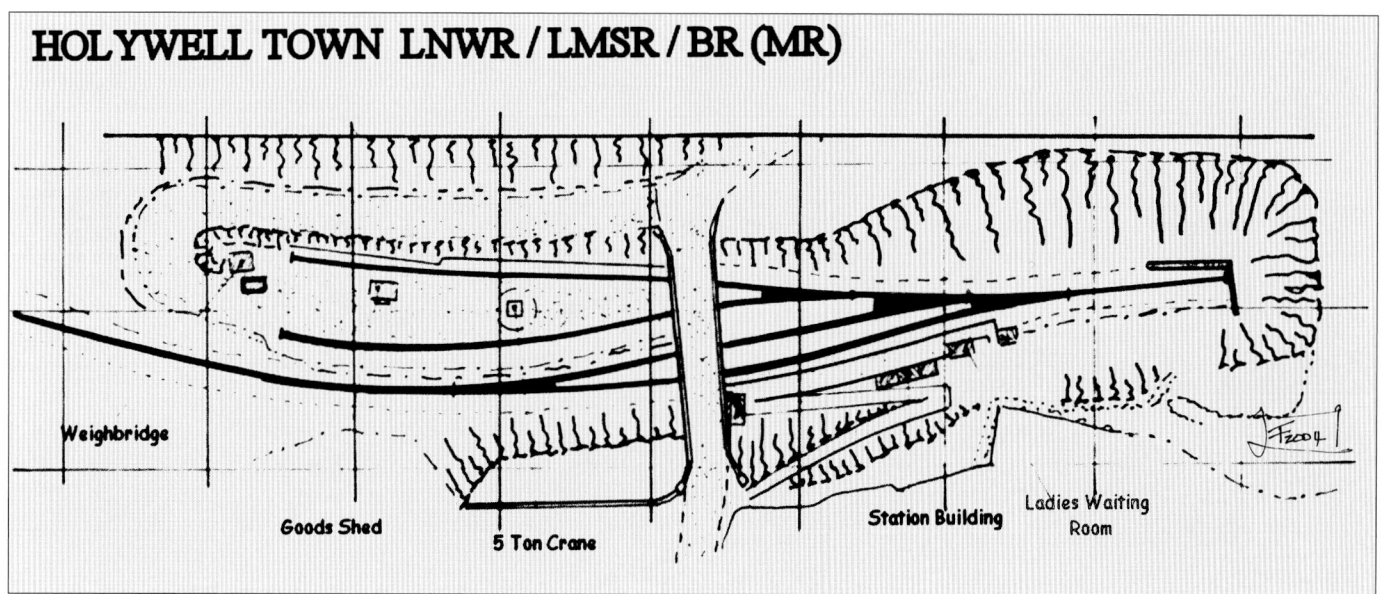

HOLYWELL TOWN LNWR / LMSR / BR (MR)

Weighbridge

Goods Shed

5 Ton Crane

Station Building

Ladies Waiting Room

Above: **A classic branch line terminus so small it can be modelled closely to scale is Holywell Town. Other small prototypes include Ashburton and Hemyock.** *Drawing by Jack Trollope*

stock up and down. It would be no more than a diorama, in effect, and few of us would consider it to be a working layout which would sustain much interest beyond the scenic work.

So consider this: what is the most basic requirement you would want from an operating layout? Essentially, most of us would want to replicate real railway operation, even if it is only in its most basic form. Assuming that there is only room to model a small part of a railway system, the starting point is clearly a station and/or yard where traffic can originate, arrive or be exchanged. We want to see trains coming in and trains departing, and also have some sort of evidence that the location serves a commercial purpose without which, in the full-size version, its construction would not have been justified in the first place.

To give the most flexible operation, it would be useful to be able to switch locomotives and rolling stock around the layout at will, since the more movements that are available, the more interesting will be the layout.

What do we need to fulfil these requirements? A little passenger station is obvious, though not essential, as we shall see later; a run-round loop to enable the locomotive to get to either end of a train is desirable; in addition to this, we could do with at least one siding, better still two, where freight can be handled and exchanged. Two

sidings, at least, are better than one, if only because you can shuffle wagons from one to the other when making up trains, and the more movements you can justify, the more fun and interest you can get from the layout. On top of this it is nice to think that there exists a full-size precedent, or prototype, for your scheme so that you can satisfy yourself, and reassure doubters, that you are not too far removed from reality.

LOCATIONS

Once you start looking for location with these basic operating requirements, you will find plenty of information in published books and magazines, but the quest does not end there. Some of the full-size sites are very spread out and profligate of space because the real railway builders had no space constraints, so a compact version of a scheme is desirable.

One example which comes readily to mind, and which will be well known to well-read modellers because it has been cited many times in the past as an ideal small prototype, is Holywell Town. The station lay at the end of a short branch from the LNWR, later LMSR and BR(LMR), main line between Chester and Rhyl in Flintshire, and did not survive for long after the Beeching Report of 1963 which led to the demise of many branch lines.

The credit for spotting this location very early on as an ideal modelling prototype should probably go to Cyril Freezer, who pointed it out in *Railway Modeller* well over 40 years ago, covering it briefly in a couple of

paragraphs accompanied by a good scale drawing on which the drawing here is based. Cyril also pointed out that it was one of the few prototype stations which could be modelled to full scale if you insisted on doing so; it fits an 8ft length or so in 4mm scale, and a mere 4ft in N.

Take a look at the plan. You will see that it is restricted in area because it fits into a cutting with an overbridge helpfully providing a visual block for scenic purposes. The line also has every indication that it may once have been intended to extend it further inland. That never happened, but it means that the same setting could be modelled as a through station if you prefer that to a terminus.

The actual setting is remarkable for being unremarkable — in other words, it is very conventional, with just a single platform to the station and a couple of sidings that kick back parallel to the run-round loop, thus making a useful space saving for the modeller. There was a goods shed, a weighbridge and scale house, a toilet block in the yard and a 5-ton crane. A path led down from the overbridge, while a service road ran down the other side into the goods yard.

TAKING ADVANTAGE OF SIMPLICITY

Now, many modellers will have seen the Holywell Town plan in the past, and may have read articles suggesting it as the subject for a model, but all too many of us will have dismissed it as being too simple. After all, there is nothing to it, is there? We fancy a

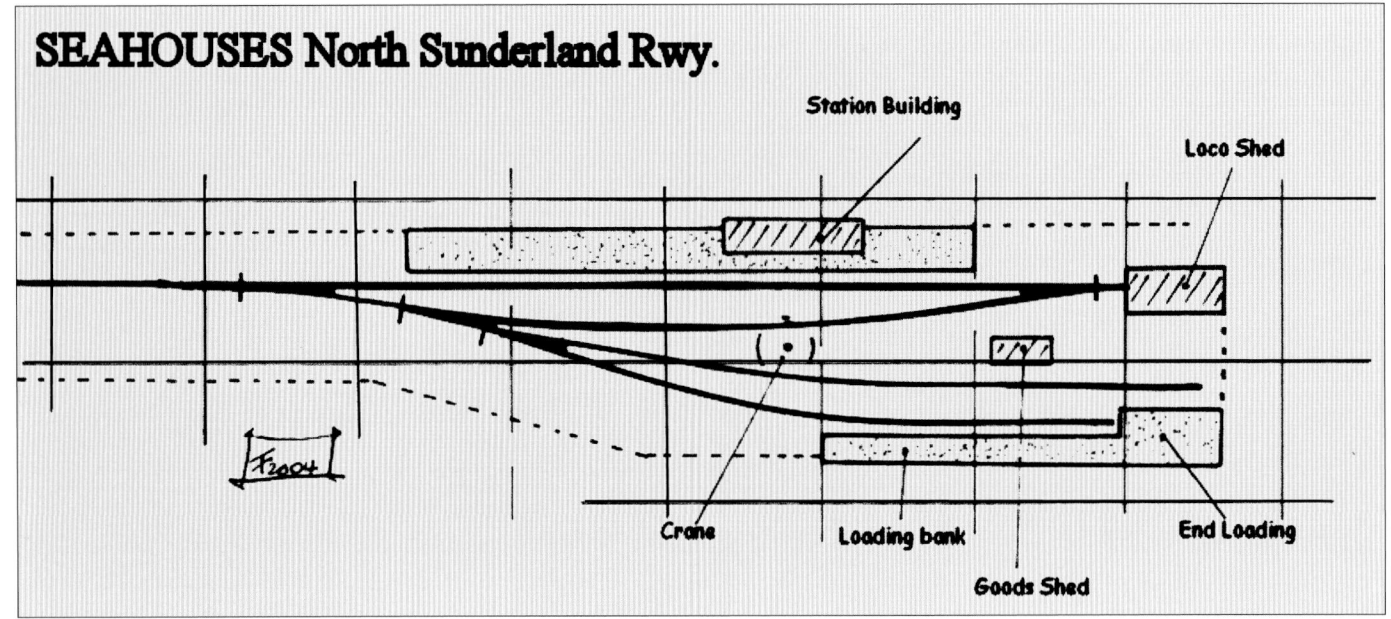

Above: **Another simple and straightforward terminus was Seahouses on the North Sunderland Railway, a classic light railway of the past which even featured a small locomotive shed and had full goods facilities. The dotted line shows the suggested baseboard area. All grids on these plans are at 12in spacing for OO/HO gauges.** *Drawing by Jack Trollope.*

tougher challenge, so we all move on to meatier articles and track plans where ladders of sidings and crossings are much more like our idea of what a layout should really look like.

However, if you suspect that the tougher challenge might turn out to be a bit too tough, take another look at what Holywell offers. Combine that with your idea of what gives you particular pleasure in a layout and ask yourself some questions. Do you like perfect running all the time, with no tedious prodding of locomotives over dodgy pointwork? Do you want a project that doesn't take years to complete? Do you want a modest outlay for track, points and materials? Think how little four points and a few metres of track will cost compared to twelve points and twelve metres of track.

If you're ready to switch to EM, P4, 2mm or any other of the 'fine scale' gauges, and would welcome an easy start, think how much more manageable minimal track requirements will be. So it goes on, for the Holywell Town track layout requires the minimum of everything but offers full branch line operation. You can run passenger trains to and from the fiddle yard (Holywell Junction on the prototype), and you can bring in and

sort out the full range of freight stock. The plan, for example, does not specifically show a coal merchant, but no doubt there was one.

The simplicity extends to layout construction. Agreed, you can do wonderful things with plywood, open-frame baseboards and all the rest, but a simple firm, flat-topped board, maybe with a ply, MDF or Sundeala covering to which you can pin a simple track formation, is still easier than anything else. To many modellers, good running is the first priority, for jerky, uncertain locomotive movement is the greatest enthusiasm killer there is. The Holywell Town track formation is a simple one with the minimum of track joints and the fewest number of points to cause trouble.

If you also want a simple scenic project, the Holywell setting can start with the track laid on a flat top; the scenery of the cutting can be made up on each side from the flat base, making it a very simple proposition, assuming that you want to replicate the setting accurately; the choice is yours in this respect. If you are a fan of the LNWR or the LMSR, you could build it to scale length as an accurate model of the real location, as a couple of 48in by 18in baseboards would form the foundation for the entire section drawn. It would make a fascinating research project as well.

Those not worried about prototype realism can, of course, play about a little. The length could come down to 6ft or so instead of 8ft and still catch the

character of the prototype. If you are unhappy about the name, make whatever changes you prefer, perhaps adding a cattle dock, coal staithes or whatever, and maybe changing the name to a sound-alike such as Honeywell Town. Another variation would be to omit the station, or render it closed to passengers, and add a warehouse or two to operate it as a freight-only branch.

Of course, given the basic track plan, you can develop it as you like to suit any period, setting, company or location that takes your fancy. You could even change countries if you are looking for, say, an American short line setting or a German branch terminus, for you can find simple track formations like this one in almost every country. If you feel very limited in modelling ability but want a layout which looks good scenically, one solution would be to use Ratio, Wills and similar kits exclusively to provide all the structures. The site could look most convincing by using the Ratio provender store and weighbridge in the yard, with the station building from the Ratio kit. The possibilities really are endless.

The important point is that, because of the simplicity of the layout, you can concentrate on getting the track laying and performance perfect, so that all locomotives run slowly and faultlessly. Point control, using whatever method you prefer, will not be too demanding. If you like hands-off uncoupling, using Alex Jackson, Sprat & Winkle, DG or Kadee and other magnetic variations

Right: **A very interesting station plan to fit an awkward space was Bratton Fleming on the Lynton & Barnstaple narrow gauge line. The 'spread' and curvature can be changed to suit a 'tighter' site. For an example of how it can be adapted, see the plan on page 34.**
Drawing by Jack Trollope

(see Chapter 3), you once again have the minimum requirements when placing magnets and so on. What is very certain is that if you succeed in making a simple layout that works very well, it will give you far more pleasure than an extremely elaborate layout which fails to live up to expectations in terms of its operating quality or its appearance, or both.

VARIATIONS ON THE THEME

Clearly, in taking up this Holywell Town idea, you can vary it in several ways to make it appear completely different without altering the amount of track needed in any way.

Take a look at the second plan (left), which shows Seahouses, terminus of the North Sunderland Railway, a light railway which was one of the few outside Colonel Stephens' empire. A book on the line is available from Oakwood Press if you want to investigate it further. As the plan shows, it is a similar terminus to Holywell Town but simpler, in that the surrounding landscape is flatter and no cutting is involved. The two goods sidings this time run in the opposite direction to Holywell, and there is an added attraction in the form of a small locomotive shed occupying the headshunt at the end of the line. You could fit this layout easily into a 6ft space in 4mm or 4ft in N, with proportionately modest lengths in larger scales.

Moving on to the third plan, you will see how the same idea was fitted on to a curve at Bratton Fleming, on the Lynton & Barnstaple Railway. The diagram shows the station as built; it was altered later. Though Bratton Fleming was a through station, you could put a buffer stop at either end if you want to adapt the scheme as a terminus; in the same way, the Seahouses plan could become a through station if the locomotive shed were moved. Bratton Fleming suggests how to use a corner site for this small layout if you are in the position of having to fit the layout into a corner, if you are going to have any layout at all.

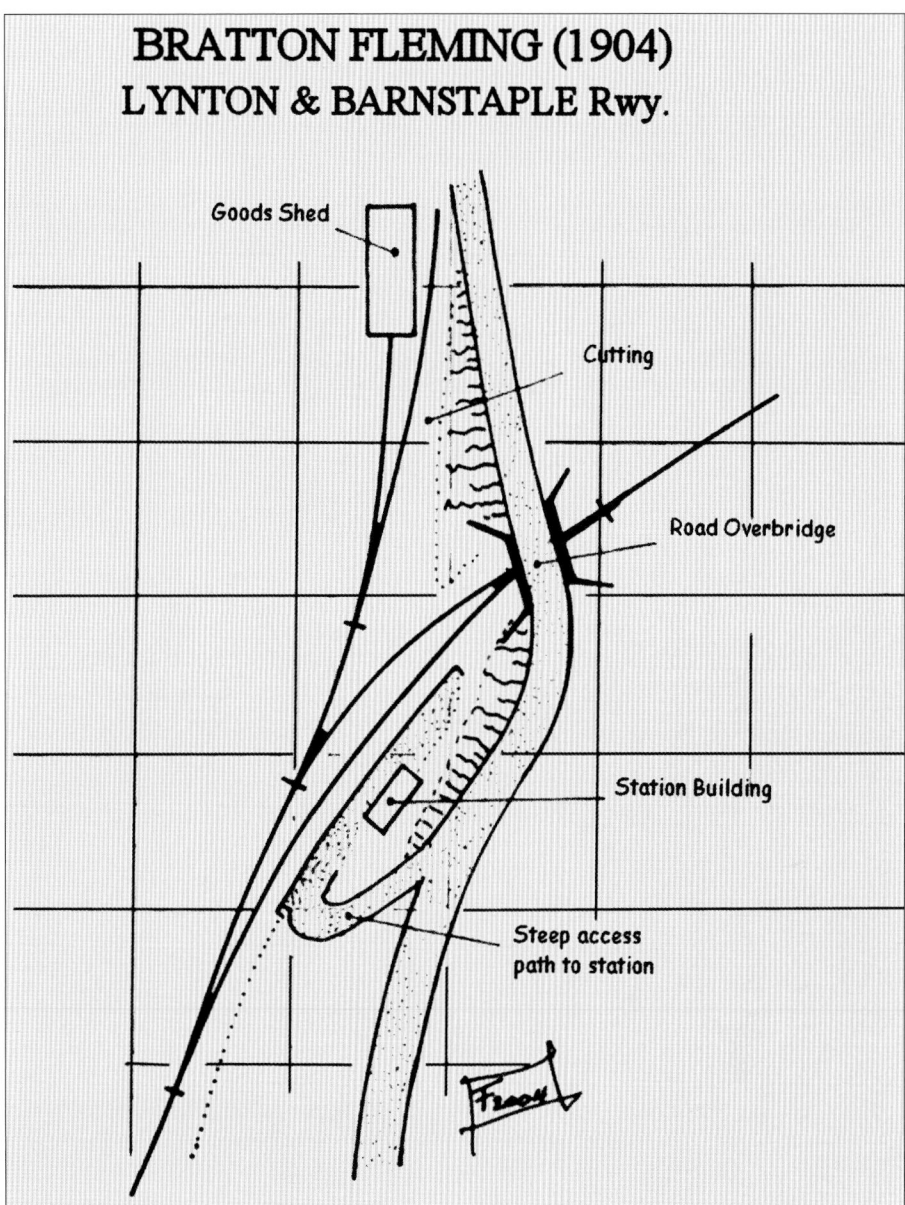

BRATTON FLEMING (1904) LYNTON & BARNSTAPLE Rwy.

Goods Shed

Cutting

Road Overbridge

Station Building

Steep access path to station

TO THE ULTIMATE

Finally, to show how the Holywell Town idea can be adapted even further — and even compressed a little more — look at the fourth plan (on page 30), a clever bit of planning by Richard Crockett for his O gauge layout 'Blakeney', which was featured in *Model Railway Constructor* for May 1986.

This was a mythical 'might have been' branch terminus on the Midland & Great Northern Railway. It has the Holywell Town track plan, with the sidings reversed as at Seahouses, but space has been saved by the use of the 3-way point leading to the sidings. The dodge could be used in smaller scales, and saves almost a whole point length. 'Blakeney' fits comfortably into a length of only 2m, very modest for O gauge

and suggesting that the equivalent figure in 4mm might easily be about 6ft. Once you go entirely freelance, of course, you can pack in all the features you like, as Richard did, to make this modest little layout idea not only very simple but also very busy!

EVEN MORE COMPACT

The foregoing train of thought is given in some detail to show how what I would call a 'conventional' small layout can be planned and built. But you can go simpler than that and make what I have previously called a 'twig off a branch' layout or a 'field of view' layout. The 'Tuning Fork' layout drawn overleaf, simple as it is, comes into both these categories. It is just a segment, clearly, of a much more

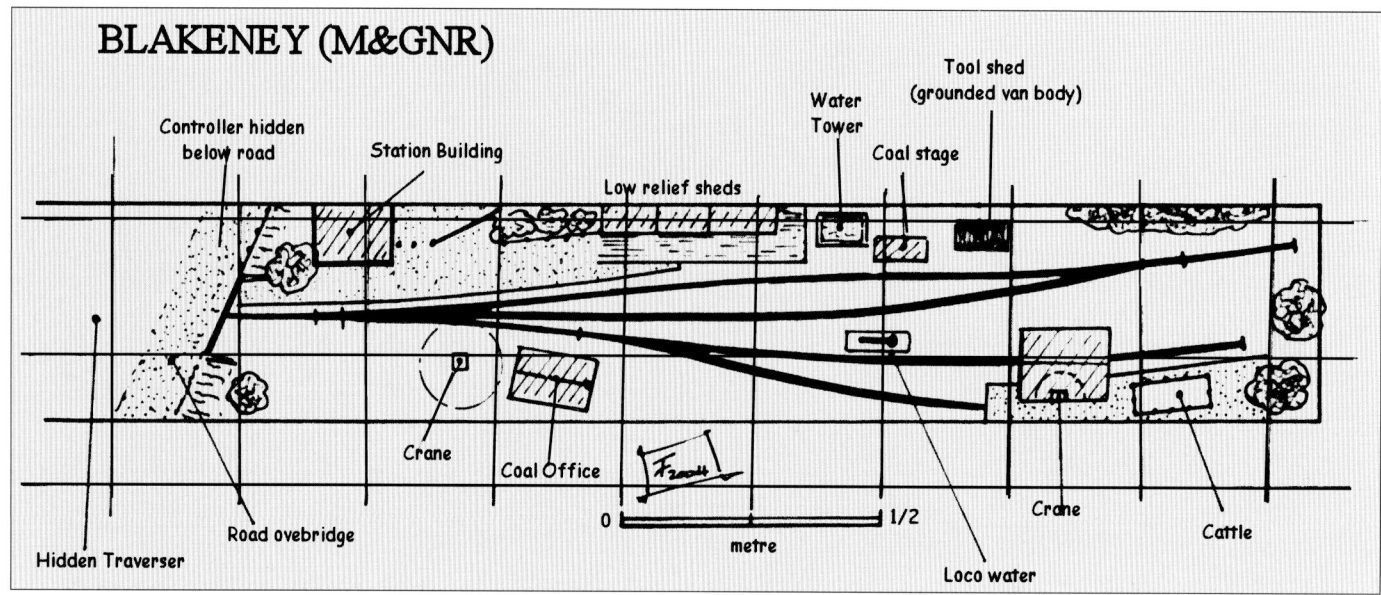

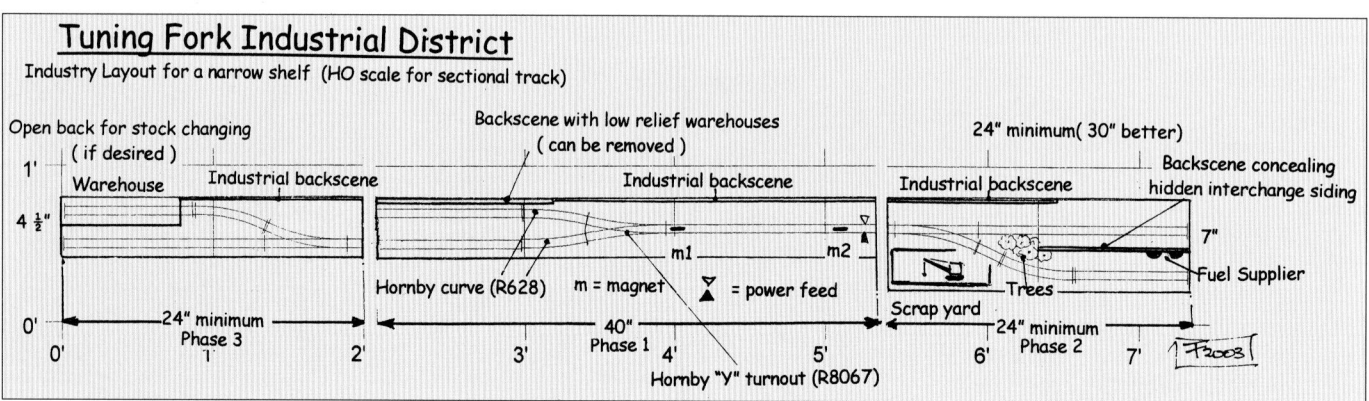

Top: The plan for Blakeney, a very compact O gauge branch terminus built by Richard Crockett which saves length by the use of a three-way point. The grid is at 25cm spacing for O gauge, but can be adapted to smaller scales. *Drawing by Jack Trollope*

Above: Plan for the 'Tuning Fork' industrial layout built by the author, and made in three modules as shown over a period of time. Phase 1 stands alone as a very simple shunting/switching layout using magnetic coupling. *Drawing by Jack Trollope*

Left: Phase 1 of the 'Tuning Fork' in action in German mode with a DB Class 333 (Köf 3) Kleinlok doing the shunting. The low relief warehouse backscene can be set either side and changed for American or British backscenes, as desired.

complex series of spurs serving local industries. You could build further modules on to it to make up more of the 'freight branch' system and I did, indeed, do that with another segment with further sidings (see the plan). But the basic 'Tuning Fork' stands alone, too, all 4ft of it, and I like to think of it as a 'field of view' layout as it encompasses just about the extent you can see in real life if you stand trackside

and watch shunting operations. This is emphasised on the layout if you operate it at eye level up on a high shelf.

You see the locomotive shuffling the rolling stock really close up and it looks uncannily realistic provided you have a nice slow running locomotive and sure-footed rolling stock (no wobbly wheels!). It always convinces me that you do not need a large layout to enjoy realistic modelling.

Small 'field of view' layouts are becoming popular these days, and American modeller Carl Arendt had christened these Micro Layouts — definition 4ft x 1ft or less, or the equivalent in area. Some very intriguing layouts have resulted and are shown (well over 200) on Carl's website carlarendt.com and in a couple of layout books he has published.

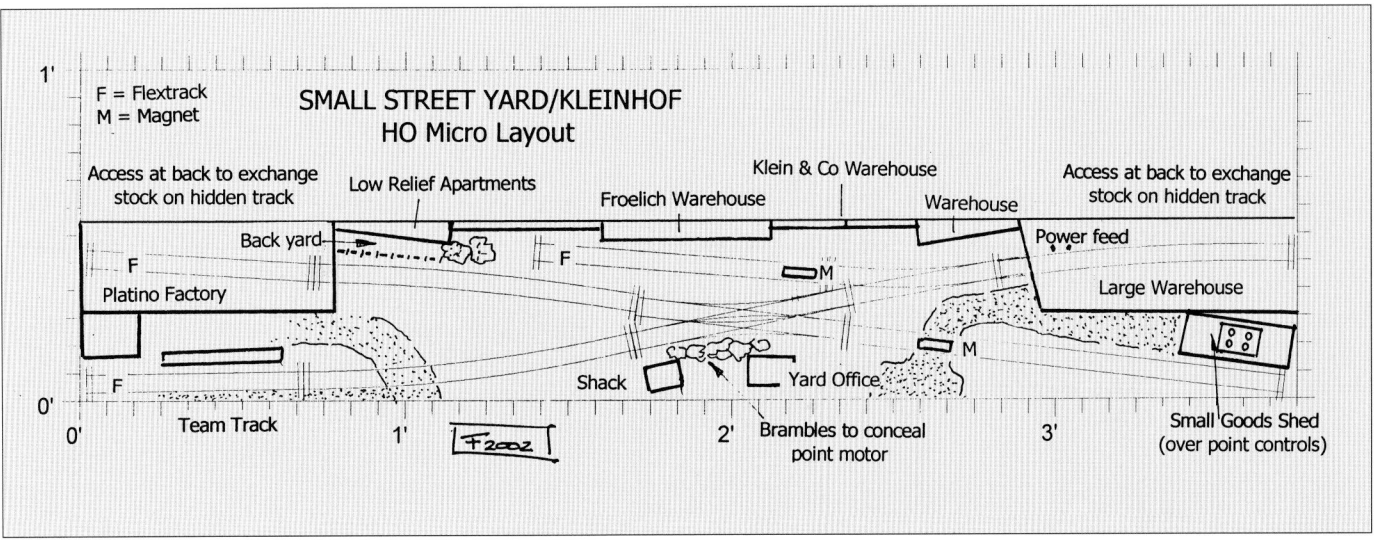

SMALL STREET YARD/KLEINHOF
HO Micro Layout

Above: **You can get an HO/OO layout in only a metre (3ft 3in) of length if you think small enough, as on the author's 'Small Street Yard' ('Kleinhof' in its German form). The warehouses each end have open backs to change over the stock. A Fleischmann double slip in the centre allows the space saving.** *Drawing by Jack Trollope*

Right: **'Small Street Yard' in action. The smooth running Atlas Alco S4 is doing the switching here. This is the right hand end of the layout drawn above.**

One result of 'Micro' thinking (or 'field of view' layouts if you like) is the disappearance of the conventional fiddle yard or hidden siding because there is no room for them. On one of my Micro layouts, 'Small Street Yard' (which is less than 4ft long in HO) I use what I call a 'virtual fiddle yard'. The tracks disappear into warehouses at each end of the layout — each just long enough for a locomotive and freight car. Then the freight car (or even the loco) can be craftily switched over by hand from behind the scenery and the locomotive (or a different loco) runs back into view hauling a different freight car, supposedly from sidings in the wide world beyond the layout. The plan and photos here show the idea and should scotch any idea you might have that an HO or OO operating layout could not possibly be fitted into less than 4ft of length! As a bonus I have made the setting neutral enough for the layout to be used in either American or German mode. The yard office is reversible, with German name (Kleinhof) and German notices on one side and American name (Small Street Yard) and signs on the other. The warehouse names are reversible, too. I could go further. The layout looks equally plausible with a Pug, a Terrier

or a BR Class 08 diesel shunter at work so this little layout has loads of potential. More examples of Micro layouts are shown here in photos and track plans.

FREIGHT BRANCHES
One limitation on modelling a conventional branch line terminus like Holywell Town, or most others, is that in real life service was sporadic. Modellers usually ignore this and run a busy service, but in real life I've only come across one country branch line, Cadolzburg in Germany, where the timetable is as busy as on most model branches. This line has a half-hourly train service, today with DMUs, and a 15-minute service at rush hours! Until recent years it had a daily freight service too. But the Cadolzburg branch happens to be a rural adjunct on the outskirts of the Fürth and Nürnberg conurbation and it carries lots of commuters, students and shoppers to and from these cities.

If you want to operate trains with an easier conscience and constant movement, then a freight branch is worth thinking about. The 'Tuning Fork' and Small Street Yards already mentioned are freight branches, of course, but you can go bigger than that if you have, say, 8ft of length or more available in OO or HO (or equivalents in other scales).

Shown on page 32 is a plan I designed some years ago for a typical British industrial or freight branch of the sort that could be seen before about 1950 in or around many cities. It is generic, of course, but has features you might have seen in places like Brentford Dock (GWR), Salford Docks (LMS) or East London.

Given the basic track plan I've presented, there are several ways in which you could develop it in the scenic and structural senses. I've indicated a few ideas, but the sorts of industries served or the style of architecture to be seen is up to your personal preference.

CANAL SIDE SIDINGS

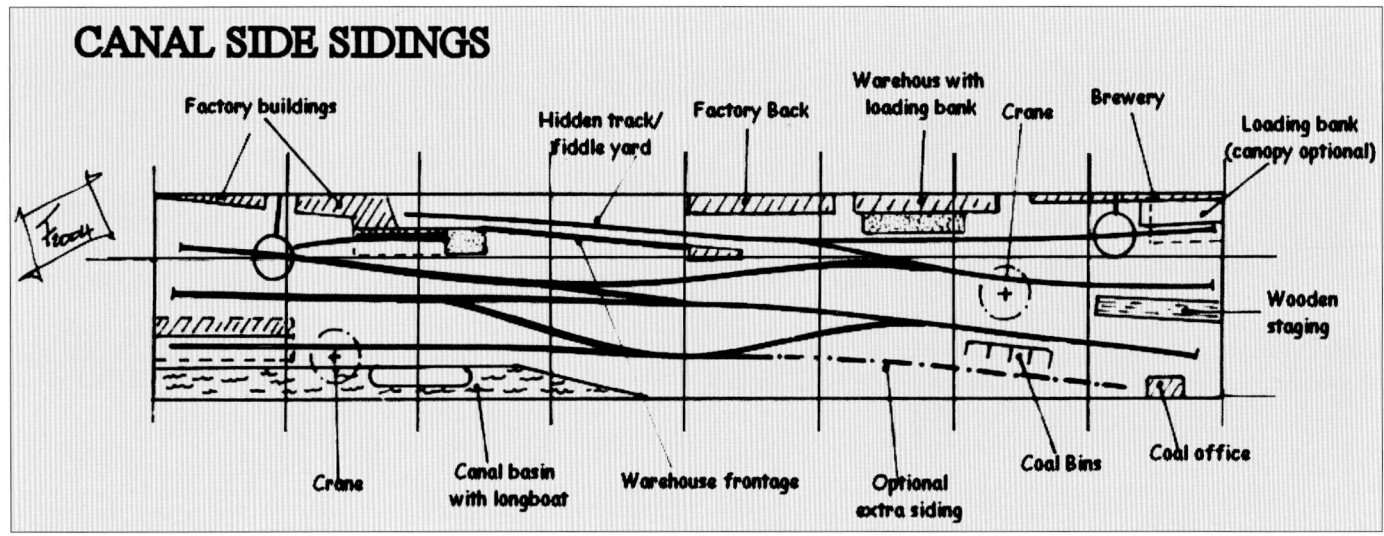

Above: **Lots of shunting and movement is possible on this layout, 8ft long in 00 or HO, with scope for atmospheric industrial scenery and structures. The wagon turntables marked are cosmetic dummies which could be omitted if desired.** *Drawing by Jack Trollope*

Left: **Real life industrial settings could be quite simple, yet atmospheric, as on this loading wharf with crane, fence and old metal advertising signs photographed in the 1970s at Ironbridge.**

In a Scottish setting, for example, you might make most structures of imposing, if grimy, stone, whereas a London or Midlands setting might be more aptly represented using smoky brick in Victorian style. Almost any sort of commercial enterprise or industry could be selected to your choice, among them being glass and bottle making, brewing, soft drinks, mills of all sorts, bonded goods (in bonded warehouses), nail and screw-making, light or heavy engineering, freight forwarding and any sort of canal-rail interchange which could include the shipment of coal, sand, aggregates, straw, steel, potatoes and much else.

An attractive, though entirely optional, feature in connection with this canal interchange could be a covered loading shed spanning both siding and canal, so that canal boats are loaded and unloaded under cover. This treatment has the added advantage that you don't have to be too precise about the lifting appliances and methods used — there was often an overhead hoist working along a beam underneath the roof in such buildings — or, if it comes to that, exactly what the goods are which are being transhipped. Another alternative might be to represent the small chutes sometimes seen which were used to discharge wagons directly into barges, either by gravity or by hand shovelling, methods which could be used for coal, sand and similar robust materials.

The facilities I've marked on the plan are only suggestions. The coal merchant, for example gives a good excuse for bringing your favourite private owner wagons into use, and the wood-loading stage behind it gives you an excuse for all sorts of general transhipments such as case oil or crates of vegetables from a van pushed up to the buffer stops. If you choose not to install a covered loading shed over the canal basin, then a narrow office store or stable block would be useful as a vision blocker for the headshunt behind, where a locomotive could lurk out of sight while a second locomotive shunted elsewhere on the layout. Not only that, but people always forget to model things like stables, obviously preferring to suggest that horses can exist outside permanently.

To keep things simple, I've suggested just a single long siding as a fiddle yard behind the warehouse scenic flat. I know that more complex arrangements are often postulated, but as you'll only be handling small locomotives and trains of two or three wagons at a time, this single long siding should be ample for handling stock either coming out of the yard or being taken into it.

There's much scope for little cameos to set the scene and suggest a lot of activity, although you too could be fiendishly clever by making a working wagon turntable: an alternative would be cosmetic dummy tables, using a base card or thin veneer 'planking'. The spurs which would go off at right angles could have dummy vans in them, built using low-relief techniques — one half end of a wagon glued inside a doorway would represent the whole vehicle, and you could equip two doorways with one kit. The capstans and hawsers which would be used to move the prototype can be modelled cosmetically too. In a like vein, the kickback stub siding off the left-hand wagon turntable gives you a golden chance to highlight activities around loading and unloading wagons.

One or two vans and/or wagons here could be modelled with their doors open, with men loading sacks, drums, crates and what have you, and ramps in open van doorways providing routes for other figures using sack barrows moving in and out of vehicles. The vans and wagons involved never move, keeping the cameos in position and providing an excellent employment for any vehicles you have which run badly or not at all. The fact that these vehicles never move rarely registers with viewers, who are much more impressed by the fact that miniature vans or wagons are actually in the process of being loaded and unloaded, a sight rarely seen on layouts where there is much movement of rolling stock but little evidence of cargoes actually being handled!

If you model an end loading bay in this area, you might consider having a lorry or trailer backed up to it, also in the process of being loaded, to emphasise that road-rail interchange does take place. If you do, make sure that you get a good example of a suitable vehicle, such as those which EFE and Lledo offer in such abundance. You can scatter a few more vehicles around the yard (horse-drawn if your setting is more historic). With all these vehicles dotted about, don't forget to include some crossings where they can cross tracks! Another option, in fact, is to pave in some of the track areas, as was done on the prototype, so that road vehicles can get about easily and can also draw up to other loading and unloading points, maybe alongside railway wagons and vans.

OTHER COUNTRIES

While canal side sidings will satisfy those nostalgic for the steam age, you can make the modern equivalents, and I give plans for two more examples here.

The first plan, on page 34, I've called Little Enterprise Rail Park, and it is based on the real life Enterprise Rail Park at Effingham, Illinois. In the USA rail freight is still big business and some modern 'tin shed' industrial estates are rail connected and are still served by sidings in the way once seen in Britain (eg. Trafford Park or Slough Estates Railway). On the plan I've put in some of the rail-served customers actually located on the Enterprise Rail Park. The estate has its own diesel switching (shunting) locomotive and its own name, the Effingham Railroad, a common American practice and an ideal prototype for a small layout.

Scenically you will not be hard pressed. Mostly these modern rail-served business parks are flat with spaces between the 'tin sheds' laid with grass or gravel, and service roads neatly done in tarmac. There is a good chance to depict 'big rig' trucks, of course, interchanging with rail at the warehouse doors. Where trees or hedges exist, they are mostly young plantings, often put in as screens or windbreaks. Big mature trees are rarely seen.

Though America is the place to see this sort of industrial railway, they once existed in Britain, and a very tiny operation of this sort still remained at Trafford Park even in 2004. There are examples in France, Germany and other countries, and this basic track plan could be used for almost any setting with structures, signage and industries served altered to match — for example, a winery in a French setting.

Finally here I give a plan for a layout which I built in 1989-90 which is still going strong — Nürnberg-Tragbar. This is only 5ft long in HO and is essentially the well-known Inglenook Sidings plan featured in *First Steps in Railway Modelling* but with an added kickback spur to allow further movement. I based this layout on the little freight yards that were tucked into odd corners around Nürnberg (and, indeed, other German cities) serving local areas and customers. Most of them have disappeared since the German railways were 'rationalised' in the 1990s, but a few remain. With endless shunting and exchanging of wagons possible, this is a very pleasing layout to operate with never a boring moment!

You could, again, set the layout in other countries if you prefer.

CAMEOS

You can add a lot of visual interest to your layout by setting up little scenes that suggest a lot of activity. Since the object of real railways is to carry traffic (eg, passengers, parcels, freight etc) many of these cameos can be centred on this. The example shown here is a forklift truck loading up a Unimog lorry, both of them 'weathered' and with properly posed figures. The other trick shown is to have a wagon or van permanently posed at the end of the siding with loading or unloading going on. A typical scene from yesteryear was the coal wagon being unloaded by men with shovels. Vans can be similarly posed with open doors and cargo being put inside. Trains stop short of these 'cameo wagons', which stay in place. Visitors will not notice that they never move away because their eyes are drawn to the realistic activity that is being simulated.

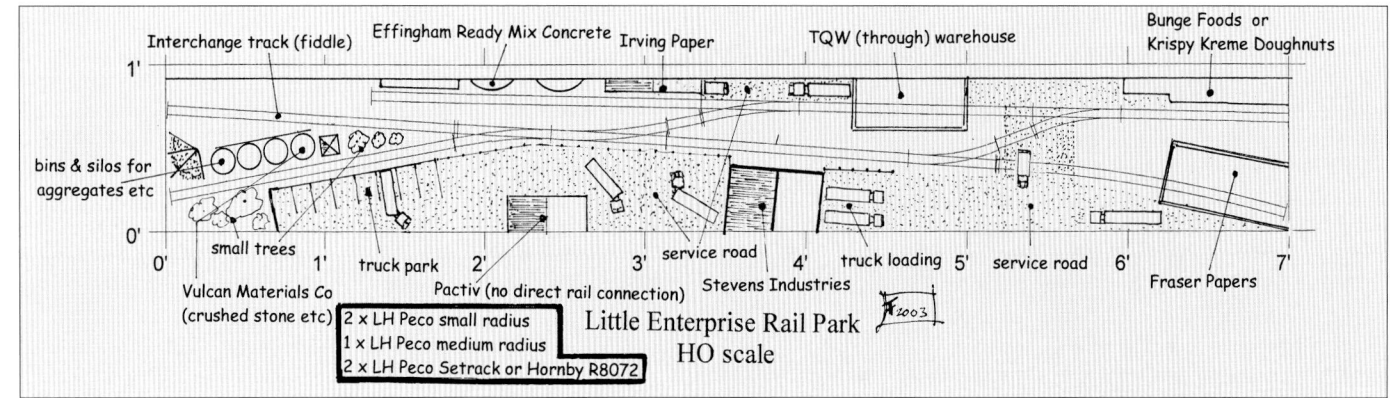

Interchange track (fiddle) — Effingham Ready Mix Concrete — Irving Paper — TQW (through) warehouse — Bunge Foods or Krispy Kreme Doughnuts

bins & silos for aggregates etc — small trees — Vulcan Materials Co (crushed stone etc) — truck park — Pactiv (no direct rail connection) — service road — Stevens Industries — truck loading — service road — Fraser Papers

2 x LH Peco small radius
1 x LH Peco medium radius
2 x LH Peco Setrack or Hornby R8072

Little Enterprise Rail Park
HO scale

Above: **Little Enterprise Rail Park** is based on the real Enterprise Rail Park, served by the Effingham Railroad (which owns just one switcher locomotive) at Effingham, Illinois, USA. This is a modern industrial estate served by rail. Actual companies on the estate are depicted. *Drawing by Jack Trollope*

Below: Very successful as a small layout has been the author's HO Nürnberg-Tragbar, based on the little freight yards which were once abundant in Nürnberg and other big German cities. It allows much shunting and movement in a very small area. *Drawing by Jack Trollope*

Bratton Fleming USA

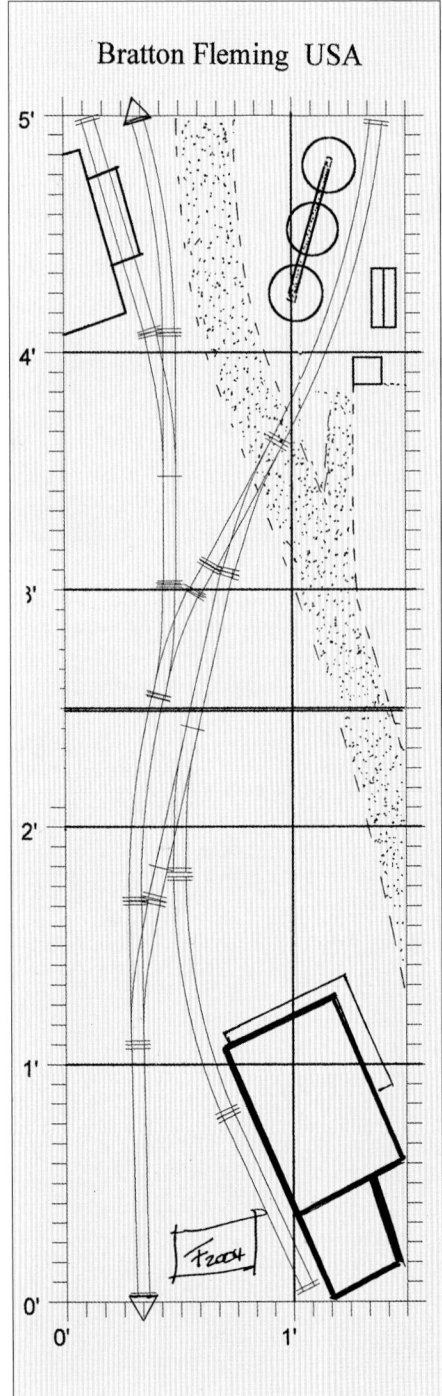

NÜRNBERG - TRAGBAR

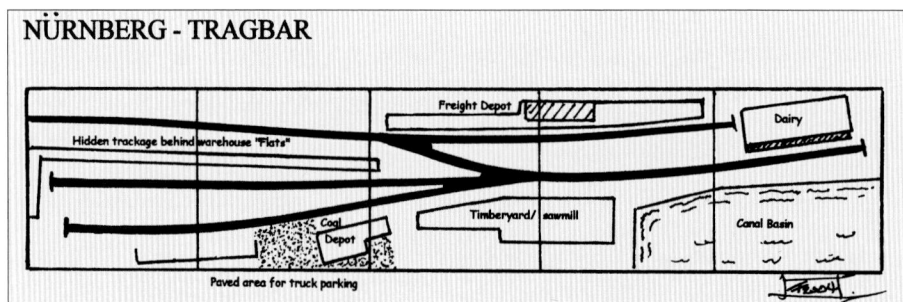

Left: **Here is a prime example of how a published track plan can be adapted to other settings.** The actual Bratton Fleming track layout shown on page 29 has been adapted (and drawn) by Jack Trollope as an American short line with a fuel depot (top right), 'feed and seed' mill (top left) and a factory (bottom right) served by spurs. It can be used as a through line as drawn, or you can put a stop block at either end to depict the end of the line. Exactly the same plan could be used for a French or German 'private line' setting, or it would make a nice setting for a British light railway in the Colonel Stephens style. An option in all versions would be a small passenger station added in the centre between the 2ft and 3ft marks on the left side.

Above: **Shunting in progress on the author's very compact Nürnberg-Tragbar German HO layout.** The sawmill in the foreground acts as a 'vision blocker' from normal low angles of view, partly concealing the movements shown here. The city of Nürnberg is shown on the backscene, again more effectively when viewed from a lower angle than this. The canal basin is just visible lower right, and the Class 360 locomotive (by Roco) is removing vans from the freight depot siding.

In *First Steps in Railway Modelling*, Cyril Freezer gives a very precise description of making baseboards by what might be called 'conventional' means. If you follow these instructions you'll end up with a good firm board and it must be emphasised that a properly braced baseboard is essential for good operation. Old hands at the hobby know this well enough, but there are still beginners who think a plain sheet of plywood or chipboard makes a sufficient base. But without bracing and support it will flex immediately and ruin the track and make running out of the question. Unfortunately some beginners find this out the hard way. So never skimp on baseboards.

LESS CONVENTIONAL METHODS

Having said all this, there are many, myself included, who find the carpentry skills involved in making very precise 'conventional' baseboards rather exacting and time-consuming. Making neat joints and countersinking screws etc is very worthy and not to be decried. And the L-girder system for baseboard framing also described in *First Steps in Railway Modelling* is well proven and ideal for large layouts where extensive landscaping is required.

But if you are making small shelf-type layouts or portable layouts where the baseboard sections would typically be 4ft long and up to 1ft wide (though usually narrower) you can use simpler methods which are quicker, easier and cheaper than the 'conventional' methods. However, if you are building a biggish layout it would be best to stay with the methods described in 'First Steps'. Something like Highfield Yard (in *First Steps in Railway Modelling*) or Tuning Fork (in this book) will fit on a kitchen table, a single bed, across the arms of a chair, on the spurs of a shelving system, on top of a bookcase, or almost anywhere else where you can stand or sit to operate it. And when not in use it is easily stowed away in a cupboard, on top of a wardrobe or against the wall in the corner.

Upper right: **The 19mm square whitewood frame for a 4ft x 1ft layout section using the methods described on this page. All joints are screwed and glued.**

Right: **You can make the light framing to any desired size. This is a 2ft x 1ft section for a corner position. It has been assembled flat on the floor to avoid any 'built-in' warp, and the power drill, screwdriver, screws and white PVA glue used in construction are also shown.**

ALTERNATIVE BASEBOARDS

Portable layouts like this can be light and handy. Recent materials can be utilised to keep the weight down and simplify constructions. The four methods I most commonly use are outlined here.

1. THE LIGHT FRAME METHOD

This actually follows the same pattern described by Cyril Freezer in 'First Steps', producing a rectangular cross-braced frame. But the wood used is the commonly available 19mm square planed whitewood, with a single screw (there is not room for more) and white PVA glue securing each join. Assembly is done on the floor (or garden path) to ensure it stays flat — you don't want a built-in warp!

This results in a light frame. You could use plywood for the top board where the track goes, but I prefer to use the Sundeala Hobbyboard that is quite widely available (Homasote is a similar material in the USA), is light, easily cut to size, and takes track pins very securely. It is simply screwed on to the framing and you are ready to go. Some

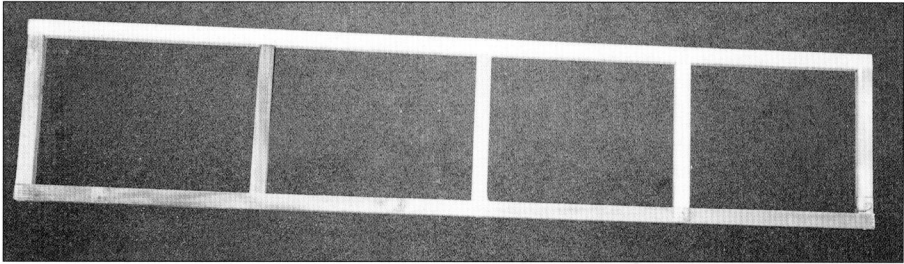

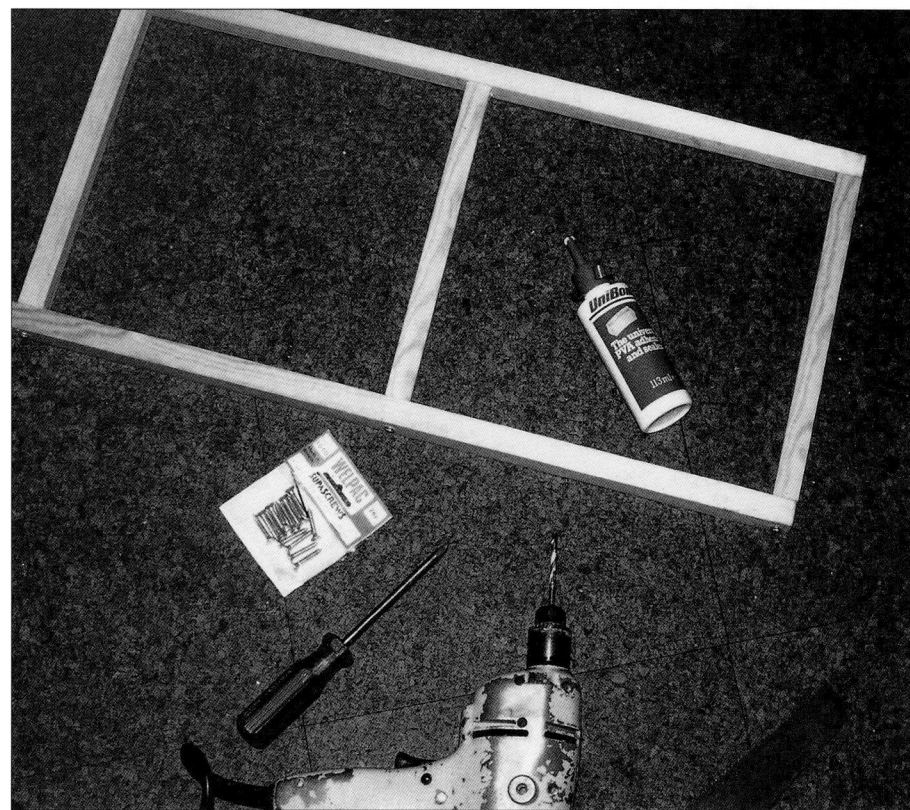

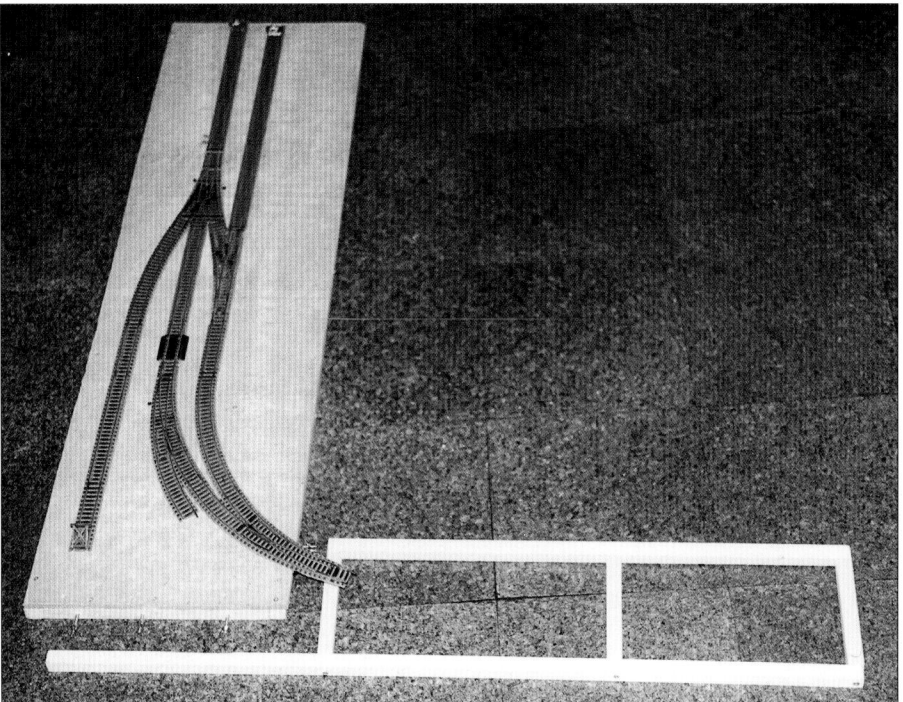

Above: **The modular nature of the light framing method of baseboard construction is shown here. On this L-shaped layout to fit a corner site, the first section has been finished, complete with Sundeala Hobbyboard top and track laid temporarily in place. The next section is assembled as framing and is positioned to show how the sections are joined (by screws through the framing) when the layout is placed in position.**

will say the framing is too light and may flex. But most layouts have a background for the scenery or back scene. This can be from plywood, hardboard or 3mm thick MDF (see below). Once it is screwed into place along the length of the framing it adds enormous strength and rigidity to the unit.

MDF (medium density fibreboard) is a fairly new building trade product which is also good for baseboard surfaces. It is cheap (from DIY shops) and small offcuts suitable for narrow layouts are cheaper still.

MDF comes in 3mm, 6mm, 9mm or 12mm thicknesses (or even thicker) but 12mm or less is suitable for baseboards. It is hard and quite rigid. The 3mm thickness can actually be cut with a sharp Stanley knife, but otherwise it is sawn. It takes track pins nicely if you drill a pilot hole (through the sleeper/tie pin hole) first. With the light frame method you can use the MDF instead of Sundeala or plywood and it works well. I usually use 3mm or 6mm thick MDF for N or HO/OO

layouts, and 6mm or 9mm for larger scales.

There is an important health warning for working with MDF. It is said to be possibly carcinogenic if fibres are inhaled, and when cutting or drilling it you are advised to wear an industrial face mask (sold in DIY stores). Alternatively most DIY shops will cut the MDF sheet to the area you need when you make the purchase.

2. THE CRISS-CROSS METHOD

When making larger area layouts or odd-shaped ones, a framing method I have used with success is what I call (for want of a better name) 'criss-cross framing' because that more or less describes its way of assembly. In this system, instead of fitting the cross-bracing between the longitudinal members, it simply goes across the top.

The dimensional idea of a 12in grid is retained as far as possible, but there is great flexibility possible in both spacing and dimensions to suit particular requirements. In essence the modular approach is still followed, and the illustrations show the assembly of a typical irregular section, a task which took less than one hour including cutting the wood to length.

There are several advantages with criss-cross framing:

1. It's quick to do — just saw all members to length.

2. You can often use 1in or 19mm square wood, so it is lighter.
3. You can actually use a mix of wood sizes — say 1in (25mm) square (or even 19mm square) for the longitudinal and 2in x 1in (50mm x 25mm) for the cross-members — as a general rule use larger wood for bigger modules.
4. You can add extra longitudinal and cross-members at will and vary the grid spacing to suit.
5. You can also add such pieces retrospectively if you change the scenic set-up on the board later on, requiring more support in certain places.
6. Though you have to take the same care to keep the assembly flat — work on a really flat floor — you don't have to worry too much about assembling the cross-members in a regular square grid. The cross-members can be put across at an angle if required.
7. There is no rule about width of cross-members. If a projecting piece is needed, just make cross-members longer as required.

Assembly is by glue and screw. It is quickest to screw down from the top since the whole lot can be laid flat and you can literally move along the grid with a power drill putting in the screw holes with great rapidity. There is a further refinement to this idea, however. This is to put the screws in from the bottom so that if you want to remove or reposition cross-members later on you can do so without disturbing the layout. For example you may want to cut a hole in the baseboard top to build a lake or valley when you get round to altering the scenery. If the screws are put in from underneath a cross-member can actually be moved a few inches to one side and re-positioned if it gets in the way of the hole you wish to cut.

Putting the screws in from underneath takes a little longer, and it requires rather more care to keep the assembly flat, but it can be worth it if you envisage changes later on. The Sundeala or MDF top can also be screwed on from underneath — then it can be moved complete from one frame to another without the need to disturb the track or scenery at all!

Make up your own mind about this. Screwing down from the top is much quicker and easier, but it does mean

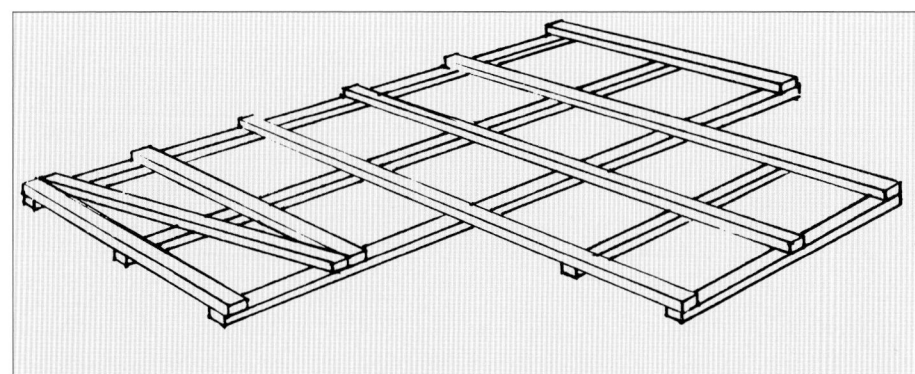

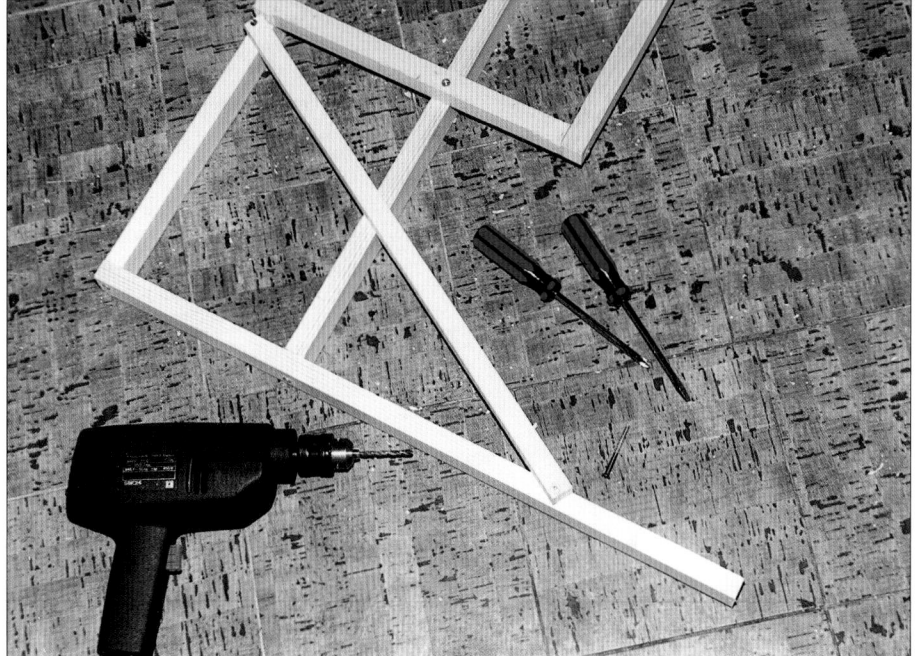

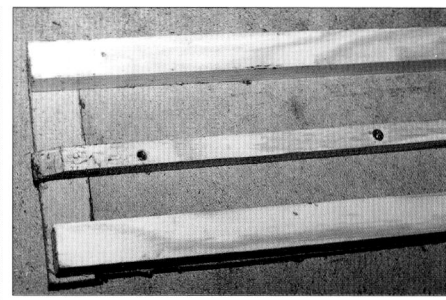

Upper left: **The diagram shows a typical assembly of an irregular shaped baseboard framing using the criss-cross method. You do not need to cover it completely with a flat board. Only the areas carrying the track bed and associated structures (eg goods yard) need to be covered with MDF or plywood strip and the rest can be covered with 'hard shell'-type hilly terrain, making this a good system to use if you want dramatic scenery.**

Lower left: **An irregularly shaped baseboard framing being assembled by the criss-cross method, in this case to fit into and turn a corner.**

Above: **A 'quick fix' MDF baseboard seen from below. A 4ft x 6in length of 6mm MDF is braced merely by a centre' spine', in this case a 12mm x 15mm wood strip, with 19mm x 15mm strips down the outer edges. This is actually the underside of the small 'Tuning Fork' layout shown in this book.**

possible disturbance for the track or scenery if you wish to alter the framework later on.

If you use the criss-cross system, plus modern light methods of scenic work (foam packing and 'hollow-shell' etc), you'll find sections made this way very light. A 4ft x 2ft section can be held and carried easily with one hand.

3. THE MDF QUICK FIX

This is the fastest and simplest way of all to make a baseboard, maybe as little as 20 minutes once you've got the materials together! I must emphasise that it is probably only suitable for narrow shelf-type layouts, though it may work on wider and longer ones too, though so far I've not tried it on other than small layouts. Struck by the inherent rigidity of 6mm, 9mm and 12mm thick MDF as purchased, I thought that narrow strips of it would not really need cross-bracing. So all I do is lay the strip (typically 4ft long by

6-8in wide for a small layout or section) and screw a 'spine' of 12-19mm square planed wood along its centre line. Then on the edges I screw other strips. That's it! But to ensure rigidity, a 3mm MDF or hardboard strip is screwed along the rear edge as a backscene board. I've made three small layouts this way, all narrow (the Tuning Fork in this book was the first) and all have been successful and trouble free. No prizes for woodwork or design, but it's cheap and cheerful and efficient as a small layout baseboard.

4. FOAMCORE

One of the materials you can now use for baseboard construction is actually intended for the display and exhibition trade. It is a polystyrene foam sheet sandwich between smooth clay-coated paper, mostly done in white, but also available in black in some ranges. Brand names include Kappaboard, Centrefoam and Fome-Cor, and I have

used the name 'foamcore' as a generic description. It comes in 5mm and 10mm thickness, sold in art shops mostly in 4ft x 2ft sheets. The 5mm suffices, and the price is modest, no more than any other materials mentioned here. You can sometimes get this free if you keep abreast of the retail trade. Supermarkets and department stores use foamcore for their special offer and promotional signs, and then they throw it away. Make friends with the shopkeeper and get it when it is thrown away!

The top expert of foamcore use is Keith Harcourt whose work inspired me. His Kappaboard Railway was the pioneer layout made from this material in the early 1990s. He has made others since, including the very compact Harris Yard USA layout.

There are several ways of making foamcore layouts, but essentially it can be used to make both the framing and the baseboard surface by cutting and gluing strips of the required size. PVA glue only is required (spirit glue would 'melt' the foamcore).

You need a good craft knife or scalpel with a new sharp blade (and change to another as soon as any bluntness is observed), a good cutting board like a sheet of Formica or close-grain ply, and good quality PVA glue. Optional are ordinary track spikes which I use to

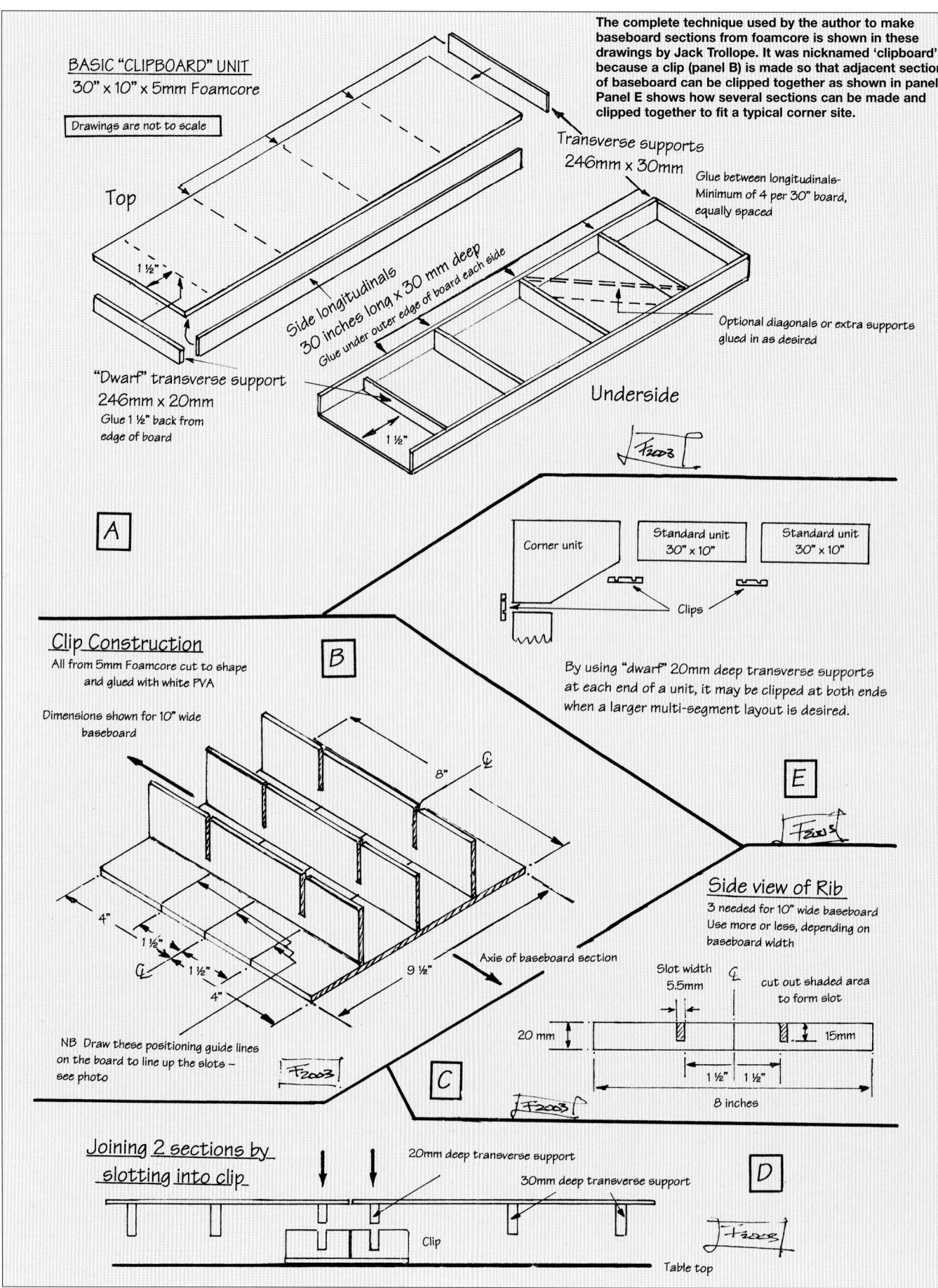

BASIC "CLIPBOARD" UNIT
30" x 10" x 5mm Foamcore

Drawings are not to scale

The complete technique used by the author to make baseboard sections from foamcore is shown in these drawings by Jack Trollope. It was nicknamed 'clipboard' because a clip (panel B) is made so that adjacent sections of baseboard can be clipped together as shown in panel D. Panel E shows how several sections can be made and clipped together to fit a typical corner site.

Top

Transverse supports
246mm x 30mm

Glue between longitudinals-
Minimum of 4 per 30" board,
equally spaced

Side longitudinals
30 inches long x 30 mm deep
Glue under outer edge of board each side

Optional diagonals or extra supports
glued in as desired

"Dwarf" transverse support
246mm x 20mm
Glue 1 ½" back from
edge of board

Underside

1 ½"

A

Corner unit   Standard unit 30" x 10"   Standard unit 30" x 10"

Clips

Clip Construction

All from 5mm Foamcore cut to shape
and glued with white PVA

Dimensions shown for 10" wide
baseboard

B

By using "dwarf" 20mm deep transverse supports
at each end of a unit, it may be clipped at both ends
when a larger multi-segment layout is desired.

8"

E

4"
1 ½"
1 ½"
4"

9 ½"

Axis of baseboard section

Side view of Rib
3 needed for 10" wide baseboard
Use more or less, depending on
baseboard width

Slot width
5.5mm   cut out shaded area
to form slot

20 mm   15mm

1 ½" 1 ½"

NB Draw these positioning guide lines
on the board to line up the slots —
see photo

C

8 inches

Joining 2 sections by
slotting into clip

20mm deep transverse support
30mm deep transverse support

D

Clip

Table top

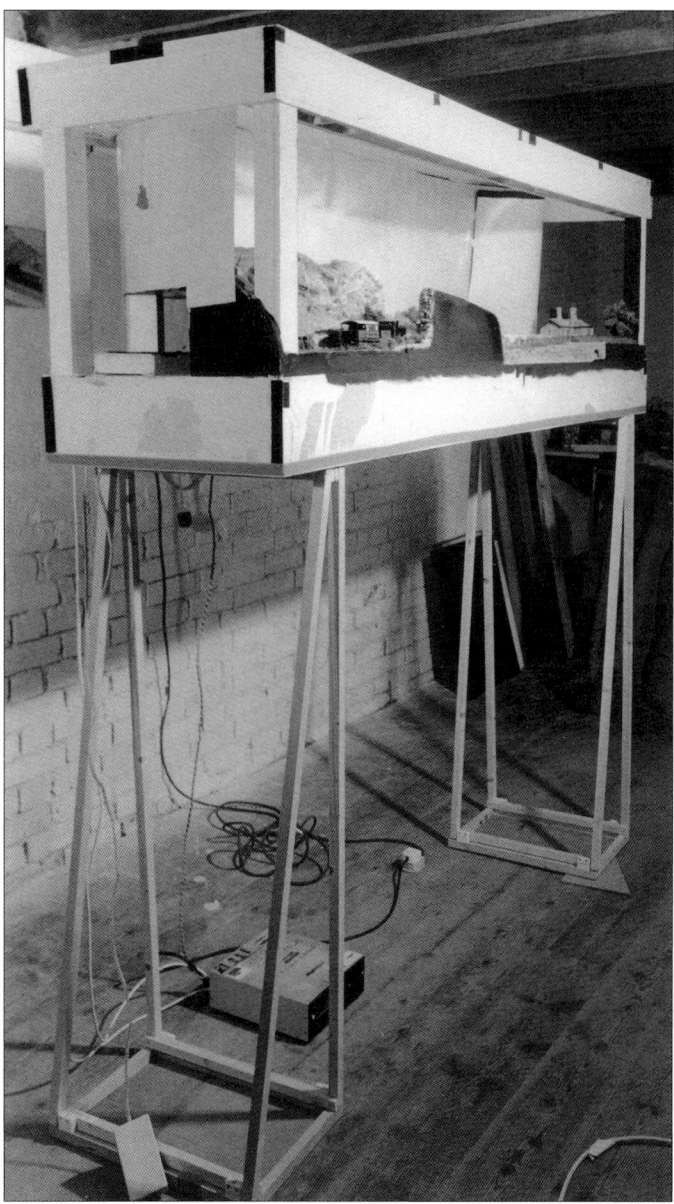

Top left: **The pioneer worker with foamcore type material was Keith Harcourt, seen here assembling his original Kappaboard GWR layout, built entirely from Kappaboard. The posts that support the fascia and lighting unit are being fitted.**

Above left: **Fitting the canopy to the uprights. The lighting unit is under the canopy, and the canopy and the uprights are also made of Kappaboard so the whole assembly is extremely light.**

Above right: **The Kappaboard layout set up on its wooden trestle supports at chest height for display at model shows, a picture that gives useful ideas to anyone wishing to present a layout attractively at a model railway exhibition.**

Lower right: **A black fascia board, also from Kappaboard, is fitted to the front of the layout and canopy, and this is how the viewer sees the layout pleasingly illuminated and displayed at a model railway exhibition. The layout depicts a small GWR terminus, and all the scenery is lightweight, too, being made from styrene packing materials. Keith has also made an American HO layout, Harris Yard, to similar size.**
Photo sequence by Keith Harcourt

THE KAPPA BOARD LAYOUT

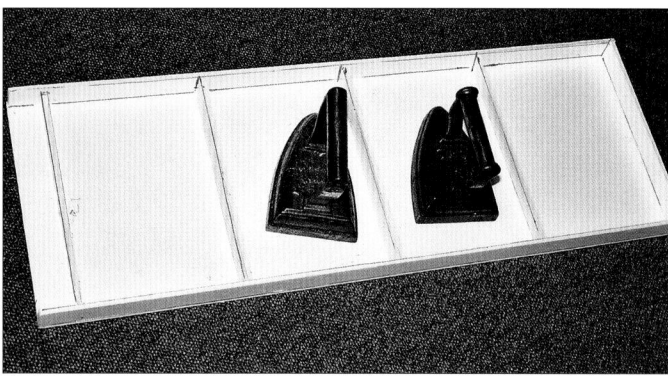

Above: **A foamcore section made as in panel A, page 38, left overnight flat on the floor for the glue to set. The old flat irons are an extra precaution to ensure the foamcore stays absolutely flat while the glue dries.**

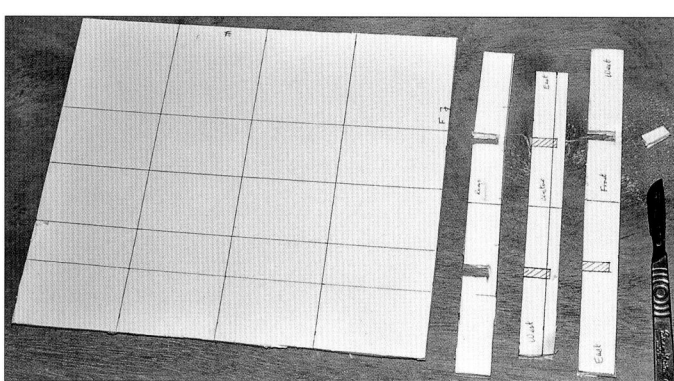

Above: **The foamcore sections cut out to make up the clip, as in panel B on page 38. White PVA glue is used for assembly and the rib positions are marked out.**

Above: **Two foamcore baseboard sections being joined together — the clip is first slotted to the ribs on one section.**

Above: **Baseboard assembly is completed by clipping the other section into place so that you end up with a long rigid board, 5ft long in this case. It is extremely light.**

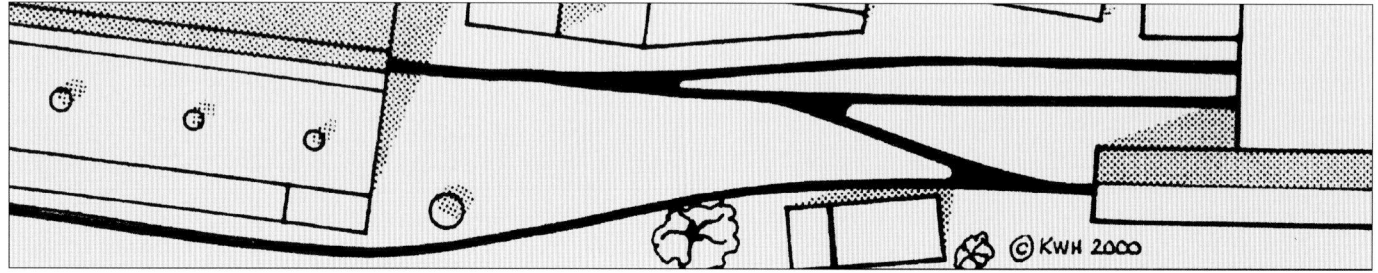

reinforce the corners and main edges while the glue sets. They just assist it, stopping any tendency for the faces to spring apart before the glue sets, and can be pulled out afterwards if desired. Also needed is a good steel rule as a cutting edge, and a ball-pen and 'school ruler' to do the actual measuring. A set square or T-square is a bonus to ensure all lines are square, but I use neither. Assembly must be done on a flat surface, the aforesaid kitchen table being ideal but with newspaper spread to catch any glue spillage. Leave to set overnight on a perfectly flat surface.

The diagram shows the basic assembly system which is strong enough to avoid sagging or distress. But if you want extra support you can add as many extra ribs or diagonals etc as you wish between the main transverse supports. It can all be cut out and glued in place in minutes.

Meanwhile you can see that once the principle is accepted it can be varied to suit your needs. I chose the 10in wide baseboard as it makes maximum economic use of a foamcore sheet, but you can make the shelf-type baseboard wider or narrower as desired.

Even a corner segment or 90 degree (or less) turn is possible so long as the section ends are kept square on. The

Above: **This is the track plan for Harris Yard, an American HO industrial-type layout built by Keith Harcourt (and drawn by him) on a 5ft x 1ft baseboard from Kappaboard in similar style to the construction shown in the pictures above.**

dimensions I worked out are suitable for both HO/OO and N. But if you want deeper sides and more generous 'clip' depth or length, that is up to you. My dimensions offer good economy and minimum use of foamcore. However, if you make a long layout in sections you cannot easily use screws or bolts to join the sections as you would with wood. To remedy this and make a way of joining sections I devised a 'clip', also shown and dimensioned in the

Right: **This baseboard for a small N gauge layout combines two methods. The framing is from wood as shown on page 35, but the top surface is foamcore sheet glued and lightly tacked to the wood framing.**

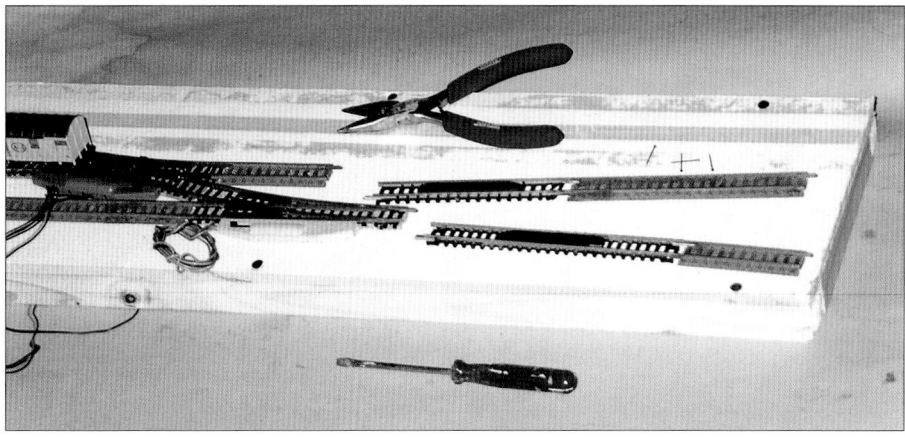

diagram, and also made from foamcore. Adjacent sections can then be slotted together to make a rigid whole.

You will not find this a strain: each module weighs 6.4oz (184g) and the clip weighs 1.4oz, so the whole layout weights less than a jar of jam! It is, however, immensely strong.

A variation on all this is that I combined the use of foamcore with the light frame method already described. I used a sheet of foamcore instead of Sundeala or MDF for the surface. Screws cannot be used, but I secured it with small tacks gently tapped through the foamcore.

OTHER OPTIONS

The four methods of baseboard construction above are those I've used in the past 10 years or more and all have worked well. But that does not exhaust the possibilities. Here is a brief mention of other alternatives.

1. PLYWOOD

This is popular and quite widely used. Typically a 'box' is made of plywood with the back and ends sometimes shaped (with a jigsaw) to give the outline of any desired landscape contours. Diagonals or a 'zigzag' pattern of cross-bracing are often used. This gives a strong but light layout and it is specially good with spectacular landscape settings — the track is on strips of plywood across the unit, leaving the rest clear to be landscaped as desired.

2. PASTE TABLES

Believe it or not, the cheap folding paste table sold in DIY stores can be used for folding layouts, and I have successfully made at least two using these. You need to 'reverse' them and add heightened sides or blocks to take the hinges. This is necessary to give depth for the scenery or structures.

3. FOLDING LAYOUTS

Following on from the paste table you can make a neat small folding layout 6-7ft long with plywood or planed wood frames and a plywood surface. Sturdy wood blocks are needed to hold the

hinges, and a carrying handle on the side (from a DIY shop) means you can fold and carry the layout like a suitcase. It is nicely dust free when folded and stored, another advantage.

The diagram overleaf shows all constructional details I have used for the small folding layouts I made.

4. FOLDING BOX LAYOUTS

These are popular with more advanced modellers who take layouts to shows. Typically two plywood 'box' halves are made which are hinged vertically at the front. The two halves fold together to make a closed box for transport and storage. The open fronts form a 'fascia' for the viewer, and lights are concealed in the top to illuminate the layout. You need good woodworking skills to make this sort of layout, and I have so far not attempted it myself!

Note that nowhere in this chapter have I mentioned chipboard. You will, however, still see it in use and mentioned in magazine articles. But it is heavy and not nice to work with. Conservative modellers will, no doubt, continue to use it and struggle with the weight involved. I don't commend it, however, and find the lighter methods described here much nicer to live with.

Above: **Underside of a plywood baseboard made by Steve Grantham for his Steinbeck HO layout. The sides are deeper than usual, at 30cm, but this is to raise it higher when set up on an ordinary table top. Note the diagonal and corner bracing. Depth can be made to your requirements, typically 3in, rather than the 30cm used here, but you have the flexibility of choice with the type of baseboard construction.**

Below: **The baseboard above, shown in the early stages of layout building, with the track and first structures temporarily in place for test purposes.**

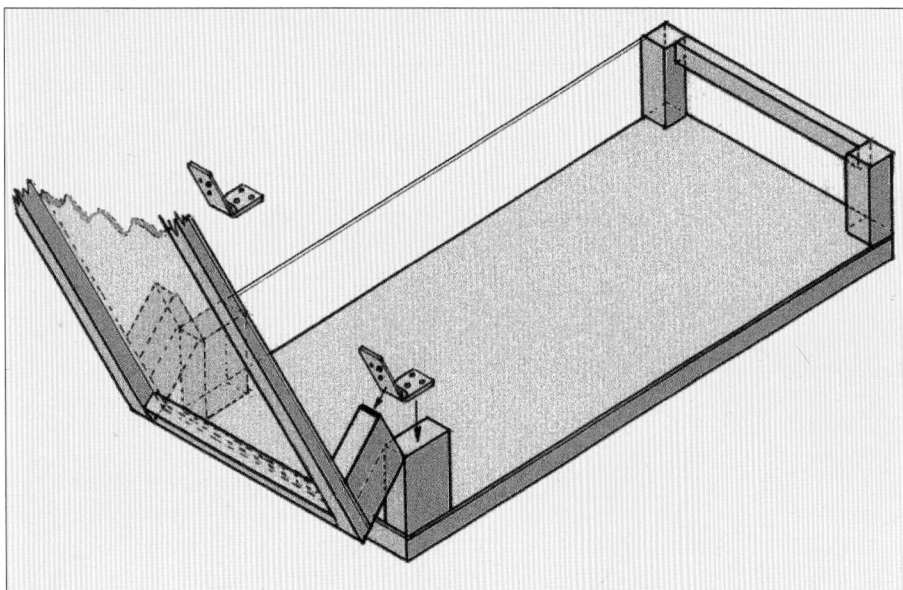

Above left: **A layout under construction in a folding paste table of the sort sold in DIY shops. Scenic work has started in the lower half and provision is made (a tunnel mouth) for running on to a second paste table. The legs are switched to the original top of the table.**

Top right: **To get sufficient depth for scenery, it is necessary to extend the depth of the paste table sides with strips of wood screwed in place. The centre hinge plates must then be fitted to the extended side pieces, as shown here.**

Above right: **Using two or more modified paste tables you can make quite a long layout that can be set up in the garden on fine days for operation. However, it is usually necessary to strengthen the folding legs supplied on the tables as they are often too flimsy to hold the layout really steady for operation.**

Left: **Constructional details for a purpose-built folding baseboard as made by the author, and drawn here by Jack Trollope. Note the hinge blocks and the need to allow sufficient depth for scenery and structures to clear when the board is folded.**

Right: **Folding baseboard made by the author using the method shown in the diagram opposite, below left. Here it is folded up before the track was laid.**

Below left: **The folding baseboard showing the hinge blocks (which can be covered by buildings when scenic work is done), with the layout part opened up. Note the line of ballast but no track across the baseboard join.**

Below right: **When the baseboard is fully opened up, the track across the join is completed by insertion of a Fleischmann extending track section (6010) which is laid over the ballast. This track section must be removed, of course, before the baseboard is folded up again at the end of an operating session.**

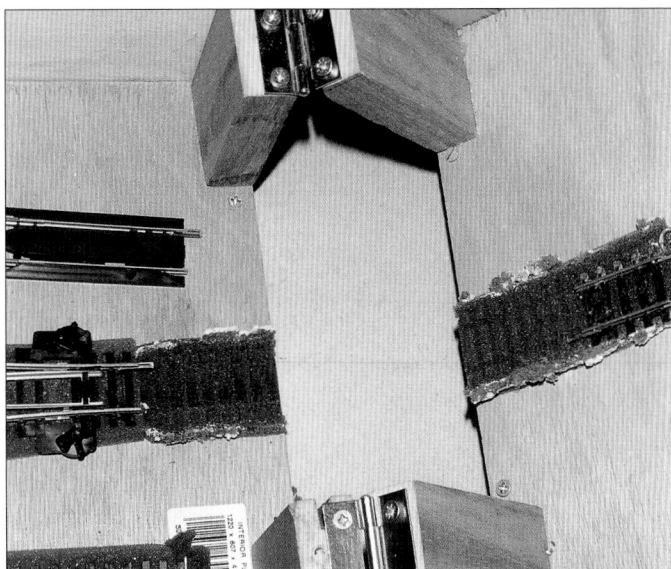

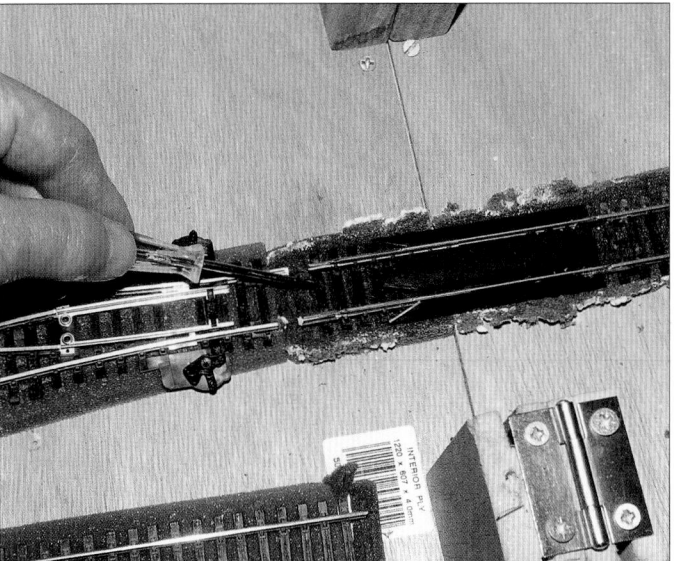

Right: **A very compact O gauge layout by Alan Wright of Inglenook Sidings fame. This is called Stephenson Sidings and follows the Inglenook Sidings track plan but is on a 6ft-long folding board, the hinge of which is visible here. The lineside hut is placed in position to disguise the join. The baseboard works in a similar way to Foldingham shown on the next page.**

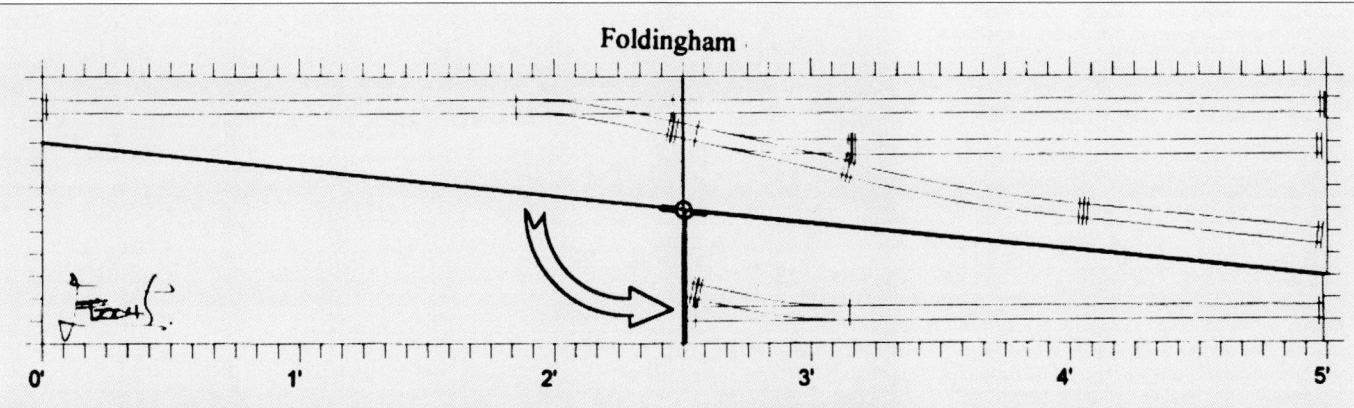

Foldingham

Above: **Plan of Foldingham by Jack Trollope — essentially a side-folding version of Inglenook Sidings. The arrow shows how half the layout swings round for storage.**

Below: **This drawing shows a further possible development with cassette-style fiddle yard and a lid for storage incorporating a stock box.**

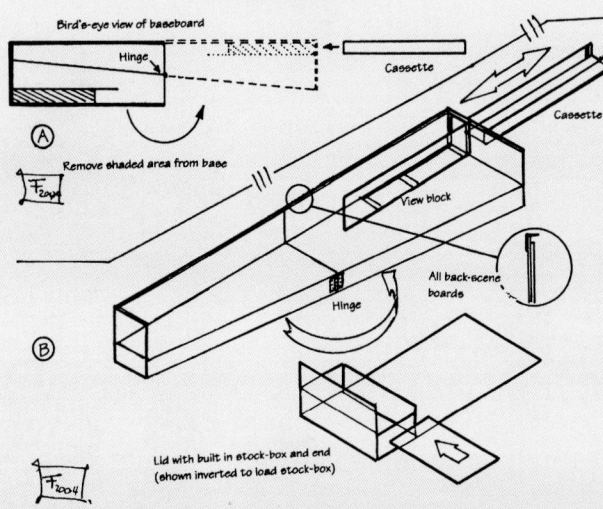

— Foldingham —

FOLDINGHAM

If storage of your small layout is a problem, one solution is to have a layout that folds in half. Most layouts that fold are arranged so that one half folds over the other, as also shown in this section. As an alternative for an Inglenook style of layout, Jack Trollope and some fellow enthusiasts came up with an idea for a side folding layout. The principle and construction details are shown in the drawings. The 'lid' with a built-in stock box is an optional extra. The track is carried over the join by using one of the sliding track sections described in Chapter 9. The first picture shows the framework folded before the baseboard was added. The second picture shows the centre of the layout with a small bungalow used to conceal the join. Another hinge with the pivot removed and replaced by a nail (as described in Chapter 9) is used to secure the layout rigid on the other side. The picture on page 43 shows the same side folding principle used on Alan Wright's Stephenson Sidings compact O gauge layout, an Inglenook just 6ft long that folds sideways in the middle. The tool hut is used to conceal the join and is removed when the board is folded. The slide-in cassette is another option which allows stock to be changed behind the vision blocker, which in practice would be a warehouse served by the centre siding. Both the cassette and the view blocker can be omitted if you prefer an 'open' type of goods yard like Stephenson Sidings.

Above: **The baseboard framing, shown folded as in the top diagram, on a version of the layout built by the author.**

Above: **The hinge on the side framing of the author's version of Foldingham. The small bungalow helps to disguise the join.**

Below: **If you have a permanent site for a larger layout, this is a good way to add braced support legs, bracketed to the skirting board. Inset right: a shelf-type narrow layout with a permanent home can be supported on strong wood brackets made like this.**

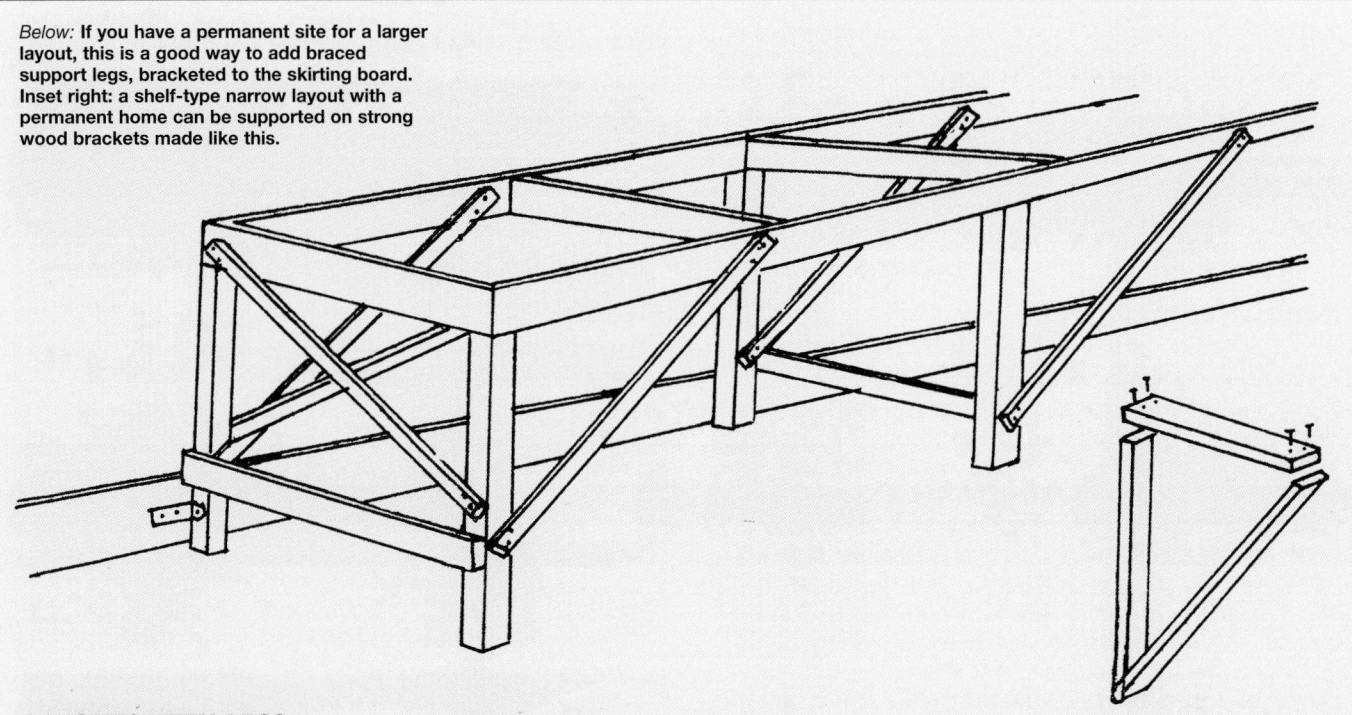

LAYOUTS WITH LEGS

Many of the very small layouts shown in this book are compact enough to set up on a table, or support on top of a bookcase, a piano or some other item of furniture. Small lightweight layouts can also be supported on spur shelving systems. If you build a bigger layout, however, you will need sturdy legs to support it, and the drawings on this page by Richard Gardner show some commended ways of doing it, including (below) the classic old 'table' layout featuring a continuous-run oval-based scheme, favoured by many. A further alternative is two or three sturdy trestles of the sort sold at DIY stores if you do not wish to make your own support legs.

Below: **A good way to support a free-standing 'table' layout of the oval-based type which might be kept propped against the wall when not in use. Folding legs and bracing struts in position (1); the legs folded and bracing struts removed (2); a method of joining two sections together with hinges and pins (3); an underside view of a single 'table' unit shows the bracing and framing arrangement.**

Folding legs

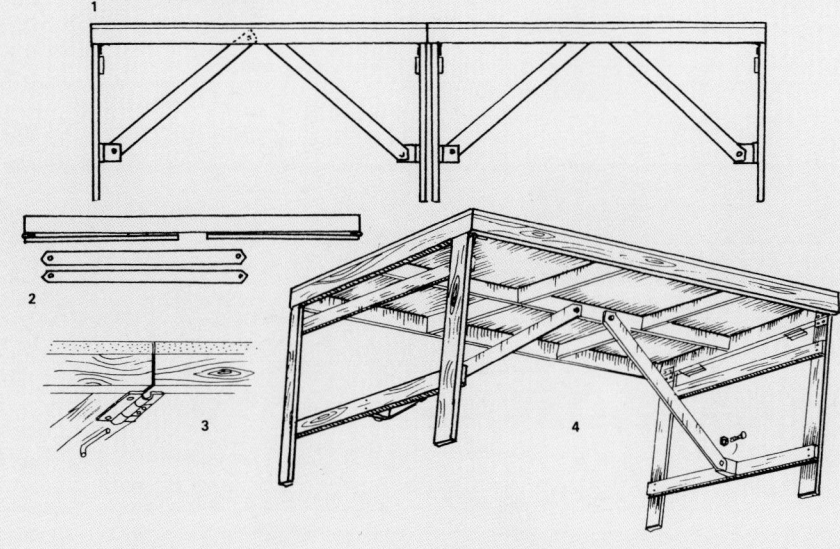

Below: **A longer folding HO layout built by the author with the strut merely in place for photography purposes to show the layout half folded. This layout, based on Arkona, eastern Germany, is 6ft long and 1ft wide when set up.**

Right above: **Stuart Robinson overcame storage problems by making a small British HO layout in three 2ft-long sections which cleverly slotted into a 2ft-square box, leaving room for the controller and accessories on top.**

Right below: **The author built a 3ft-long version of Inglenook Sidings in N gauge, called, appropriately enough, Wunyard. It fits inside a purpose-built plywood box just over 3ft long, with a screw-down lid. The layout and rolling stock go inside, with the backscene removed and laid on top. Thus secured it can be taken to model shows on public transport and is completely dust and damp free when stored out of use.**

EXTREME PORTABILITY

A surprising number of enthusiasts put off building a layout, using the excuse that they lack the room for one. Strictly speaking that may be true of a conventional layout of the 'traditional' kind. Those who live in small apartments, modern small houses, bedsitters, or live away from home certainly face a challenge, but it is easy to overcome by thinking small. Several very small but satisfying layouts are shown in this book, and while they may not satisfy your ambitions for the layout of your dreams, they do at least let you do some practical modelling and run some trains. Most small layouts, too, can be extended as you get more space. For example, since the little Tuning Fork layout was drawn for inclusion in this book it has already been extended to four times its original area, but even so still fits into a length of 4ft 9in — the extension was mostly sideways! But it started off as just a Y-point and two sidings. It stands on end in a cupboard when not in use.

The alternatives are folding baseboards, also featured in this book, and they have a pedigree going back to 1926 when A. R. Walkley made his famous 'Layout in a Suitcase'. Further alternatives are shown here — layouts that fit inside their own boxes for storage and transport and take up very little domestic space indeed. The author has another N gauge harbour layout that fits inside a 3ft-long sturdy cardboard box, and quite a few enthusiasts have built small layouts that fit inside guitar cases and the like. Just to prove that there is no limit to compactness and portability see page 93 where there is a layout built on a 12in ruler!

Right: **A very high standard of modelling on the O gauge Port Warren layout of Twickenham & District Model Railway Club. The beautifully made and painted Stroudley LBSCR Class D 0-4-2T in full Stroudley livery is shunting wagons on the quayside which captures the late 19th century atmosphere of tall warehouses and cobbled streets.**

While a few model rail enthusiasts are quite happy to see locomotives running on track laid on bare baseboards, for most of us the pleasure comes from having our train run in a realistic scenic setting. This is the true 'world in miniature' that delights both the builder and the viewer of the layout.

Scenic work is that part of the multi-disciplined model railway hobby that demands some artistic sense and skill to be successful and convincing. Not everyone will have this talent to start with, but with even minimal experience it will come. Essentially scenic work is the true creative part of the hobby. Locomotives and stock are fixed as they come, but the scenic setting for these models has to be made by you from materials to hand, either raw materials used imaginatively or scenic products made by the trade. In practice most of us use a mix of the two to arrive at our needs. However, the good thing about scenic work is that you can alter and revise as you go along, at any time in the life of your layout. This is commonly done, even by long-time modellers. As your skills increase you may get better at making trees, texturing surfaces, depicting rock faces or whatever. You can go back over your earlier work and simply give it a make-over with the old trees replaced by new ones, grass re-textured, roads re-surfaced and so on. To a certain extent you need to do this anyway, for all scenery wears with time — grass gets 'threadbare', trees work loose, colours fade, surfaces are chipped bare and so on. Just as you need to maintain and service locomotives and stock from time to time, so you need to attend to the scenery.

Scenic work is a huge subject and, indeed, whole books have been written about it. In *First Steps in Railway Modelling*, Cyril Freezer gave a very thorough coverage of long-accepted and well-proven ways of landscaping layouts. You can follow those methods with confidence, but there are plenty of other methods, some of which are in the 'short cut' or 'quick fix' category,

Right: **The Linfield Junction layout of Richard Gardner is a good example of accurate detailing and setting to a precise period, in this case British Railways of 1960-2, a nostalgic and popular modelling era for many of today's modellers who were youngsters at the time. This 00 gauge layout makes full use of the many models of the period produced by the trade.**

SIMPLER SCENICS AND QUICK FIXES

and may well be more suited to the smaller, more compact home layouts that are popular today.

It is not possible in a book of this size to cover every aspect of scenic work, but on the following pages the most important simple or 'quick fix' techniques are covered. The first item covered here is a variation on the way of making hills described in *First Steps in Railway Modelling* but features a few alternative ideas.

LIGHTWEIGHT HILLS THE EASY WAY
When you start building a layout, you usually get the track laid and ballasted and the next task is to add some scenery. Most layouts need hills on them somewhere and the pictures here show an easy way to do the job. Obviously this is not the only way, but this version is light and strong, and remarkably quick.

Essentially all you do is cut a lot of strips 12-25mm wide from old breakfast cereal boxes and make a criss-cross pattern to whatever gentle contours you need, having first put a profile board the shape of the hilltop along the back of the baseboard. Over the criss-cross you lay strips of scrim, a

material used in dress-making that you can usually buy at clothes shops, tailoring shops or department stores. You can do all this yourself, but the firm of Set Scenes makes it even easier by making packs of pre-cut strips and scrim for instant use. Over the scrim you simply paint (with an old paint brush) a layer of modelling plaster, and only a thin application is needed. It all dries as a light hollow shell. Add some brown or black powder paint to the modelling plaster when you mix it to 'kill' the whiteness of the plaster so that later chips or cracks won't show up stark white. Once the plaster is dry, paint it ground or grass colour, and glue on ground scatter in the usual way.

Also available is a plaster-impregnated scrim which is wetted and applied in the same way, obviating the need to paint on the plaster yourself. Hornby are among the makers of this, item R8070.

Peco produce a variation of this idea called Landform in which the criss-cross support is pre-formed and the scrim is included. All you do is cut it to size with scissors, pin or glue the support in place and proceed from there — even easier. It's worth trying this method if you are

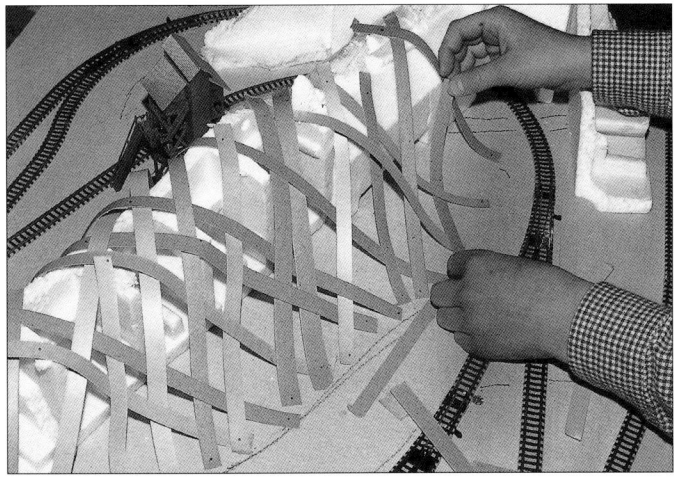

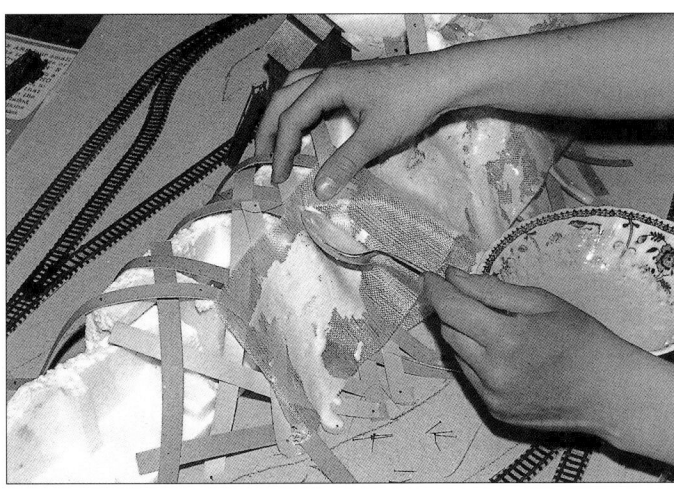

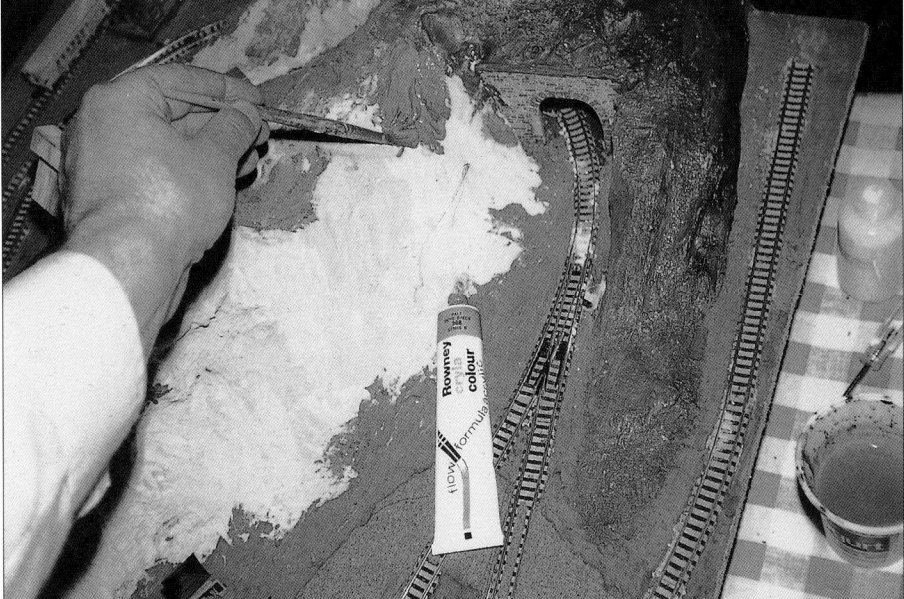

Above left: **Making lightweight hills, also known as 'hollow shell', in the way described in the text. Here card strips are pinned in place.**

Above right: **Over the card strips , lengths of scrim are placed, with modelling plaster added over the top.**

Centre left: **The plaster is now dry on the same hillside, and the ground colour is painted on using acrylic paints.**

Lower left: **This is the same hillside after texturing. Lineside huts have been added alongside the track, as have some trees. On the extreme left a rocky outcrop has been modelled by inserting a piece of cork bark into the plaster hillside as it dried.**

new to scenic modelling or want to try a method that is different.

More recently Australian modeller Geoff Nott has demonstrated on alternative method. Here ordinary chicken wire, sold in hardware stores, is used instead of the card strips. Over this you position sheets of kitchen paper which are 'painted' into position using ordinary PVA white glue. Several layers of kitchen paper can be used if necessary to build up a smooth or neat surface. No modelling plaster is used with this method, only the PVA glue. Obviously you need a large pot of this and a paint brush to apply it.

It is worth mentioning that chicken wire can also be substituted for the card criss-cross strips in the first method described, and the scrim and plaster is applied over the wire.

Whichever method is used, leave everything for at least 24 hours until the plaster or glue surface is dry before applying scenic texturing and finish.

If you only need low hills, old egg boxes of the usual moulded card sort can make quick and easy supports. Cut them into top and bottom halves, but 'stack' them or trim them shallow to give height variation. Pin, glue or tape

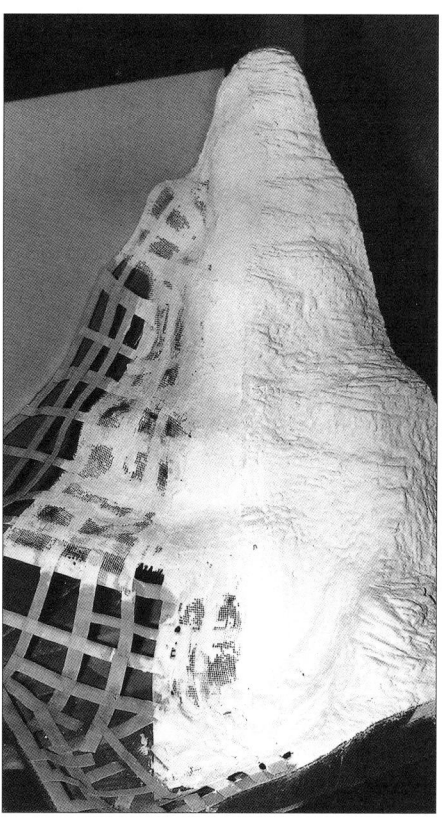

Above: **You can work in various effects while modelling plaster dries. The quarry loading area on this 009 narrow gauge layout has been surfaced with modelling plaster pre-coloured brownish-grey with added powder paint. Now an old plastic glue spreader is being used to simulate ruts and cart tracks in the surface before it dries.**

Right: **A demonstration model made some years ago by Set Scenes to show that quite tall hills and**

mountains can be made the 'hollow shell' way using the card strips, scrim and modelling plaster it supplies from its stand at model shows.

Below: **Imaginative modeller Paul A. Lunn did this drawing to illustrate some of his good ideas for cheap and simple scenic methods, notably the use of old egg boxes and toilet roll or kitchen roll tubes for supporting landscape work. Typical applications of other scenic products are also shown.**

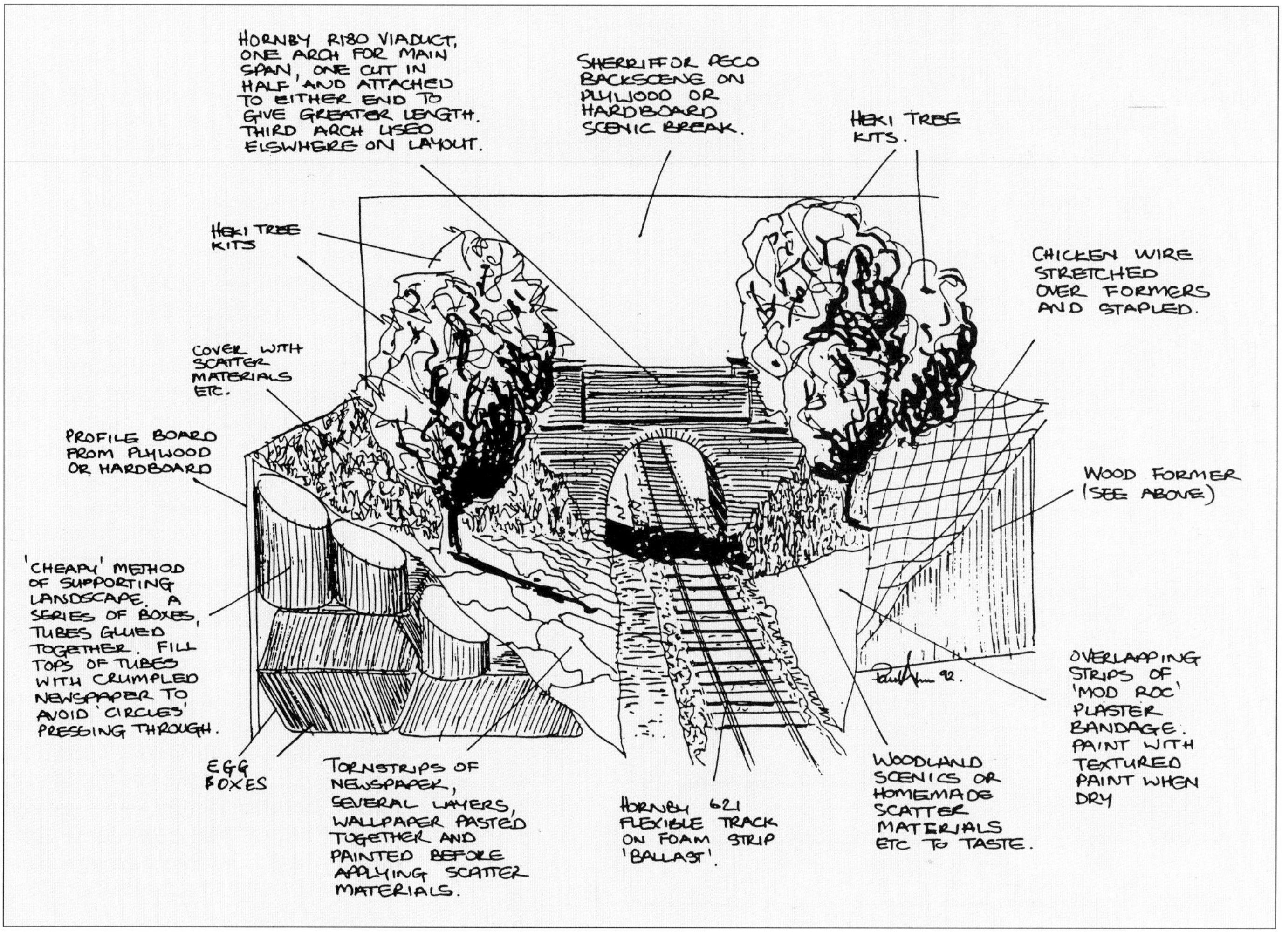

HORNBY R180 VIADUCT, ONE ARCH FOR MAIN SPAN, ONE CUT IN HALF AND ATTACHED TO EITHER END TO GIVE GREATER LENGTH. THIRD ARCH USED ELSWHERE ON LAYOUT.

SHERRIFF OR PECO BACKSCENE ON PLYWOOD OR HARDBOARD SCENIC BREAK.

HEKI TREE KITS.

HEKI TREE KITS

CHICKEN WIRE STRETCHED OVER FORMERS AND STAPLED.

COVER WITH SCATTER MATERIALS ETC.

PROFILE BOARD FROM PLYWOOD OR HARDBOARD

WOOD FORMER (SEE ABOVE)

'CHEAPY' METHOD OF SUPPORTING LANDSCAPE. A SERIES OF BOXES, TUBES GLUED TOGETHER. FILL TOPS OF TUBES WITH CRUMPLED NEWSPAPER TO AVOID 'CIRCLES' PRESSING THROUGH.

OVERLAPPING STRIPS OF 'MOD ROC' PLASTER BANDAGE. PAINT WITH TEXTURED PAINT WHEN DRY

EGG BOXES

TORN STRIPS OF NEWSPAPER, SEVERAL LAYERS, WALLPAPER PASTE'D TOGETHER AND PAINTED BEFORE APPLYING SCATTER MATERIALS.

HORNBY 621 FLEXIBLE TRACK ON FOAM STRIP 'BALLAST'.

WOODLAND SCENICS OR HOMEMADE SCATTER MATERIALS ETC TO TASTE.

Above: **German scenic firm of Noch makes a clever system called Terra-Form consisting of plug-together plastic and wood rods that enable a lightweight landscape framework to be built up quickly. On this demonstration layout the framing is covered with grass mats to depict rolling hills.**

Below: **Using layers of expanded polystyrene scrap to built up the basis for a round hill. They are joined with white PVA glue.**

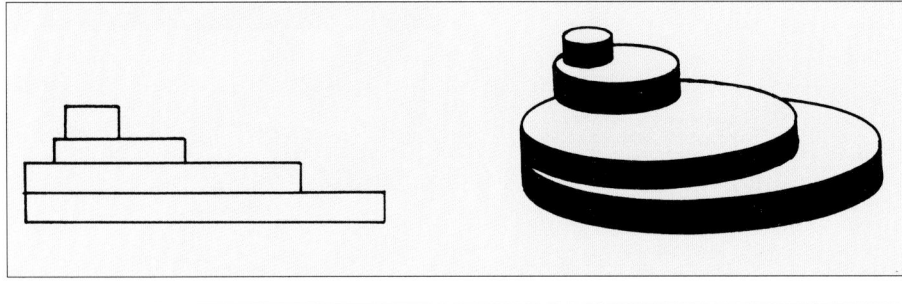

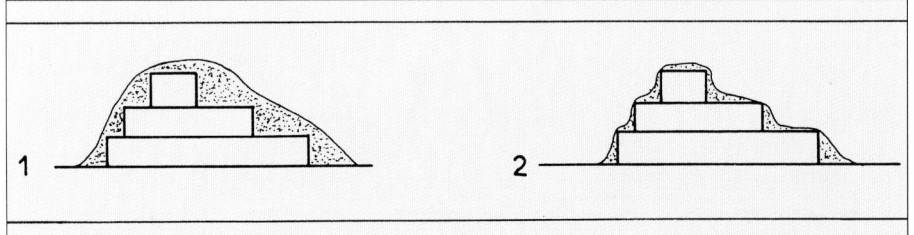

Above: **The polystyrene layers can then be covered with modelling plaster to form contours as desired, in this case for a rounded hill or a stepped hillside.**

Below: **To build up cuttings, or hills against the back of the layout, do the same procedure as above, but line up the layers to form a flush rear face.**

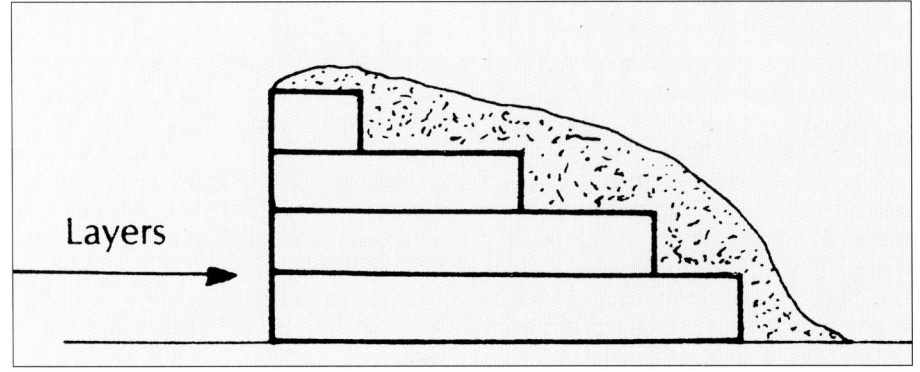

them to the baseboard surface, then lay on the scrim or kitchen paper layers and finish off with modelling plaster or white PVA glue as before.

USING EXPANDED POLYSTYRENE

This technique is quite recent, and uses expanded polystyrene to make up shapes. This material can be purchased, is sold also in the form of ceiling tiles, and is available as scrap from packaging. The advantage is that it is easy to cut, easy to glue (use white PVA), and very light. It is a potential fire risk, but when coated with emulsion paint and/or modelling plaster this risk is greatly reduced, and the surface finish then matches terrain modelling in the conventional style.

A good large knife (such as an old kitchen knife or a Stanley knife) is best for slicing polystyrene. It makes a mess of granules, however, so cover the floor and table with old newspapers to collect the debris.

The principle is easy enough. Just build it up in layers to give a contour effect as shown here. Pins, nails or glue secure the layers. When the glue is set, simply cover with patching plaster or modelling compound as shown here.

Note that rock faces or strata can be depicted by breaking off tiles to give rough edges, while large blocks or polystyrene may be cut complete to form cuttings, low hills, etc.

MAKING ROCKY TERRAIN

Rocks and mountains are popular on model layouts. They are spectacular scenic features, and they give an excuse for the steep gradients and cramped situations prevalent on many small layouts. Obviously they also provide an excuse for the tunnels giving access to hidden sidings and fiddle yards.

There is quite a wide interpretation of what constitutes a rocky terrain. It doesn't necessarily mean high mountains. There are plenty of lowland areas where there are rocky outcrops. More commonly, however, a mountainous area is modelled. To give an illusion of depth a scenic background depicting mountains can be used on a shelf layout, with only the foreground actually modelled in relief. Firms such as Peco (UK), Faller (Germany) and Walthers (USA) all produce mountain backscenes depicting terrain from their respective countries.

Above: **Cutting an expanded polystyrene block to form a section of steep cutting on the corner of a layout. Note the old newspaper used to catch the waste granules of plastic.**

Below: **A light coating of modelling plaster, pre-coloured with powder paints, is then applied. After that apply texture and vegetation etc as for other scenic bases.**

Above: **The polystyrene block is further shaped to the desired contour, then painted over with household emulsion (from a small sampler pot) to stop it crumbling and reduce fire risk.**

Below: **These diagrams show a poor random way of depicting rocky outcrops, on the left, and a more plausible way of positioning the outcrops on the right, suggesting a degree of stratification.**

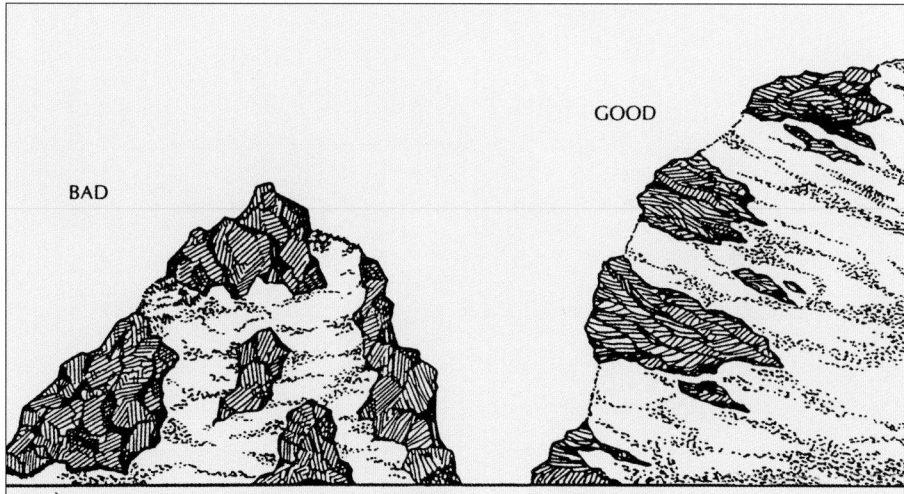

If you build an actual rock face, however, it is best to go for height and bulk to make it believable. A small mound, however rugged, will not be so convincing as a craggy cliff-like depiction of part of a mountain.

The rock often appears only as outcrops from a grassed surface. In its simplest form the rocky outcrops can be modelled from broken pieces of expanded polystyrene stuck into a wet plaster surface prepared as in the previous section, or the rocky surface can be worked into the plaster covering as it dries. A stiff paint brush and a scriber of some sort can be used to give the rocky cliff surface as the plaster dries, cutting ledges and strata layers by horizontal working with the scriber.

Moulded rock sheeting is available and would be suitable for small surfaces, particularly of the vertical type. Cliff faces or cuttings, however, are very easily depicted by cutting and/or layering polystyrene blocks and giving a coating of modelling compound as required.

A favourite method, much used for rocky faces, is cork bark, sold in some model shops and also by florists. Most of this bark has a realistic striated surface and looks remarkably like a rocky texture. Obviously this is easy to use, and is often big enough to be free-standing.

It is possible to mould your own realistic rock face. One way to do it is to use crumpled kitchen foil and press it on to the modelling compound while it is drying. Removing it in good time before the plaster sets will give a good 'rock face' texture caused by the creases in the foil. Some modellers have used casting resin to make cliff and rock sections, with pieces of coal or real rock used to make a master surface in the rubber mould. This gives an excellent realistic effect if you can master the technique.

The illustrations show some examples of scenic treatment for rocky terrain.

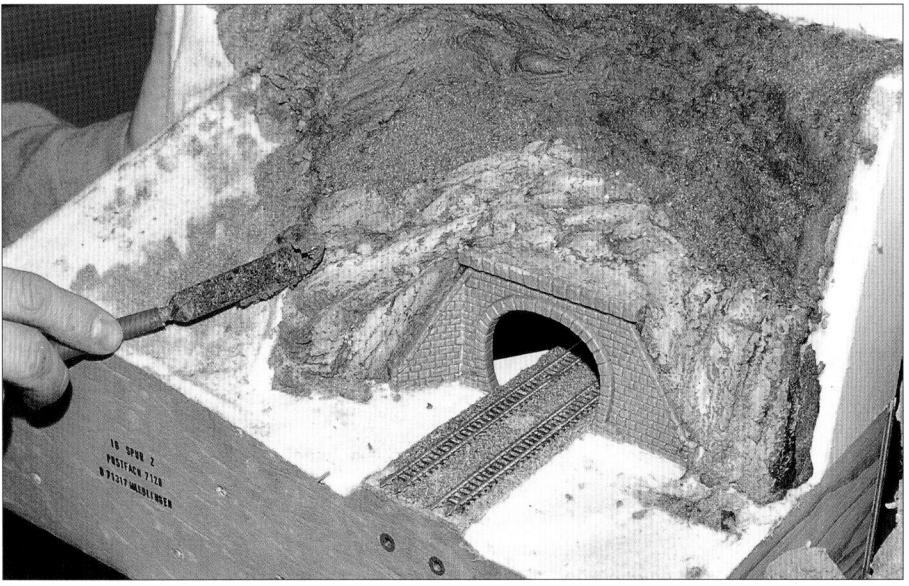

THE SIMPLEST BACKSCENE

The backscene is important because it serves the same function as a backscene on a stage, film or TV set. Your layout may carry nice scenic effects, of course, but a layout occupies a finite space, typically a table or shelf-shaped baseboard. Beyond the baseboard area we suppose the adjacent terrain to extend on to infinity just as real scenic views do. But this cannot be done on a small model railway baseboard, so the scenic backscene is used to suggest that behind the model railway the terrain continues.

Some skilled modellers paint their own scenic background and this can certainly be done if you have good artistic abilities. But if you cannot paint your own there are printed backscenes available from several model railway firms, among them Faller, Auhagen, Busch, MZZ, Bilteezi, Peco and Townscene. Most are done in large and small sizes to suit different model railway scales, and there are a variety of scenes including mountains, fields, forest, seaside, industrial townscapes, village streets and city centres.

If you have not tried making backscenes before, the simplest method is covered here and shown in the photographs.

The backscene can be painted on a stiff strip of any desired height, but for a small layout use a height of at least 6-8in (150-200mm). Thin plywood board or 3mm MDF can be used, but the smooth side of hardboard is equally suitable. The backscene board is first cut to the desired length and screwed in place along the framing of the back edge of the layout. Then mark an ink line along the point where the backscene board meets the baseboard top. This is to ensure the background is level and is positioned

Top left: **Making a rocky hillside above a tunnel mouth in the most conventional way, using modelling plaster applied with a spatula or old kitchen knife, and fashioning some stratification as the plaster dries.**

Centre left: **A very good example of convincingly made rocky terrain on a demonstration layout made by Heki, a German firm of scenic accessory makers. The tunnel mouth is one of many types available commercially.**

Lower left: **A nicely made rocky hillside with retaining wall of stone at its base forming a natural backscene on a German HO layout.**

so that it actually lines up with the baseboard.

The backscene board is then removed and laid flat on the worktop. The entire board is then painted down to just above the marked line in 'sky' colour. You could use ordinary light blue or grey-blue paint for this, but a quick and inexpensive way is to use a sampler pot of emulsion from a local DIY shop. They are cheap and you can get 'sky blue' or similar pale blue/grey shades. The paint can be applied straight from the pot, but if you have some white poster or acrylic paint, squeeze some into the sky blue paint on the board and work it in horizontal strokes. It does not have to be uniform as the sky is often 'streaky'. When fully covered, including the board edges, set aside to dry.

In the example shown, two Peco landscape sheets for HO/OO are being used and the desired sections are carefully cut out all round with scissors. In most scenic sheets (but not all) the sky is already printed in place. But even if it is, it is still a good idea to cut out the image from the sky. This is because when you glue the scenic sheet to the backboard it is very easy to get air bubbles under the image. On the ground area these can be disguised by bushes or trees etc, but in the sky area they stand out only too prominently and look very unrealistic.

The cut-out ground area can now be glued to the sky-painted backboard using white PVA glue. Ensure the glue is carried right out to the edges and that no gaps are left to form air bubbles. The scenic sheet is lined up on the datum line, then pressed down using an art roller. If you do not have an art roller, use an empty milk bottle or a coffee jar instead, or even an old rolling pin. Make sure any air bubbles are eliminated when you roll the backscene flat. You

Top right: **On the author's HO East German layout, Büchow, only the low relief station building and the inn in low relief at the right are 'solid' structures. The rest of the town is made from MZZ backscene sheets.**

Centre right: **Typical of the useful backscene aids available are these American cut-out 'flats' for HO by Walthers which can be arranged as required for background use.**

Lower right: **If you have the artistic skill you can paint your own backscene as done here by Richard Gardner. In front of it Richard is scratch-building a viaduct, and this view, without the front facing in place, shows how it is done.**

SIMPLE BACK SCENES

For small layouts of the narrow 'shelf' type, making a backscene is quite an easy task, even for a beginner. These pictures show the process of doing it, stage by stage, using Peco printed backscenes as the basis, with additional foreground items added. Surprising 'depth' is achieved even with this basic method of working.

Upper left: **The smooth side of a hardboard strip is used. The pencil line shows the baseboard frame depth and gives a guide for straightness. Light blue emulsion paint depicts the sky, with streaks of acrylic white painted over it while wet to tone down the blue.**

Centre left: **The printed sky area is cut away with scissors from portions of two Peco backscenes which are to be merged together. The backscene segments are then glued with white PVA glue to the backscene board, using an art roller to eliminate air bubbles.**

Below left: **The backscene board is then screwed in place to the baseboard framing. As it backs a goods yard area, low relief warehouse structures are now glued to the backscene. Do not glue them to the baseboard; this makes the backscene board easy to remove if changes are made later.**

Below right: **The completed section with low relief structures fronting the backscene. The vertical oil tank is actually cut from a Faller kit catalogue illustration and glued to the backscene, and the water tank at right is a low relief model (actually only half a tank!) also glued to the backscene.**

can 'cut and mix' to get variety. The backscene shown is actually made up from two different segments from Peco sheets carefully butted together, so it has a degree of individuality and is not exactly the same as the original printed sheet.

With the backscene board screwed back in place you get an immediate impression of extra depth, even before any of the foreground scenery has yet been added. Even if you do not try any more advanced scenic work, do at least make a simple backscene like this to get away immediately from the 'bare' look of an incomplete layout.

CREATING YOUR OWN BACKSCENE

An alternative to using a commercial printed backscene is to create your own. In fact, on a long layout you might have a mix of 'home-made' and printed backscenes, depending on your needs.

For this easy technique proceed as before with a ply, hardboard or MDF backboard screwed to the rear edge of the baseboard. Also, as before, paint the backboard as blue sky, using quite pale blue and white. Paint it on horizontally, rather darker towards the top, with white paint streaked and run into it to lighten it towards the bottom. Variations could include a touch of grey if you want a winter sky, or a little pink, which, if not overdone, gives a warm hue to the sky.

When the backscene paint is dry, use old card (such as the inside faces of food cartons) or thick lining paper and cut three rows of undulating hills. You could, if desired, cut them to depict three mountains rather than hills. Paint

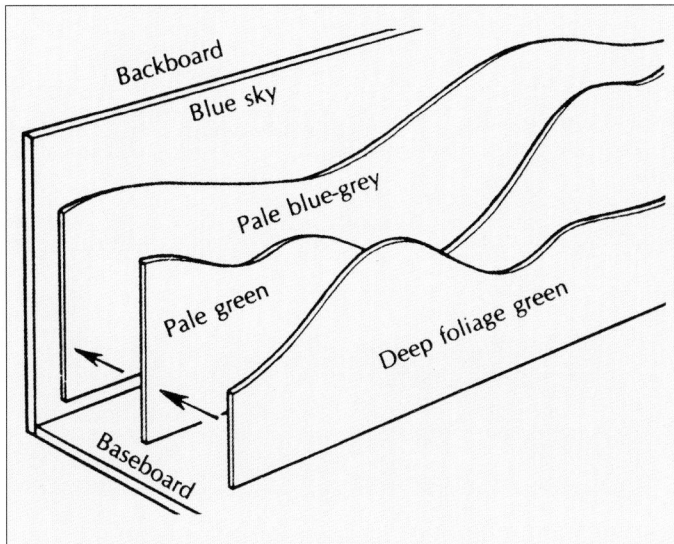

Above: **A simple way of making your own backscene by cutting out profiles of hills from card or thick paper and layering them, after painting, in front of the sky backscene board.**

Below: **Trees can be cut from printed backscenes and glued in place to vary the appearance or to make it look more wooded. But you could draw and paint your own, using this diagram as a guide to shape and colouring.**

Above: **An actual example of the layering technique shown in the diagram is seen here installed on an OO gauge layout.**

Below: **A very fine example of a realistic backscene made by Julian Andrews who cut out suitably sized cottage pictures from calendars and brochures. They look very 'solid' but are actually flat on the backscene board.**

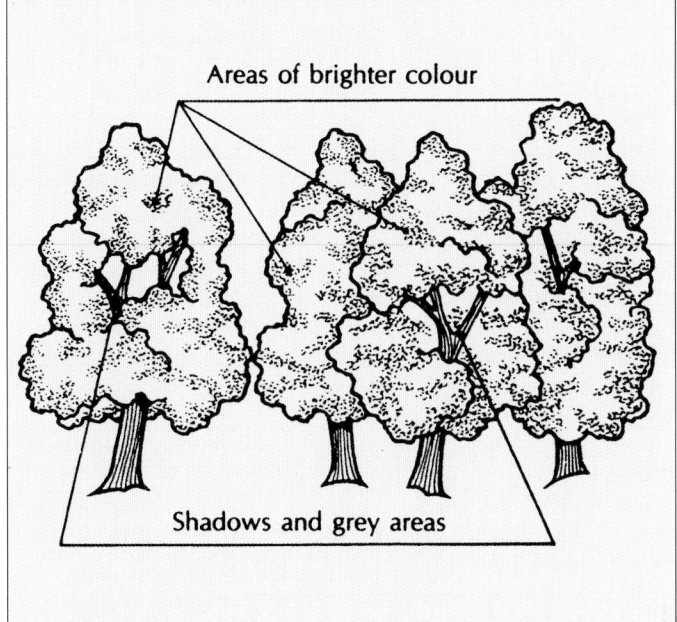

the three different layers pale blue-grey, pale green, and deep foliage green, and glue them in layers to the backscene. This is the simplest way of making a backscene with apparent depth, particularly if you have only limited artistic ability. The use of layers is actually more effective, than simply painting the hills in place on the backscene.

As a digression the importance of the variation in colour of the hills should be emphasised. Because of atmospheric conditions distant terrain looks 'bluer' and generally lighter than close terrain. This you can verify from observation. Hence when reproducing terrain on a backscene the hill colours are graded as outlined above to get a similar effect of distance.

This gives an alternative to the painted backscenes available which are easy to use but become very well known and familiar on all too many layouts. Hence a 'home-made' variation, unique to your layout, may have appeal to those who seek something more original.

There are many ways of using commercially available backscenes, however, to give something different from the material as presented. The backscenes themselves may be cut and re-arranged so that they no longer exactly resemble the original printed version as sold.

In Great Britain there is the Bilteezi range of scenic sheets which includes hill and terrain sections which may be cut and glued in layers to the sky background. In Europe the Swiss company MZZ offers a similar range.

Right: **Effective scenic work by Stuart Robinson on his British HO layout. There is only about 4in of depth here, just enough for the wagons, siding, coal drops and dozer. The wall behind the wagons, and the industrial buildings, are all flat on the backscene (which hides a fiddle yard behind) but the illusion of great depth is created.**

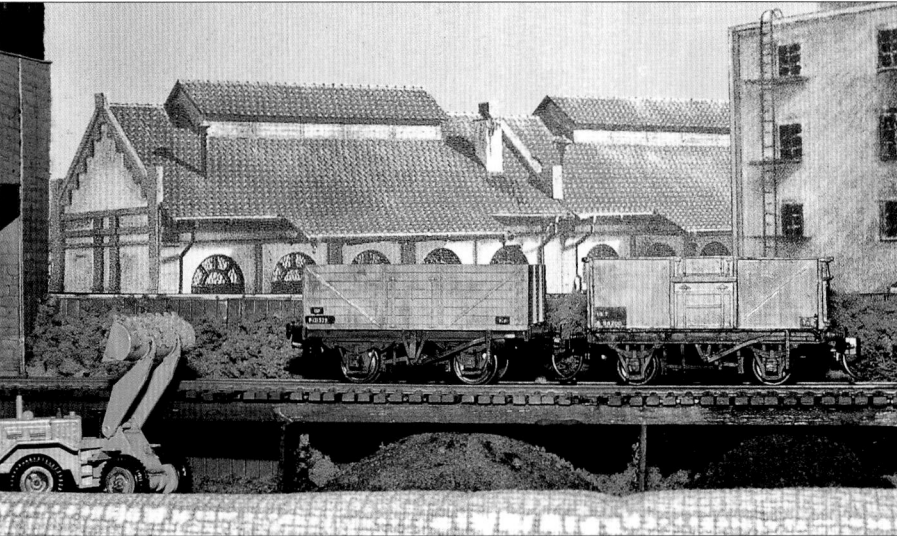

A further variation on this theme is to cut suitable parts from magazine, calendar or travel brochure illustrations for overlays in the same way. If you look around you will see many examples of illustrations in colour which may have a use in model railway scenic backgrounds. The main requirement is that the illustration should be matt. Glossy illustrations will reflect light and thus destroy any illusion of realism. It is possible to spray suitable, but glossy, illustrations with matt clear varnish if you are happy to spend money on the aerosol of matt varnish. This will overcome the reflection problem.

Once the basic terrain is depicted on the backscene you can add all sorts of foreground features, also in the form of overlays. For example, trees can be painted separately or in groups on stiff paper, and cut and glued in place. However, you can again cut suitably sized trees from colour illustrations and pre-printed backscenes and glue them in place. Structures can be similarly cut out and glued individually to a flat backscene.

Structures as part of a backscene are almost always very effective. Sometimes it is possible to combine a low-relief structure with a scenic flat so that they all appear to be part of the same building. For example, a covered loading bay is fully modelled over the track, while the rest of the factory is depicted solely by a flat cut-out stuck on the backscene. Many of the card cut-out buildings available, such as

those made by Bilteezi, Metcalfe, Superquick or Builder Plus, can be adapted additionally as scenic flats merely by cutting out individual front or back walls and gluing them to the backscene. These adapted flats lack perspective, of course, but as they are full scale for your model they are best used to depict immediate background structures alongside the railway. Parts of plastic kits can be used in a similar way. Another technique is the use of a specially taken colour photograph. This is quite feasible if you own an SLR or digital camera. Find a small building you want on the layout, photograph it front-on in good cloudy bright or light sunlight weather, and ensure there are no vehicles or people in the way. You may need to get a print to the size you need, but for an average building an ordinary enprint gives more or less the correct scale for N and a 30% enlarged print matches HO. There are the ordinary options offered by the photo processor, but specify 'matt' rather than 'gloss' prints.

POINTS TO REMEMBER

There are several 'tricks of the trade' that help to make any sort of backscene or scenic flat arrangement more effective. The diagram here shows the best treatment at corners — curve the backscene around it. If for any reason you can't, use a clump of trees in the corner to disguise the right angle. A variation on the problem is also shown. Again plenty of model trees in front of the backscene at that point, with higher ones in the actual corners, would be an alternative treatment.

As noted earlier, with scenic backgrounds we are creating an illusion of distance — or, at least, attempting to do so. In this connection there are often minor problems to overcome. One of

Below left: **Corners are best treated by taking the backscene in a curve around them. Taking the backscene into the actual corner can destroy all the illusion.**

Below right: **Avoid taking roads or footpaths etc straight into the backscene. It is much better to curve them around and let them 'disappear' behind trees or bushes, as shown on the right.**

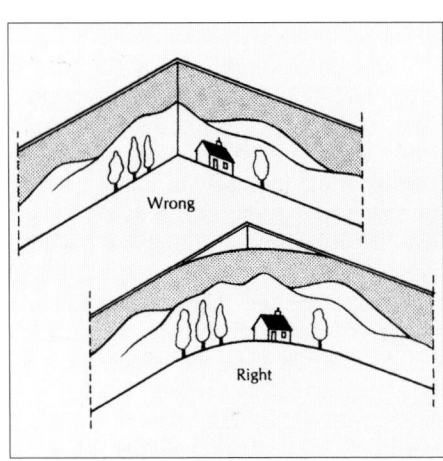

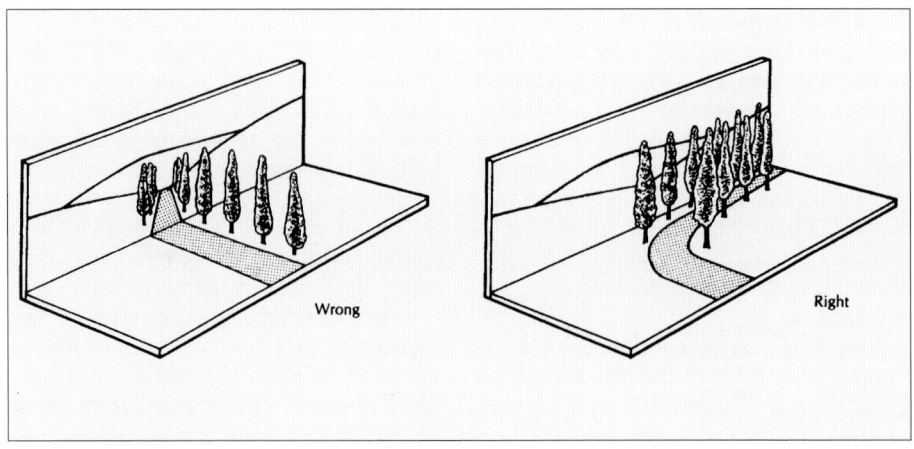

the most common is perspective. This is not much of a problem if the backscene shows only countryside or a town, but when you come to depicting a road disappearing into the distance you may encounter the visual problems. In theory a road in the foreground should merge smoothly into the road continued on the background, but in practice it is difficult to maintain this illusion however much you try. Instead of trying to depict the road on the background, curve it round in front of the backscene and 'lose' it among the trees. The improvement is obvious from the diagram.

GRASS AND SCRUB

Much scenic work relies on visual 'suggestion', as is often the case also with theatre sets. A few house fronts may suggest a city street, even though they are literally flat fronts with nothing behind them, and an expanse of green with just a few fronds of grass painted clearly at the front may suggest a meadow — even though the artist has not painted every single blade of grass.

In scenic work, the 'suggestion' starts with the grass and the vegetation. You will have a relatively large area to cover (even on a small layout) and the usual material used, as we all know, is flock powder. This is readily available in numerous ranges from most model shops. Obviously flock powder cannot depict individual blades. So with flock power the rough texture and colour is substituting for individual blades of grass and simply suggesting an expanse of grass. If it is to do this successfully it is essential to concentrate on the texture and the colour. Flock powder (or 'scenic dressing' as it is sometimes called) comes in many colours and textures from rough to fine. In the old days it was common for modellers to dye sawdust or old dry tea leaves green and use these, but this immediately illustrates the problem — they are far too coarse to look anything other than what they

are. So today's flock powders are much finer. Which grade you get depends on your preferences, but for N or Z gauges the truly fine powder variety is essential, for anything heavier looks too rough for any sort of grass in these very small scales. With OO/HO or O gauges you can vary textures because the scales are big enough to differentiate between coarse tussocks, meadow grass and the finer grass you might find on verges and in sheltered woodlands.

Colour is most important. Some of the ranges offer flock powder that is far too bright. Most modellers chose to build their layouts in a spring or summer setting, when grass is at its lushest and thickest. However, a lot of grass is yellowish rather than bright green, tending to be darker in well-watered areas. From the shades available you should find what you think is suitable. Like an artist, however, develop your powers of observation before you get too far into a project.

Just go and look at grass. It is something taken for granted, but if you stop and study it you'll note the sort of things to remember when modelling it. Note how it tends to grow higher against fences or walls, to spread out over footpaths if unchecked, to grow against the walls of buildings or between paving stones. Depict all this in your model.

In N scale a 10cm long blade of grass would be only 0.6mm long! In OO/HO it would be 1mm long. These are useful measures to remember when choosing a grade of flock powder.

The other material which gives an effect of individual grass blades is Noch Streugras. A Streugras dispenser contains 'green grass' fibres electrostatically charged so that when 'squirted' on to a glued surface they stand on end and give the effect of vertical blades of grass. The idea is clever and effective, but as with grass mats, you get a uniform effect which is

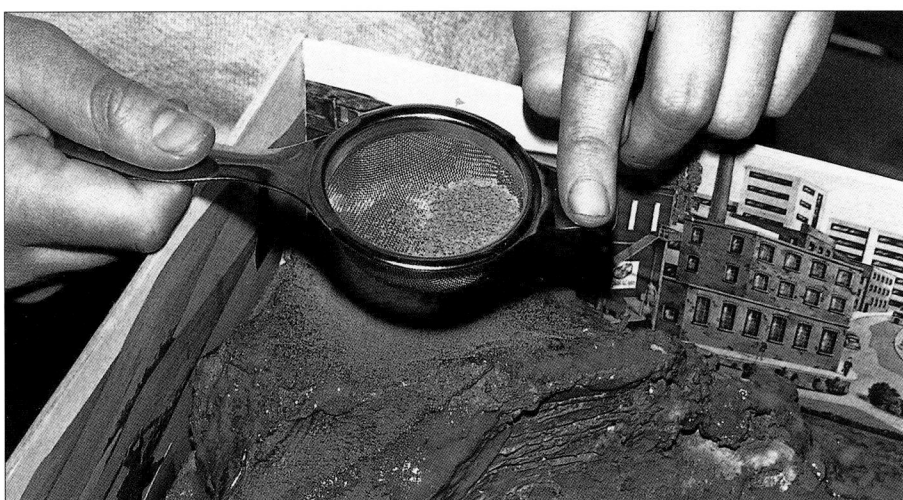

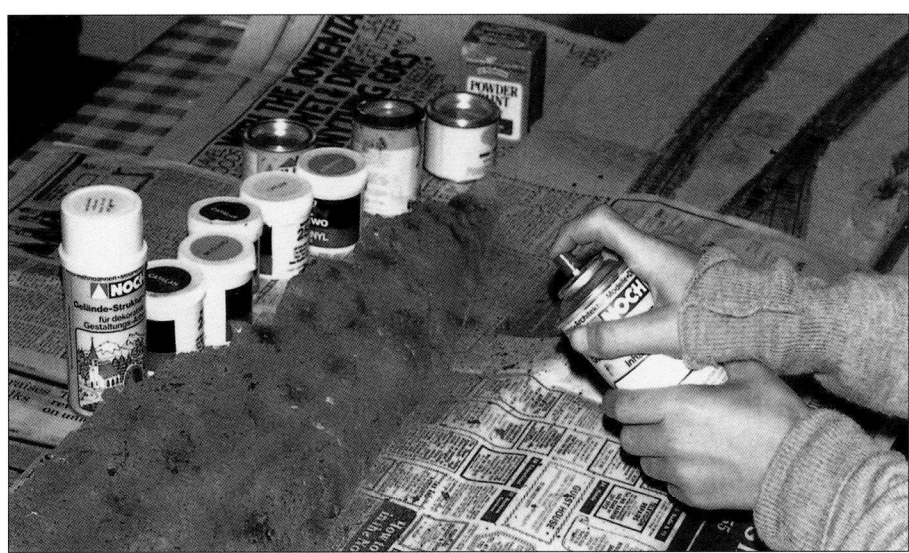

Upper right: **Fine texturing is essential for grass effects in N or Z. A good way to ensure only the finest scatter material gets on to the surface is to use an old tea strainer for sprinkling which will stop coarser powder falling through.**

Lower right: **Noch Streugras comes in aerosol form and gives a realistic effect with actual grass blades visible in HO. Here it is being applied to a cutting but the track area is masked off with newspaper to prevent the spray falling on the track.**

not always what you want. However, Streugras does present another area of choice.

Yet another option well proven over the years dates back to the days before modern scenic accessories were available in such quantities. With this method ordinary surgical lint is used. It is first dyed grass green using a suitable domestic dye as sold in department stores. The ground surface is prepared and painted grass green. When it is dry the whole area is painted over with ordinary glue. Allow this to get slightly tacky, then press the surgical lint flock downwards on to the glue. When it is dry, pull off the sheet of lint. It leaves the flock behind, stuck in the glue. A realistic 'grass' texture results, usually a little lumpy in the characteristics way of wild grass. This is a favourite method of treating prominent foreground areas of grass, such as railway embankments.

VEGETATION

The representation of undergrowth can be done in several ways and, indeed, it is a good idea to mix all of them as real undergrowth is of several species of plant.

Very readily available, also in varying colours, is what is known as ground foam. This is actually plastic foam 'minced' up into small pieces. It is very suitable for depicting undergrowth of the clover, thistle and plantain variety that tends to grow in clumps against fences and walls, and in between rail tracks.

Another material is the Woodland Scenics foliage supplied in its tree kits. There is always some left over and this is ideal for shredding into small pieces and using for taller undergrowth.

The other common method of making undergrowth of the much denser variety is to use rubberised horse hair. This is available from Set Scenes, but is also obtainable elsewhere, and may be found in old discarded pillows and the older type of mattress and upholstery. If is ideal for bushes and the hazel or bramble type of growth. Before gluing it in place, smear the small teased out clumps in white PVA glue and dip them into flock powder to add the leaves.

Some modellers make much use of traditional carpet underlay, either teased out into clumps and fibres to depict bushes, undergrowth or all grass in the small scales, alternatively dyed grass green and used for areas of rough grass in the larger scales like G or 1.

Finally there is the idea of using teased out lengths of green garden string, either stuck into the ground plaster work while it is wet or stuck into pre-drilled holes. This is a realistic way of depicting such growths as elephant grass or reeds etc. A similar effect can be obtained by using what is called 'Moss Look Liner' for hanging flower baskets, sold by garden outlets. This makes rough clumpy grass for large scales, or it can be teased into individual strands to make tall grass or undergrowth for the small scales. It comes pre-coloured in grass green.

TREES

Unless your layout is set in a barren or derelict landscape it is going to need trees of some sort. This is another vast subject area which you can approach from several levels. Some modellers are pedantic about model trees, demanding the highest fidelity and accuracy. This is a worthy objective, but making perfectly detailed model trees is not within everyone's ability. You can

Upper left: **The small plastic scoops that come with ice cream tubs are worth keeping. They are handy for dropping flock material into very precise positions such as the corner of this paved area. Note the use of old jam jars to keep scenic flock powders.**

Lower left: **Flock powders and other surface texturing materials (eg scree, sand, small stones etc) can be positioned 'dry', then 'glued' into place by flooding them with diluted white PVA glue (to milk consistency) dropped pipette fashion from a thick drinking straw. The glue here is in the egg cup. Leave overnight to set.**

see the skills required at some of the larger model railway shows, where model tree making is often a popular and instructive demonstration theme.

The rest of us depend on tree kits or ready-made — or more primitive home-made — models. The good news is that virtually all the companies in the structure and scenic business make tree kits, or ready-made trees. Look in the Faller, Auhagen, Busch, Noch, Heki and similar ranges for these. In recent years there has been a move into depicting actual tree species even in these popular lower price ranges. There are more highly detailed tree kits in the up-market range such as Woodland Scenes and Anita Decor.

Most tree kits offer a plastic (or sometimes soft metal) trunk unit and branches, with foliage material to tease out, shape and glue to the branches. You can improve these at once by painting the tree trunks in a more realistic greyish 'bark' colour. As supplied, some model tree trunks are a shiny brown plastic which can catch and reflect light in an unrealistic way. Branches can be variably positioned, and heights can be varied, so trees from kits need not be uniform.

Most model shops stock ready-made trees that come at very reasonably low prices, and when you need plenty of trees these are worth going for. Many of these are generic rather than specific types, but en masse they give a good effect. Even some of the ready-made trees these days are very realistic with

Above: **Firms such as Woodland Scenics make ranges of very high quality trees in kit form depicting actual species. This picture sequence shows the making of a model tree, from bare trunk to full foliage, from a Woodland Scenics kit.**

Right: **Readily available at low 'budget' prices are several makes of fir trees of generic kind. Their appearance can be improved by smearing them with white PVA glue, as is being done here.**

Lower right: **The tree smeared uniformly with glue is then rolled in a pot of ordinary scenic flock powder and comes out looking much better textured than it appears when purchased.**

good leaf effect. Check out your nearest model shop for these. Most of the really cheap ready-made trees can be much improved by repainting the trunks in the 'bark' colour, and brushing white PVA glue over the foliage. Then dip the tree into a saucer of green flock powder, roll it, shake off the excess flock, and you have quite a good 'leaf' effect. This can be done optionally on deciduous trees, but it is essential on cheap model fir trees (such as the good low price Jordan type), for without this treatment they look like Christmas cake decorations!

You can make simple but generic trees from suitable garden twigs or even the grape stalks that look wood-like (not all grape stalks are suitable — some are too green and soft). Use the foliage fibre left over from tree kits, teased out and glued with white PVA to the twig or grape stalk 'branches'. The result is a cheap and cheerful tree that looks quite reasonable if used well in the background.

WATER

There are many ways to depict water. For some years various clear resin-based kits have been available. A recent good brand is Solid Water. Basically you mix, pour and leave to set. You can get waterfall and 'rapids' effects etc and it is all covered in the kit instructions.

For ponds, lakes, rivers, etc others have favoured glass, clear acetate sheet, crumpled cellophane, over card painted bluish-grey, and other similar methods. Kibri includes useful slightly rippled plastic 'water' sheeting in its big scenic and structure range. For dripping pipes, running fountains, etc, a favourite trick is to stretch out clear plastic sprues from kits, heated over a candle flame and pulled out until the desired diameter for the 'pouring water' you want is achieved. Then cut a length and glue it on the end of the pipe or

duct from which it is supposed to be running.

Puddles and ruts filled with water (as on farm tracks etc) can be depicted by pouring out suitable blobs of clear gloss varnish and leaving it to dry. Of course, for this the surface must not be porous, otherwise the varnish will just soak into the baseboard and disappear!

But my favourite 'quick fix' way of depicting water — which I use almost always — is clear gloss varnish over a suitably painted base. Most small layouts only have room for a nominal area of water, typically a canal or harbour basin with jetty, or a canal lock, depicting just a small portion of a bigger water area on the edge or end of the baseboard.

The method here is to cut a sheet of 20 thou or 40 thou plastic card to size for the lock or basin. Glue it in place at 'water level'. Then paint over it in gloss

paint to give a darkish blue-black for inland water or green-blue for sea water (there is a lot of variation possible) and leave to dry. Over this paint clear gloss varnish, leave to dry hard, and apply at least two more coats. The more gloss clear varnish you apply, the 'wetter' the water will look. It will give realistic water reflections, too. If the gloss ever dulls — as it may do with time — simply refresh it with more coats of clear gloss varnish.

Whichever way you depict water you can then glue on the surface driftwood, canoes, boats, water weed (from flock powder), reeds (from teased out green string), and even swans or ducks (from castings) as desired.

SCENIC MATS AND OTHER SURFACES

Experts tend to look down on scenic mats and say they look 'toy like'. But ignore this. They only look 'toy like' if the mat is glued or pinned perfectly flat to the baseboard and everything else — track, structures, accessories, etc — is placed on top of it. If you use scenic mats sensibly they can save much time (and money, come to that, for they are reasonably priced) and are clean and easy to use.

Of course, scenic mats are not the answer to all your scenic needs, for you still need to model any cuttings, cliff faces or other steep or high features in the usual way. But where the ground is relatively flat, as is usually the case around station and yard areas, then scenic mats can come very much into their own. To take the easy one first, roadways, car parks or yard surfaces can be depicted by cutting strips to suit your need from the Hornby R8066 (tarmac) or R8067 (granite) sheets or similar equivalents. You can paint roadway markings on these as required once the roadway is laid in place, but if you are not too good at this, the Busch range includes a pack of road markings transfers to cover every requirement, including car parks. For country lanes or cross-country paths etc the cork mat can be used, but its appearance is improved if you give it a brownish-grey wash of acrylic paint to take away the 'clean' look of a fresh cork mat.

The widest use of scenic mats, however, is for depicting grass surfaces, for which the light, dark and meadow green mats are available from

Above: **Various clear acrylic-type 'water' kits are available, such as Solid Water. This sets with a realistic effect, especially if 'running water' is to be depicted, as with these rapids.**

Left: **The water running out of the culvert pipe here is made from clear plastic sprue stretched and bent to shape over a candle flame — a well-known trick. The water in the stream itself is depicted by layers of clear gloss varnish painted over a 'muddy' base colour.**

Upper right: **Excellent use is shown here of scenic mats, with grass mat for the verges round the office block, and sheets of embossed cobble stone for the surface of the yard. Note the use of tree foliage material to depict ivy climbing the wall.**

Lower right: **Firms like Noch and Busch produce a huge range of ready-to-lay roadway, rolls, paved areas, crash barriers, road markings, zebra crossings and pre-printed car park sheets to suit the smaller scales, and a selection for HO (which also suits OO) and N can be seen here.**

both Hornby and the German makers noted below. Also worth getting are the cobble, sett, roadway and paving sheets from Faller, Auhagen, Noch, Busch and others for road and yard areas. Clearly if you really need to depict a smooth, flat, grass surface, then the grass mats are ideal as they come. Such areas as garden lawns, bowling greens, tennis courts, crazy golf pitches, cricket pitches, football pitches, suburban road verges, recreation grounds and so on are usually flat and well tended, so the light green scenic mat can be cut to size and glued flat to the baseboard. An art roller or coffee jar should be used to ensure that mat areas are really flat without any air bubbles that may later result in an unrealistic 'bump', say, in the middle of a model tennis court. You can use white paint for any sports field markings you need.

Most grassed areas, however, are uneven and slightly undulating. Provided you have a suitable surface you can use grass scenic mats for most heavily grassed areas. On flattish areas of land, for example, as may be adjacent to tracks in a station or yard area, you can use the mats cut to the required shape, but instead of gluing them direct to the flat baseboard surface, glue down a few scraps of card, styrene, sheets, balsa offcuts, etc first. When the grass mat is glued over this surface it will undulate in a realistic way.

You can extend this to quite elevated areas of land. A lot of rail cuttings or embankments are quite neatly grassed in real life, and if you use styrene block or card formers for cutting/embankments etc, the grass mat can be glued on as the top surface, quite roughly so that it is not perfectly flat but again undulates slightly. On these angled surfaces you can hold the mat in place until the glue dries by pinning it with tacks or track pins.

Gently sloped or higher ground that is well grassed, as in downland areas, can be similarly covered with grass mat. On one layout I made, a high level area was roughly shaped from a block of styrene packing, complete with roadway, and the grass mat was cut to shape and glued over the styrene, again using pins or tacks to hold it in place while the glue dried. For all this glue work with scenic mats, use white PVA glue, for this will not attack any styrene or plastics you may be using in the general scenic work.

Once the grass mat is in place, it will look far too new or 'perfect' for true realism if left exactly as it is. The exception, of course, will be lawns or sports pitches that intentionally look 'perfect'. The next task, therefore, is to go over the grassed areas to add a bit of undergrowth, rough clumps, bare patches, bits of tree stump or log, rubbish, rocky outcrops, trees, bushes, walls, hedges or whatever else your own idea of scenic development calls for. Add patches of rock from cork bark or coarse ballast, or even rough garden pebbles; scrape the grass mat surface gently with a blunt knife blade to 'roughen' it a little, or even try pouring clear varnish into dips to depict puddles of rain or waterlogged areas. Ideas for using grass mats and the various paving, cobbles, sett and roadway sheets are limited only by your

Above: **Many recent structure kits from Europe come with parts ready painted and weathered, an example being this German coal merchant's depot in HO from Pola which is complete with barrows, coal sacks and dummy coal. Note also the embossed sett sheet used as the roadway.**

imagination.

MAKING BETTER BUILDINGS

Nobody in our hobby these days lacks for buildings in HO or N. They are found in abundance in every large model shop, most of them in plastic kit form but also as card cut-outs in ever-growing numbers. Almost everything you need — including stations in all sizes — can be had without too much trouble. Kits are easy to assemble too, and even a lot of the card kits are simpler than you might at first think. Anyone with basic modelling experience can assemble them. Though the selection is much more limited, there are kits, too, for TT, O, 1 and G scales, and the same care must be used whichever scale you work in.

The problem is that very many modellers take the kits for granted. They certainly look good just stuck together out of the box, and it is not difficult to do this. However, this can also be a let-down. Even on layouts at model railway exhibitions there are all too many badly or indifferently made structure kits. We have all seen shiny plastic roofs, daylight showing through a big model factory from side to side, and good looking old buildings only too obviously perched on the ground with shadows showing underneath where the foundations should be! Without making an over-long list, the errors mostly noted are: unpainted plastic roofs and walls, badly applied glazing (or none at all), mould marks showing anywhere, and 'flash' too, 'hollow' see-through buildings, buildings not 'bedded in', walls painted in 'solid' colours so that the brick or stone effect is largely obliterated by paint, scenery visible through the backs of low relief buildings, and lack of guttering, downpipes and other details.

Before assembling a kit straight from the box and fitting it on the layout, spend some time looking at it first to see what it does or does not provide. Some very recent kits come with a weathered finish (which may include a painted brick effect) and all sorts of interior detail, though most are simply 'shells' with all external detail but nothing inside. Most German-made kits are pre-coloured in that the walls are moulded in brick or stone colour and the roofs are slate or pantile colour, with contrast colour doors or window frames, but there are some older kits where all parts are one basic colour.

Before any assembly begins remove any flash, mould marks or other imperfections with a file, emery board or craft knife. The first important part is to get a realistic finish. What makes a building look great is (1) elimination of the plastic sheen, and (2) visible mortar/cement coursing between the bricks. You can do both these jobs in one by the method shown. Before you assemble anything, take each wall in turn and paint it all over in acrylic matt white or very light grey. Use a big brush for this and do the walls one at a time.. As soon as you have applied the paint, wipe it all off again with a pad of kitchen paper so that only the light colour remains between the courses of bricks. On a few occasions, where a building is in yellow brick, you might want to use a dark grey for the coursing, but with grey/red brick/stone the white or light grey is required. The faint smear of paint left when you wipe off all the surplus paint also takes the shiny sheen off the plastic and it really does look like matt brick. If you do nothing else suggested here, try this and be amazed at the increase in realism!

Roofs can be given a similar treatment. In this case use matt black or dark grey and put a generous wash all over the roof mouldings, then wipe it all off again. The black will run into all the crevices between the tiles and will be left behind when you wipe off the paint. This will again eliminate the shiny plastic sheen, make the roof detail stand out, and give it a realistic weathered look. You can use ordinary enamels for this, but it is much better to use water-based acrylics, of which the Humbrol type can be commended because it comes in well-sealed pots and keeps well without drying out. The acrylic paint is soluble so you can quickly wash it off and start again if dissatisfied with your first effort. Also you can clean the brushes in water afterwards so long as you do not let them dry out.

Only after all the walls and roof parts have been weathered should you get on with actual assembly — weathering after assembly is much more difficult.

Detailing may well be needed outside. Most kits come with roof guttering and downpipes, but some do not. In the latter case you'll need to add them, and if you check out your nearest model

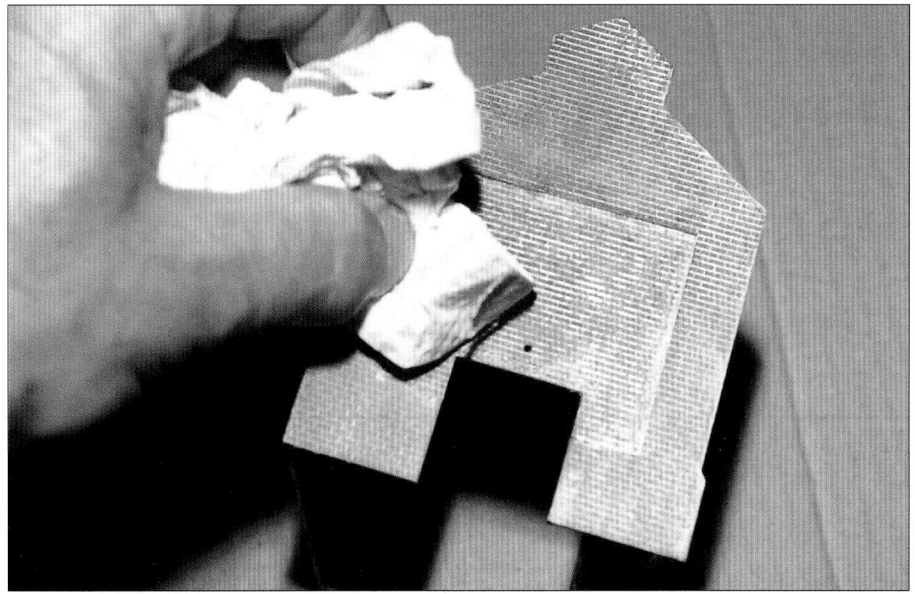

Top right: **The photo sequence here shows how mortar/cement coursing can be better depicted on model brickwork in plastic kits. First paint white or light grey acrylic paint all over the wall.**

Centre right: **Immediately wipe off the paint with kitchen paper. Do each wall in turn and do not give the white paint time to start drying.**

Lower right: **The model completed, with the coursing suggested between the bricks and the plastic sheen of the walls toned down. This is the familiar Dapol (originally Airfix) engine shed for 4mm scale. The windows are glazed and the downpipes added.**

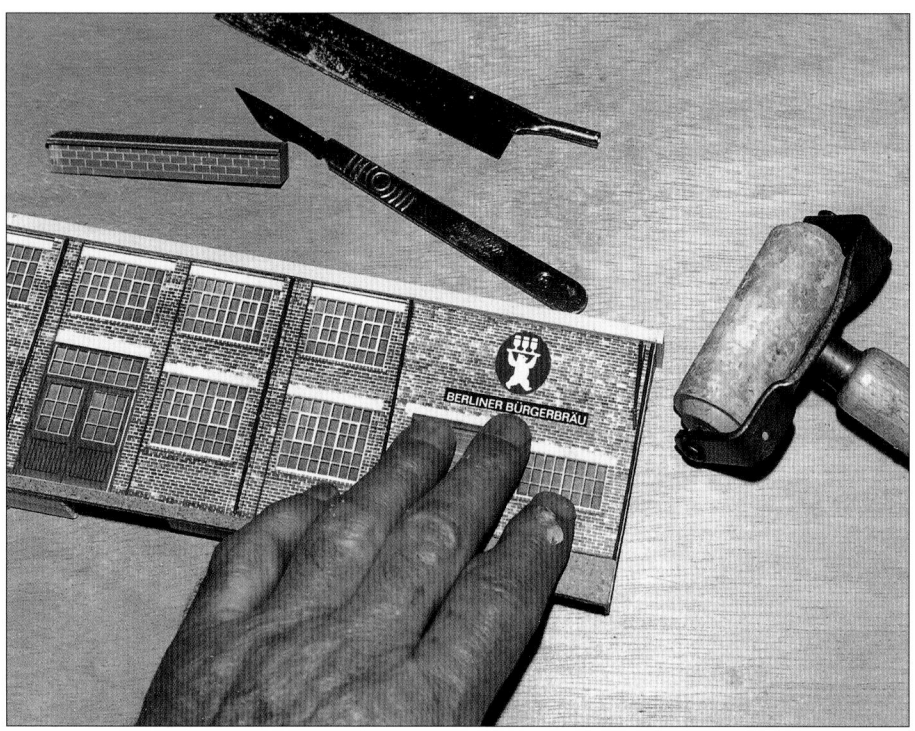

Above: **Card cut-out kits are very adaptable. This is the well-known Bilteezi factory being used to make a long low-relief warehouse rather than the square building intended. It is glued to sheet balsa, using all the walls flat. It is the 3mm version for a TT layout.**

Below: **The low relief warehouse complete and in position. A loading bank is added on the front and the printed downpipes have plastic rod downpipes glued over them to give a better effect.**

shop you'll find accessory packs by Wills, Ratio, Faller, Pola and others which provide a generous supply of pipes, gutters and other useful bits for detailing buildings. Card cut-out models may have the downpipes just painted on, or may lack these parts. Here, again, you can used the plastic detailing sets to provide them. On the card kits with printed downpipes, glue the plastic downpipes on top of them. On most card kits you can alter doors and windows to be 'open' as you go along.

This brings us to interior detail. If you open up card kit doors etc or set open doors and sliding doors in plastic kits you reveal interiors. Most models are hollow inside and you can often see right through them. To overcome this, cut card floors, interior walls, and floors for upper storeys. You need spend no big money on this. Scrap card will do, such as comes from cereal packets or the backs of writing pads or scribble pads. You can draw in planking if desired but it does not need to be precise so long as it gives the impression. After all, when the building is complete you cannot see much of the interior, but you must be able to see 'solid' walls rather than light showing through the opposite windows. Many kits these days have printed curtains for windows (and interiors for shop windows), but you can used coloured paper where no printed curtains are provided. If the window glazing is poor or over-thick, use clear plastic sheet instead, again often found as scrap such as the front of some cartons. Some kits have thick black paper liners, too, which is necessary only if you plan to light the interiors. If you don't use this lining you will find that any inside bulb glows through the plastic with loss of realism, but if you do not plan to illuminate the layout this is one measure you can ignore.

Finally, the other big let-down is lack of bedding-in effect. However nicely you have made the model, it looks ridiculous if it is only too obviously placed flat on the scenery. The trick here is either to allow a recess into which it can fit — for example leaving a gap behind the card paving in a street — or running white PVA glue round the base area where the structure is fixed in place, and sprinkle grass scatter material or ground form in the glue so that it looks like the grass or weeds that grow round the bottom edges of most buildings.

Above right: **Kit parts can be used to make entirely different buildings. Here the sides and faces of a Kibri loading tower, plus the front half of a Wills barn kit, have been used to make a low relief 'feed and seed' merchant for a country station siding. The loading bank is from scrap parts, and the adverts come from accessory sheets.**

Right: **The same model seen from behind shows that thick card or balsa sheet, painted dark grey or black inside, is used to blank off the back of the model so that no light shines through to ruin the illusion of a 'solid' building.**

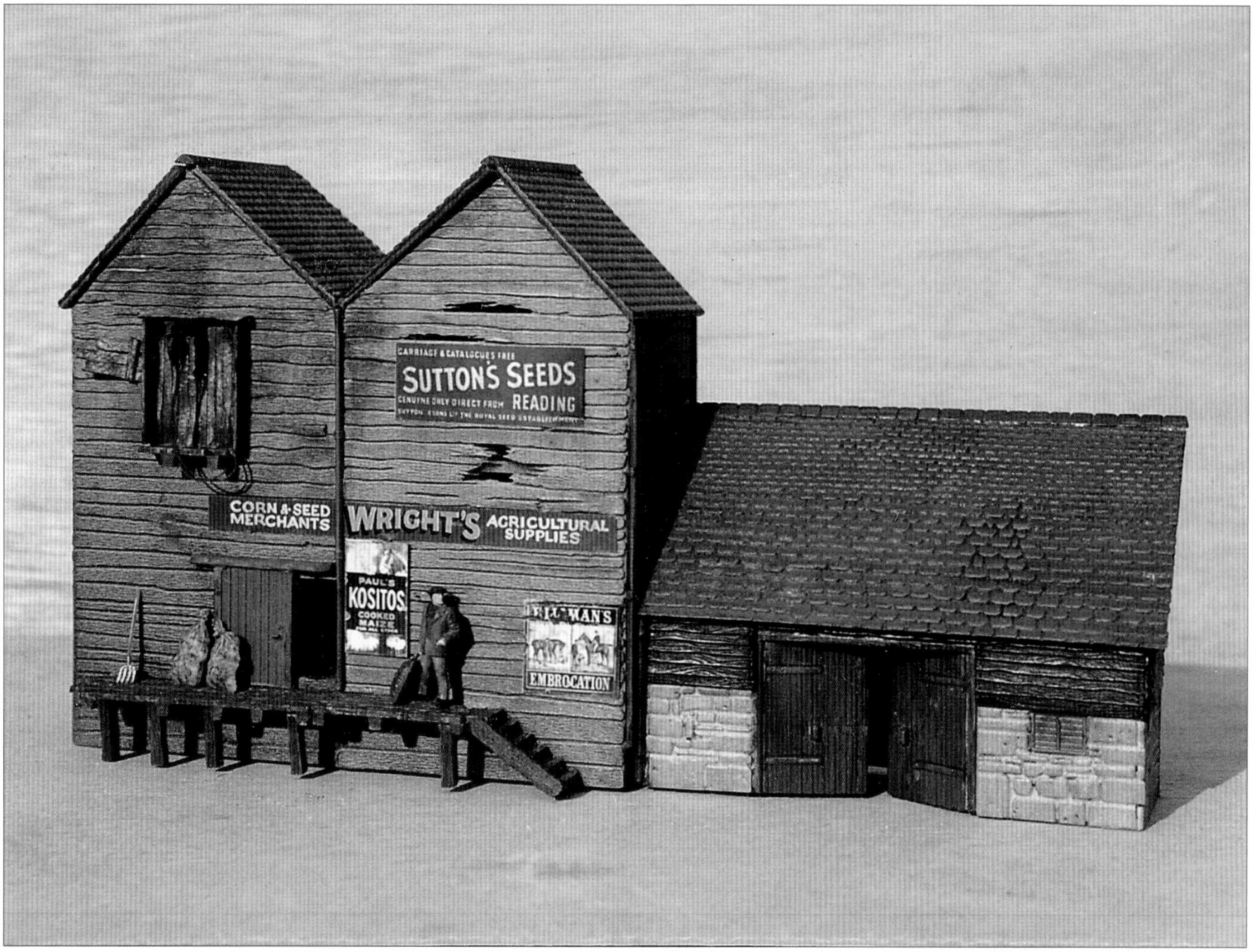
CARRIAGE & CATALOGUES FREE
SUTTON'S SEEDS
GENUINE ONLY DIRECT FROM READING
CORN & SEED MERCHANTS
WRIGHT'S
AGRICULTURAL SUPPLIES
PAUL'S
KOSITOS
COOKED MAIZE
EMBROCATION

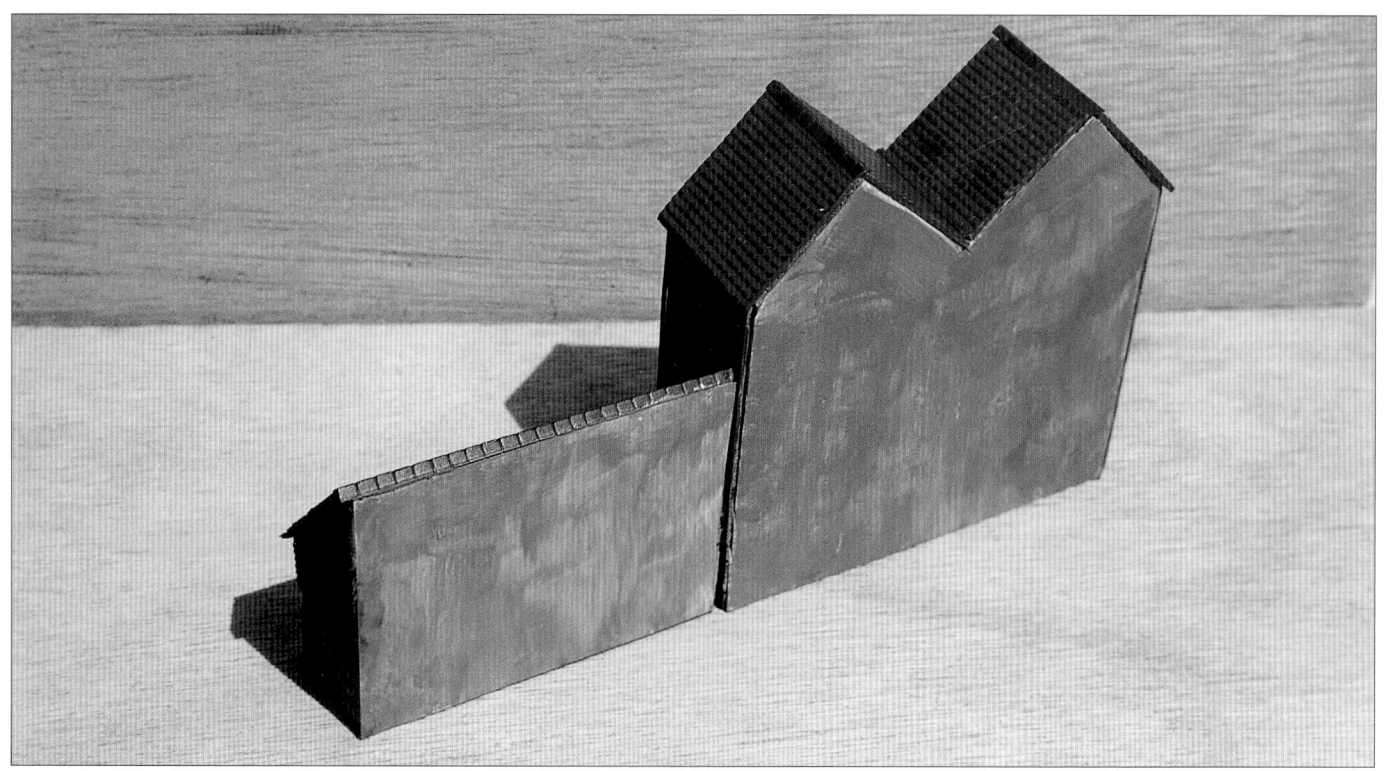

CHAPTER 7

TRACK AND BALLAST

Track is so familiar that most take it for granted. Because over 80% of hobbyists favour HO or OO gauge (16.5mm), developments in the trade have tended to be concentrated on this, and the biggest selection and variety is in 16.5mm gauge.

Sectional track is the basis for whole systems produced by all the leading manufacturers and is supplied also in the train sets that form the starting point in the hobby for many beginners. Most readers of this book will already have used sectional track and it needs little more comment here, save to say that all ranges have a fixed geometry which is not standardised, so lengths and radii may vary between makes. Some ranges, such as Hornby and Peco Setrack, do match in most

respects, but this is exceptional. However, the discrepancies can be useful if you are making up a layout from sectional track, because the different lengths and curve radii may be ideal to make up the formation you need to fit the area.

One thing I do with 16.5mm track is maintain a reserve 'bank' of straights and curves specifically for this purpose. Thus if a Hornby straight section is too short to fill out a siding I find a longer one, say by Mehano/Model Power, which does. You do not have to spend much money collecting these reserves, for secondhand track pieces are sold quite cheaply at shows and in some larger model shops. An assortment of short sections of various makes — the shortest sections they do — is also

useful for filling out sidings and station layouts.

Staying with 16.5mm gauge HO track, at the basic level a 'scale looking' rail known as Code 100 is used. This refers to the rail height of 0.100in (2.54mm). In scale terms at 1:87 or 1:76 scale it would depict the very heaviest weight of main line track. However, when weathered with 'rust' paint the rail section looks 'lighter', and Code 100 track certainly looks acceptable and satisfies most modellers. When this track is used for narrow gauge the scale becomes larger (such as 1:43 for On16.5) so the track is proportionally 'lighter' in relation to the stock running on it.

In recent years there has been a move to produce track with a rail section closer to real scale height. This has resulted in HO track with Code 83 rail (0.083in high) from Roco, Atlas, Tillig and others, and an even lower Code 75 (0.075in high) from Peco in its Finescale series. There are some adaptor rails or joiners to allow Code 100 track to be used with lighter section rails. In N gauge, Code 80 is usual, but Peco does a Code 55 Finescale track and this has a much better appearance.

Moving on from purely sectional track, all the leading makers have produced lengths of flexible track, typically in yard or metre lengths, that can be used to make much gentler curves with prototypical transitions. This flex-track can be used at will with the sectional tracks. One good point is that all the Code 100 tracks join up whatever the make, as do Code 83 tracks. Flex-track (and indeed sectional tracks if you wish to shorten them) can be cut with razor saws or the specialist rail-cutters that are available. Most makes have holes in some sleepers (ties) to take track fixings, and those that don't, usually have 'blind' holes that can be pierced out to take the pins.

Track fixings come in at least three types: spikes, pins and tacks. It is worth getting packets of each, for different

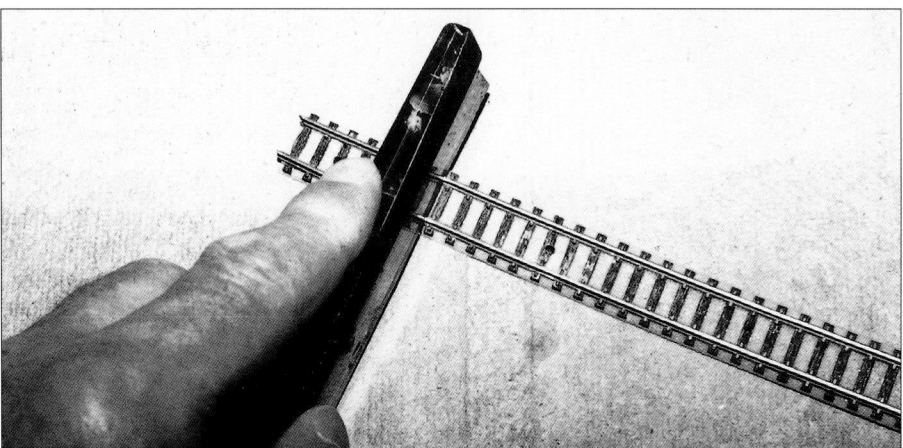

Upper left: **The advantage of flexible track (flex-track) is that it can be cut to any length to suit your track formation. Track cutting tools are available but you can also use a razor saw, as here with Fleischmann N gauge track.**

Lower left: **Track pins are easily pushed in with pliers, but in harder boards (like MDF) you may need to drill a pilot hole first. The track here is ballasted by the insulating tape method described on page 73.**

baseboards have different needs. Pins are best for Sundeala and similar soft boards. Spikes work well with 3mm MDF or Sundeala, and tacks are best for plywood and thicker MDF. In both latter cases drill out pilot holes for the tacks before pushing the tacks down with pliers.

Rail joiners are attached to most sectional track lengths, though rarely to flex-track. But packs of joiners are sold separately for all ranges. The rail joiner is a key piece, not only for holding sections together but also for carrying the current. Always replace any bent, buckled or corroded rail joiners (you may get derails or 'dead' sections if you don't) and always double check that the join is correctly made. Sometimes the joiner runs below the rail it is supposed to join. It's frustrating to find this out after all the track has been pinned down. These matters may sound obvious, but even old hands can overlook them. Run rolling stock over every rail join when you are laying track to ensure all is smooth and level.

DISCREPANCY BETWEEN HO AND OO

In 16.5mm gauge almost all track is actually scaled for the international HO gauge (1:87 scale), except for some with larger sleepers intended for On16.5. Most modellers in 4mm scale (1:76), which also uses 16.5mm gauge track, overlook the discrepancy and go along with the HO proportional track. If you don't like this, the firm of SMP produces 1:76 scale (4mm to 1ft) 16.5mm gauge track which has British-style bullhead rail section on sleepers scaled to true 4mm to 1ft scale which are obviously bigger than the HO sleepers. You cannot get ready-made OO points, however, but SMP make point kits which are fairly easy to assemble.

OTHER GAUGES

All the above comments refer to 16.5mm gauge, by far the most common. But the same remarks apply to all the other common scales and gauges. You can get sectional and flex-track for Z, N, TT, S, O, 1 and G scales, but outlets may be more limited, as will available units. However, there are specialist retailers for all gauges even though you may have to get some by mail order. Specialist track makers like

Peco (and less importantly Tillig) produce in several gauges, including narrow gauge. If you are interested in the less popular gauges it is a good idea to get hold of the catalogues of Peco (and relevant makes like LGB for G scale) to see what track units are available.

Peco, and other firms, often have full-size illustrations of their points which are very useful to have to hand when planning your layout, as you can work out what units you need before you buy them.

WEATHERING TRACK

A key task is to make shiny new track look more realistic by weathering it to give it the dirty or rusted look seen on real track. This is easily done by painting the rail sides, fixings and sleepers/ties in a dirty brownish colour. Some paint ranges include 'track colours' specially for this, but earth brown or dark earth shades, or even matt black with a touch of brown added, will do equally well. It is easiest to paint the track before you lay it, but on a small layout where all track is accessible, it is also possible to do it with the track in situ. A medium chisel edge brush is handy for the painting job. You'll get paint on the top of the rail, too. Wait until it is dry, then rub off

Above: **Weathering track the conventional way with a brush and dark earth paint on the sides of the rail. The sleepers (ties) also need weathering and this can be done in the same painting session.**

Below: **This track formation has been weathered and a track rubber is used to clear unwanted paint from the rail tops. On this ballasted Profi track the sleepers (ties) and plastic ballast base have also been weathered.**

the top edge of the rails only with a track rubber until the shine is restored. Check or guard rails should be painted on top, too, as the wheels don't run over them.

Be particularly careful not to let paint run inside the rail joiners, or get on to the moving blades or pivots of the points. It is surprisingly easy to 'gum up' moving parts or destroy an electric circuit with only a smear of paint in the wrong place.

A further option in finishing the track is to do some slight 'dry brushing' of the sleeper/tie tops to bring out the moulded grain and adding greasy black on sleeper/tie tops at plates where locomotives might stop or rest. However, this does not need to be done until after the track is in place.

BALLASTING THE TRACK
One task which some put off, or never do at all, is track ballasting. We all know that properly ballasted model track looks superb, but not everyone is confident of doing it properly.

Don't despair. There are messy ways of ballasting and there are simple ways of ballasting. And better still, in the most popular scales there is the option of ready ballasted track. If you choose the right prototype, such as some old-time American logging or backwoods lines,

or some industrial narrow gauge lines, you can omit the ballast. They simply laid the track flat on the ground and ignored the ballasting. These are isolated examples, however, and ballasting can't be overlooked if you want realistic track.

Clearly you can solve the ballasting problem fairly easily by going for one of the ready-ballasted track ranges in HO/OO or N. The cost is higher but you can trade that off against the time and hassle — if that is how you regard it — of ballasting ordinary track. In my experience, this track is very durable due to the extra strength and rigidity given by the ballast base, so you should get a lot of use out of the higher first investment. If you do a careful job of weathering the track and ballast, the fact that it is ready-ballasted will not be obvious. The ultimate reward here is when a visitor asks: 'How did you ballast the track?', not recognising it as one of the commonly sold ranges! Much of the secret is in careful weathering work, but also in bringing the edge or the scenic work right up to, and even level with, the ballast edge. This eliminates the straight edge of the ballast, just as the weathering eliminates the 'plastic' look. When these ready-ballasted tracks first came in, some modellers said it looked too 'toy-like' (or words to that effect), which may be true when it is fresh out of the box. The modeller's art here is to do the weathering and scenic work that eliminates the 'toy-like' look.

READY-BALLASTED TRACK (HO/OO)

FLEISCHMANN PROFI
This is the most widely available in Britain and other countries. In my experience it is also the best. This must be qualified by the fact that I have more experience of this than any other make. It is also worth pointing out that the good engineering ensures that secondhand stock is also excellent and can save you a bit of money if your budget is tight.

Fleischmann managed to make the ballast rather discreet in the sense that it is not highly shouldered or prominent like most other makes and therefore blends more easily with scenic work and does not need any special treatment in yards or station areas. They also kept the dimensions and geometry compact without it looking too obviously so. Hence 3-way points, double-slips, etc don't take up too much length. These more complex point units are also well engineered and electrically sound and do not, in my experience, cause any of the problems with stalling etc that occurs on some other makes of track. The electrical system used by Fleischmann is excellent; for example, deep rail joiners 'buried' in the ballast give a good electrical bond and hold the track tightly together. All the wiring is simple and colour coded and if you follow the diagrams and colours you need to know nothing much of electrical or wiring theory to be in business!

If you change layout ideas, nothing is wasted since all can be unpinned from the baseboard and it is ready to use over again. Some of my track has been in constant use for over 20 years and is as good as ever in running terms. The problems have been very few.

The tie-bars and plastic levers inside the points are a weak feature that in a couple of cases have made the point inoperable when they become dislodged. You can overcome this by turning the point upside down, releasing the tabs on the baseplate, and carefully relocating the movement with tweezers. But if you don't do this very gently and accurately you could be in worse trouble, so if a point movement gives up on you it might be better to contact your nearest Fleischmann dealer for servicing advice.

Below: **Fleischmann HO Profi track carefully weathered, with the built-in ballast base not too obvious. Note also the adapted Bilteezi factory and the East German political poster hoarding masking off the exit to the fiddle yard.**

In general this is a very dependable system, which can be made very realistic with good weathering. A bag of matching ballast chips is included in the range which can help 'spread' the ballast scenically in, say, areas around crossovers etc.

ROCO-LINE

Roco's 'new generation' track to Code 83 came out in the 1990s and also offers a ballast base, in grey or brown plastic, which is hollow underneath so that all the wiring can be carried inside, and point motors can fit under turnouts too. This is a good visual bonus. In Britain it is stocked by the larger Roco specialists. The track can be detached from the ballast. Roco literature shows that the ballast base can be trimmed where points need to abut etc and it all looks straightforward to use. However, I have no direct operating experience but those who have speak highly of it.

As supplied, Roco-Line comes with a heavily shouldered but accurate German-style ballasting which is how it would be out on the main line. But for yard or station areas it seems you have to do a lot more scenic work to build up

Top right: **Bachmann EZmate HO track showing built-in ballast base.**

Below left: **Rocoline HO Code 83 track with ballast base.**

Below right: **Kato HO Unitrack showing joiner clips and point wiring in ballast base.**

the ground to get it level with the ballast. With Profi track this is not so necessary as the ballast is much lower to start with. The joins between track sections are also rather more prominent because there is more ballast on view — hence more effort is needed to hide the joins.

The big advantage of Roco-Line is the lighter Code 83 rail, rather than the Code 100 used by Profi, and this might influence your choice.

BACHMANN EZMATE

Comments on this are rather restricted, based on observation rather than experience, because it is very difficult to find on sale in Great Britain at the time of writing, though it is in some Bachmann train sets and is available to order. EZmate looks quite good as it comes, though the ballast base is rather angular and would need quite a

lot of 'scenic levelling' to look more natural. The colour is a variable grey, which some might like to 'lighten' a little when weathering. The connections are very strong and rigid, again with wiring take inside the hollow ballast base. I have been told it is good and easy to use, and there are some useful pieces in the range, such as complete crossovers etc.

KATO UNITRACK

This Japanese track for HO has never been sold on the British market at the time of writing but is available in Japan, the USA and other countries.

It is, however, of superb quality with rail of about Code 75, and close-spaced American-style sleepers (ties) with 'spike'-style rail fixings. The realistic grey ballast is hollow to allow internal wiring runs, and the fixings are very strong and electrically good. The

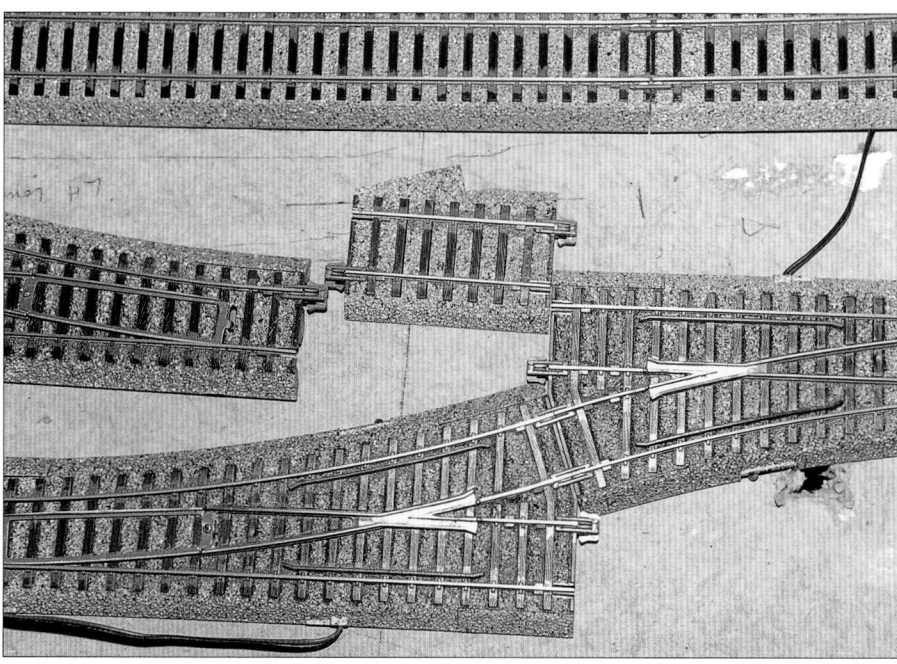

shouldering is rather high, however, as with EZmate (though not as high as Roco) so a fair amount of scenic levelling would be necessary in yards and station areas. There are nice point levers for remote control, done rather like the handles in real electric signal boxes, and these can be ganged together. The electrics, in fact, are very easy to set up, and it is all done with typical Kato quality and thoroughness.

The drawback on this Kato HO system is that its geometry is extremely rigid. It is fine for neat ovals with passing loops and sidings as familiar from train manufacturers' layout plan books, but it is extremely difficult to achieve any sort of naturalistic 'transitional' effect because there are no flexible lengths or extender sections (as there are with Profi).

READY-BALLASTED TRACK (N)

FLEISCHMANN PICCOLO

Almost all the comments made about Profi track apply to its smaller N gauge relative which actually preceded Profi in production. It is as durable and foolproof in all respects as Profi. There are a few more visual disadvantages. The point motors are the same as HO and therefore take a bit more effort to hide if you do not use them in the inverted mode that Fleischmann suggests. And the Code 80 track is relatively heftier than Code 100 in HO. However, careful weathering will make it look a lot less conspicuous (as indeed it will with Code 100 track in HO).

KATO UNITRACK

Unlike the HO version, the Kato Unitrack in N is sold in the UK and comes with brown or grey ballast base. Because there is a bigger choice of track radii and lengths than with the HO version, however, it is very much easier to get a naturalistic 'transitional' look to the track. All the comments about quality and ease of setting up made about the HO version apply here, and you can buy it with confidence. A good visual point is that while Code 80 rail seems to have been used, the rail section is finer than most others, giving a much lighter effect to the rail which is always welcome in N.

FOAM-BALLAST STRIP

This is the most widely available accessory for depicting ballast. Hornby, Peco and others make this, and Peco have point bases to match for both HO/OO and N. You can even get it for gauge 1 track by Märklin. The secret of success here is to disguise the hard edge with scenic work, and to weather it with a brown/black acrylic wash to eliminate the obvious foam appearance. I have used this on several layouts with success, even though some say it lacks realism and crumbles with age.

I have so far had not deterioration on layouts, probably because they are stored out of direct light and in equable domestic temperature. For example, my Nürnberg-Tragbar layout was built in 1989 using foam ballast, and it still looks pristine with no sign of the foam ballast crumbling or coming away.

The most recent development of this type of ballast strip gives it a quite realistic stone-chip top coating. It is made in Germany by Noch and is called 'Real Stone Pre-Ballasted Foam Underlay'. It is advertised and sold in Britain by On Tracks.

BALLAST BASES

These are essentially styrene sheets moulded with recesses to accept the sleeper mountings of sectional and flexible track and coated on top with a realistic ballast chip finish. It has to be

Above left: **As is evident from this view, the 'heavy' look of N gauge Piccolo ballasted track is much reduced when the track and ballast is weathered with dark earth paint.**

Lower left: **Kato N gauge Unitrack in use, showing the 'lightness' of the rail section which is a visual advantage in this scale.**

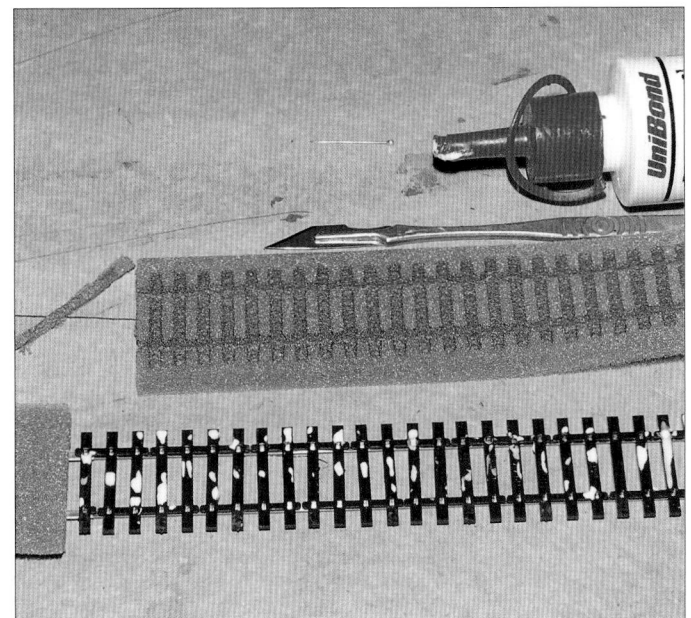

Above left: **An example of the use of the commonly available foam ballast base. The track is best held into the ballast by a little white PVA glue smeared on the bottom of the sleeper (cross-tie) base.**

Above right: **The appearance of foam ballast is much improved if you paint all over it with a blackish-brown watery acrylic paint mix.**

Right: **Foam ballast base can look quite realistic if carefully laid and weathered, as shown with Peco Code 75 track on the Nürnberg-Tragbar layout. Note the mast in the middle which carries CCTV security cameras to monitor the yard, a detail worth remembering for modern era layouts.**

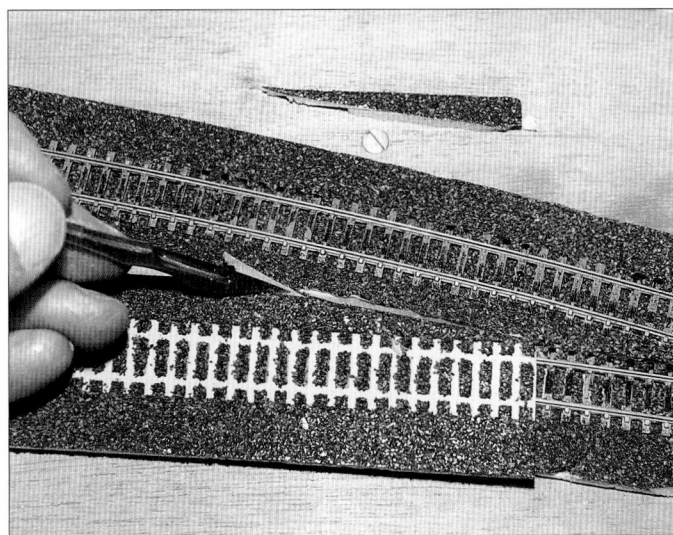

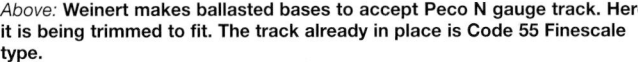

Above: **Weinert makes ballasted bases to accept Peco N gauge track. Here it is being trimmed to fit. The track already in place is Code 55 Finescale type.**

Above: **Merkur ballast base with Märklin HO track fitted in place. Ballast bases in the same style are made for other makes of HO track, too.**

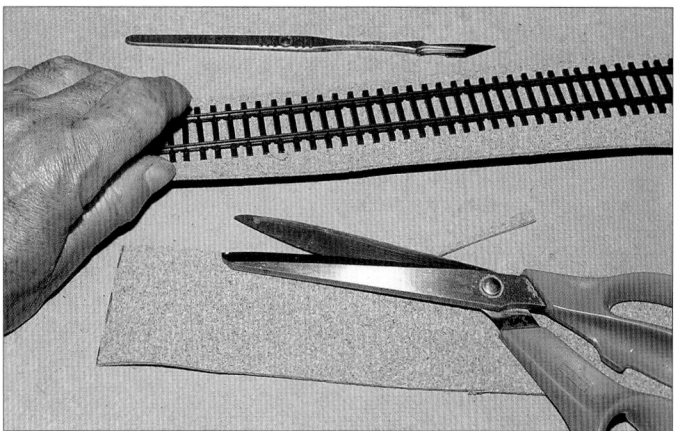

Above: Tillig pre-weathered track being laid on a cork sheet base, prior to bonded ballasting.

Below: Before ballasting starts the area under points is painted 'ballast colour' because bonding must be kept away from moving parts, so the ballast is thin in that area and the paint makes this less obvious.

Above: Before ballasting begins, check all the track and if necessary add cosmetic sleepers (ties) to fill gaps, as is being done here. The point lever here is from the Caboose Industries range.

Below: The loose ballast, granulated cork in this case, is now brushed and shaped into position prior to dribbling the bonding agent dilute white PVA glue) over it in the same way as illustrated with bonded texturing on page 58.

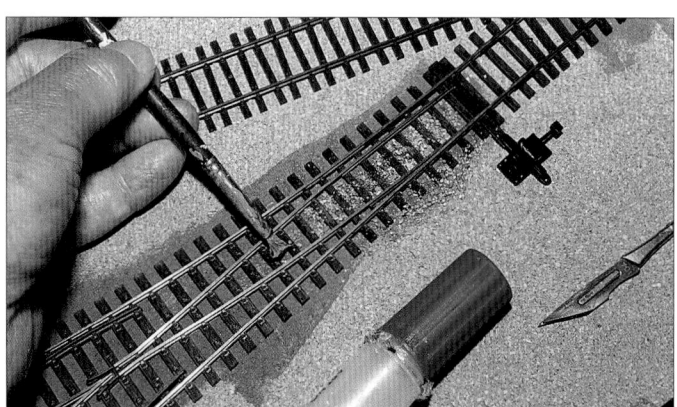

made for specific ranges, however, because almost every make has slightly different sleeper spacing or width and all makes of turnout differ and need dedicated bases.

The overall concept and design is clever, with allowance for double track and optional shouldering by removing concealed strips at the edges. Another German product, it is made by Merkur in HO (and N where appropriate) for such ranges of track as Roco and Märklin and also for LGB G scale track. Only the latter is available in Britain, however.

Another German company, Weinert, makes a very similar product to fit the Peco HO/OO N and 12mm track, and this is available in Britain via Three Point Five Models. Prices are reasonable, though higher than foam-ballast strip.

Excellent realism is achieved and it works particularly well with Peco N gauge track.

BONDED BALLAST

This is the method the experts say is the one to use, and to be honest it is the way ballasting is done on virtually all the top class layouts. It is actually quite easy on plain track, though it can't be rushed.

Essentially you pin down the track preferably on cork underlay, then drop the ballast loose around it, using a brush to get it evenly distributed and shouldered. A section at a time, it is then sprayed with a 'wetting agent' of water with a few drops of washing up liquid added. A cheap plastic spray bottle can be used. Meanwhile white PVA glue is diluted with water in proportion about 20:1 in an old cup or small bowl. Using a drinking straw in pipette fashion, pick up the PVA solution, drop it along the centre line of the track and the solution spreads through the wetted area. Leave overnight to dry. The glue dries transparent and the ballast chips appear to be loosely laid, just like the

real thing, though they are actually held in place by the transparent glue solution. If any of the ballast seems loose to the touch when dry, repeat the application.

The trickier part comes when you ballast around turnouts. Immense care is needed as it is only too easy for some of the PVA solution to stay on the tie-bar, pivots or mechanism and set it all solid so that the turnout is inoperable.

Veteran modeller Andrew Knights suggests a variation whereby the white PVA glue is replaced by acrylic matt clear varnish. Mix it to a consistency such that when dribbled on to a dry metal sink top it spreads out evenly on contact. No wetting agent is needed with this. Use the pipette method to apply until the ballast is visibly milky in appearance, then leave for 24 hours to dry out.

An advantage of the acrylic varnish is that it is easier to remove from rail tops and turnout parts if it strays off the ballast.

Upper right: **The bonded ballast is now left to dry out hard, usually overnight, but the opportunity is first taken to push any 'washed out' ballast back into place using a spatula. Note the level crossing made from card strip but with an uncoupling magnet in the upper track.**

If you want the effect of weeds growing in the track, drop suitable flock powder or ground foam into the ballast before the glue or varnish is applied.

You can use ground up cork, ballast or crushed stone ballast with this bonded ballast method, but several modellers have pointed out that stone ballast can add quite a lot of weight to a biggish layout, so cork ballast may be preferable.

Before leaving this subject, you can use this 'bonded' system with diluted white PVA glue in all scenic work, not just for ballasting. When flock powder or ground foam is laid over the surface for texturing the vegetation, apply the wetting agent with a spray, then pipette the diluted PVA glue over everything, and it will all set in place just as the ballast does. You can add small rocks and scree etc among the vegetation too, and it will all stay solid but look 'loose'. Go back to the previous chapter to see where this applies. It is a better option than merely sprinkling flock powder over glue.

COMMERCIAL BALLAST SYSTEMS

Two well-known commercially produced ballasting systems have been available for years and may appeal as alternatives to the bonded ballast system.

(1) Tracklay, done for HO/OO and N, provides adhesive underlay strip on which the track is positioned, Ballast is then pressed in place around the sleepers and tracks.

(2) Brush-it-On provides ballast packs in various grades to suite the different scales, and you then add water to an adhesive bonder. You make the mix and apply it by brush or spatula. It can be a messy process but the finished effect is good if properly done.

'BOGUS BALLAST'

Just like others, I used to encounter problems with the bonded ballast method, mostly when it came to points. However careful I was, something invariably got gummed up and caused trouble. There was also the time factor, so I thought about other simple methods. Recalling early lessons in

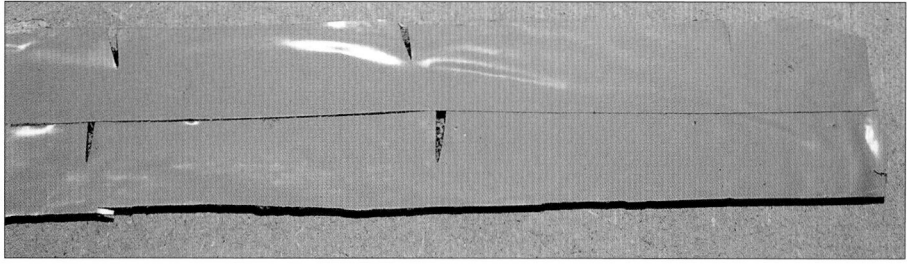

Above: **The first step in making 'bogus ballast' is to weather the track and sleepers, then turn it upside down and run two ½in strips of grey or brown insulating tape along it (for HO/OO) or one strip (for N).**

Below: **Turn the track over again and sprinkle the cork granulated ballast over it and press down with your fingers. The ballast will adhere to the sticky side of the insulated tape. You have effectively made your own pre-ballasted track. Points can get the same treatment.**

camouflage, I realised that merely suggesting the presence of ballast might work. My first experiment here, which I have used quite a lot since, was extremely simple. For HO/OO you need ½in-wide insulating tape in grey or brown, preferably grey. For N you need a single strip, but for HO track you need two strips side by side. Assemble a section of track formation, having first weathered the rails and sleepers by painting them and cleaning off the rail tops. Turn the track upside down and put the tape strips in place underneath the sleepers. Then pin the track in place in the usual way. The sticky side of the tape will be visible between the sleepers. Now just add granulated cork ballast, a pinch at a time, with your fingers, to cover all the visible sticky areas of tape, and press it firmly down. Afterwards shake any excess off on to newspaper for later use. My favoured ballast was Arnold item 1930, even better looking for HO than it was for N. However, it is hard to find this now, and you may have to settle for other granulated cork ballast.

An advantage of this system is that it is completely 'clean' and it seems durable, too, for I have track ballasted like this over 15 years ago and none of the ballast has fallen off. You can just unpin and re-use this track again, leaving all the ballast strip intact, and in this respect it is quite like the ready-ballasted track. If any insulating tape does come away, say, when you lift track for re-use, it is easy to do over again to make good, for example, a few torn inches.

The other 'bogus' method I have used in more recent years is even simpler. Noting the rolls of 'granite' and 'brown stone' scenic sheets among the grass mats in most model shops, I bought some to experiment with.

All that is done here is to cut strips of the material to ballast width and pin it down under the track when laying, having first weathered the rail and sleepers with paint. For turnouts or crossings, just draw round the unit on

the underside of the mat and cut out the shape. Again this is entirely 'clean' and track can be lifted at will for alteration or replacement. The added trick here is to build up the scenic surfacing to conceal the edges of the ballast sheet and then add a bit of build-up by gluing loose ballast along the edges of the sleepers, on the outer edges but in between a few of them too. This means that if anyone looks close to eye level they don't just see a flat sheet of matting but some undulation as well. If you are modelling a branch or yard you can also add some scenic scatter to depict grass and weeds growing between the sleepers, the more the better for a 'backwoods' line. Just dab in a few drops of PVA with a cocktail stick and drop bits of scatter on top of the glue. This all adds to the illusion and it seems to have fooled most visitors into thinking the whole lot was

Above left: **The second 'bogus ballast' method uses strips of granite or tarmac finish scenic matt pinned down below the track when the track is laid.The track is weathered in the usual way.**

Above right: **The same method is here being used with American S gauge track, in this case using the Hornby granite finish scenic matt as a suitable texture. The gaps in the cross-ties will be filled cosmetically when the ballast work is finished.**

painstakingly ballasted whereas it is all strips of scenic mat pinned down under the track.

Several of the leading scenic companies produce these mats in ballast-like textures in various colours, really intended to depict roadways, I think, but quite convincingly as 'bogus ballast'. Two I have found particularly good are in the Hornby range. R8067 works well with HO, S, O and 1, while R8066 looks best with TT, N or Z, but is fine for HO/OO too. The Hornby product is widely sold in the UK, but there are other similar makes.

New track developments come along all the time. For example, Peco has recently introduced a range of American-style HO track in Code 83 with ties and rail fixings to American standards.

Left: **You can use the 'bogus ballast' method with insulating tape and granulated cork ballast in any scale or gauge. On the author's small Felin-Dre EM layout, the SMP flex-track used has been so ballasted.**

MORE REALISTIC LOCOMOTIVES AND STOCK

One area of the model railway hobby where you can get a lot of extra pleasure and interest is in the simple improvement of the models themselves.

Perhaps because the standard of today's railway models is so high, a great many modellers seem to accept them as they come, and all too many models seen running on layouts are literally in 'straight out of the box' condition. You may not notice this — and seemingly few do — but next time you see layouts running at model railway exhibitions, check out how many locomotives are running without any visible crew aboard, how many passenger trains have no passengers, and how many freight trains are running empty with no visible loads unless the manufacturer of the model provided one. And this is just a start. How many of the models show no sign of wear, weathering or use? How many have moulded-on plastic handrails and lack details like running lamps and foot steps etc?

How many buildings lack drainpipes, curtains, open doors or windows, or have gaps between wall and ground? How many cars, buses or trucks on the roadways have drivers, passengers or loads? Or licence plates and tail lights, or a modest amount of weathering rather than shiny black tyres?

The chances are that the answers to all these observations are negative for the most part. Look at your own models. How many of these fit the descriptive state above? Don't worry if some, or even all, of them do, for you are in good company.

THE REAL THING

I dwell on this to show that there is more to building and operating model railways than simply buying models in the hobby shops, setting them on the track and running them. Though the description 'ready to run' (RTR) is commonly used to describe most modern model locomotives and stock, they will look even more realistic if you spend a pleasurable evening or two working on each one to make it look more true to life.

Much of this may sound obvious, but not everyone thinks about it, it seems.

Upper right: **Check out photographs of the real thing to see how locomotives and stock get dirty or weathered in service. Often you can use a picture as a guide to weathering a model, Very typical is this BR (ex-LMS) 3F 'Jinty' 0-6-0 No 47295 in service in a rather grubby state in 1962.** *Photograph by Arthur North*

Lower right: **There are exceptions to every rule. Here is a gleaming freshly painted DB Class 360 diesel shunter being checked out before making its first test run after overhaul at Nürnberg MPD in 1995. In service it will soon acquire a patina of dirt, however.**

Look at real rail equipment in use (or images of it in books and videos) and you'll see that nothing is shiny and gleaming unless it is fresh out of the paint shop — which is how most models come RTR. Even brand-new equipment starts to get dirty wheels and chassis as soon as it makes its first run. Most stock is dirty to some degree, varying from filthy to merely weather stained from the rain. On locomotives wheel, bogie and frame sides, and valve gear and motion on steam engines, all become a sort of grimy brown/black, and the bright metal seen on some model wheels and motion is rarely seen on the real thing, the exception being wheel treads and the wheel faces on some modern coaches which are kept clean by disc brakes. Diesel or electric locomotives may have dirt thrown up on their fronts, and exhaust and grime

Above: **An example of a very grimy hopper wagon photographed by Arthur North in the late 1980s shows the sort of dirty finish you could reproduce on a model.**

Below: **This Fowler 2-6-4T from Hornby in its Super Detail range shows all the latest standards of fine detailing (including sprung buffers in this case) and is supplied with a very nice weathered finish.**

staining on roofs and cooling grills as well as oil or water runs on the body or belly tanks.

It is true that most modern locomotives, coaches and multiple-units look reasonably clean, at least on sides and ends where they go through the washers, but it is rare to see them completely spotless all over.

Rolling stock with a lot of lettering on it — such as private owner wagons old style and new — is often too dirty for all the lettering to be read. On some of the pre-World War Two private owner wagons that still survived into the 1950s and 1960s only the odd word or letter was fully legible and they were never so impeccably clean in service as those you see running on most layouts.

MODEL INTERPRETATION

Reflecting this real life appearance on models is pleasant fun. Some of the model manufacturers have clearly listened to modellers' comments on the subject in recent years, for they are increasingly going for the sort of 'in service' realism described above. Almost all new models of both locomotives and rolling stock produced

in the past few years have their wheels (and sometimes handrails) blackened, while steam outline locomotives also have the motion blackened. This is a big visual improvement that immediately eliminates any 'toy-like' gleam. Better still, both Hornby and Bachmann in Britain now regularly release 'weathered' versions of all their new models in 4mm scale, which overcomes the 'shiny bright' problem outlined above. But as yet this is far from a universal option and on many models any 'weathering' effects will still need to be applied by the owner, for there are still plenty of older models around, both new and secondhand, that are not so treated.

Modern models, both British and overseas, in all the common scales, also now benefit from provision of masses of fine detail that enthusiasts could have only dreamed about ten years or so ago. We now find locomotives with every handrail and small fitting either in place or as 'add-on' accessories in a pack in the box. The cabs are fully glazed and, indeed, fully detailed. Some of the latest diesel locomotives in OO and HO also have opening cab doors, see-through grilles, and even adjustable cooling grilles. All detail fittings are mostly separate pieces factory fitted, and today's production sophistication (mainly due to manufacture in Chinese factories) allows details to be matched to the actual locomotive depicted, so you get several different detail variations (and appropriate finishes) on locomotives of the same class. Even buffer beam detailing like steam and brake pipes and scale couplers are included, as is all visible chassis detail.

You can truly say 'we've never had it so good' as far as modern model

releases go. But even with these you may want to make a few additions, such as adding real crushed coal glued in tenders, crew figures in the cab, and occasional missing details such as the canvas draught screens fitted on some cabs etc. These would be made of rolled or gathered up strips of tissue paper, painted blackish/brown and glued in place in case you wondered.

WEATHERING WORK

Having said all this, it still leaves many more 'last generation' models on sale and on layouts that were manufactured before the modern standards evolved. Typically these may have moulded-on foot grips and handrails rather than real wire fittings, limited cab glazing or none at all, shiny wheels, no cab interior detail, some fittings not depicted at all, or any combination of these shortcomings. And, of course, they won't have been produced with a weathered finish.

You need only the usual basic model tools and paints to transform these models into something better. In other words scalpel or craft knife, a razor saw, small screwdriver, small files, emery boards, small hand drills or powered mini-drill, glues, a selection of brushes, and paints. Modern acrylic paints are easiest to use, but the old oil-based paints are fine too. I use both types. In addition, you could do with some plastic filler (Revell-Plasto is widely available) and as far as paints go, Humbrol and Tamiya acrylics and Humbrol and Revell plastic enamels are commended, not only because they are of high quality, but they are also sold in most countries where there are model shops.

Most readers of this book will have done some sort of practical modelling or plastic kit building already, I imagine, but if you haven't, then get a box for the tools and another for the paints. Suitable small boxes are sold cheaply in most DIY or hardware stores. You'll also need both acrylic and enamel thinners and gloss and matt clear varnish, either acrylic or enamel, or both. For colours you need black, white, dark earth burnt sienna, light and dark grey, buff or stone, or any variations on these. A selection of the small size brushes in OO, O and 1 size, and small chisel edge brushes are also needed. Those in squirrel hair are modestly priced and good for the job.

INSPIRATION FROM THE PROTOTYPE

When you detail and weather a model locomotive it is essential to check out the prototype from reference books and photographs. The Southern Pacific Alco S4, pictured above switching at Ogden, Utah, in 1974, was the starting point for painting and detailing the Atlas HO model of the Alco S4 below. The model did not come in this finish. It was painted by the author using the picture above (and others) as a guide, and with SP decals from the Microscale range. The worn faded grey finish was closely copied. However, detail work included filing the rivets from the model cab, replacing the moulded hand grips on the hood with wire hand grips, adding crew in the cab, sunshades and armrests for the side windows and repositioning some fittings. Details varied between locomotives, however. No 1820 (above) had number boxes ahead of the cab, but 1809 (below) did not.

Some modellers who have never tried weathering before are afraid to start, and others say that weathering will spoil the secondhand value of the model which is why they keep it shiny bright. The answer here is to get a 'working locomotive' you can weather (you'd only need one or two for a small layout anyway) and keep any you think you might later sell in their boxes and in the cupboard!

If you use acrylic paints there is no great fear of failure. If you don't like the weathering effect you've just added, or have overdone it, the paint is water soluble and can be washed off immediately so that you can have a second try. Obviously every model is different so the following comments are generalised. But on all models start by painting wheels (except the treads) blackish/brown (unless the wheels are already blackened), and valve gears, motion and bogie/track sides can be lightly brushed over with a mix of matt brown and black. Some paint ranges include 'track grime' and these can be used as an alternative.

A wash of thinned matt grey/brown soon takes the newness out of wagons and locomotives, but another way with wagons is a quick paint over with black paint (using a large brush) after which all the paint is immediately wiped off again with kitchen paper. In either of these methods paint runs into and get left in planking, nooks, crannies, hinges, etc, giving a realistic dirty appearance to the model.

Acrylic paint allows further touches. Here you can use pre-wetting. For example 'paint' ordinary water along a solebar, underframe or axle-box. Then touch the end of the wet area with your brown/black mix on the end of the brush. Like magic, the paint will run along the frame or sidebar etc to give a very lifelike grimy appearance. 'Runs' below rain gutters and down the side of cylinders or waste tanks can be similarly applied like this. All paints should be matt, but an exception would be oil runs on diesel locomotive fuel tanks or on tank wagon filler caps and sides, where gloss black (or brown/black) gives the best effect.

Solid black engines always present a visual problem. Very often, unless your layout is well illuminated, the fine details don't show up and from some angles you get a black 'void' because no light is reflected or no shadows stand out. Look at pictures of real black locomotives and you'll see that only those fresh from the paint shop look really black. Once in service the patina of grime makes them look grey and the details become very visible. Some modellers overcome this by painting over black locomotives (either steam or diesel) with matt black paint to which a little white is added, but a 'quick fix' alternative is to use Tamiya XF-63 German Grey which gives the same effect. Paint over any numbers or lettering, but immediately use a second brush to wipe the paint away so the number, lettering or logo shows through, realistically as through a patina of dirt and grime. The modern weathered-finish black locomotives don't need this treatment.

The latest model coaches on sale have fully coloured interiors. But older ones tended to have simpler single colour moulded inserts. These can be improved by painting in contact colours, say brown or blue for the seats, and buff or light grey for the rest. On most coach models you can disassemble them sufficiently to get at the interior. While you have them apart glue in a few seated passengers at window seats — no need to overdo it, for only a few heads visible at windows of passing model trains overcome that 'empty train' effect seen all too often on layouts.

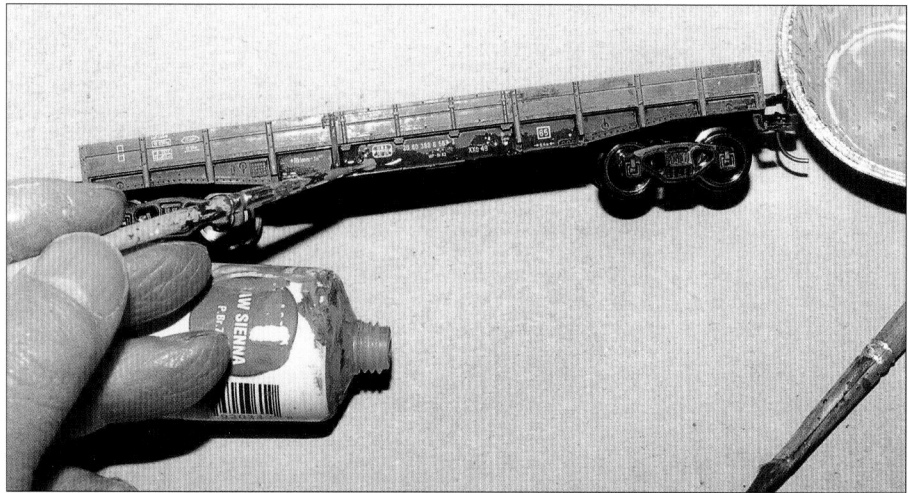

Upper left: **Very effective heavy grime and weathering on OO gauge models of the standard BR brake van and 16-ton wagon. These models have also been fitted with three-link scale couplings.**

Centre left: **Weathering a German HO bogie wagon, using the 'pre-wetting' method described in the text to run a dust and rust effect along the solebar with a touch of raw sienna acrylic paint.**

Below left: **Some suitable paints for weathering work include Tamiya acrylic model paint (large pot), Humbrol acrylic paint (small pot) and Jo Sonja acrylic gouache (tubes), but there are other brands. Colours suitable include dark earth and other brown, black, white, light grey and terracotta etc. Also shown are chisel edge and pointed brushes.**

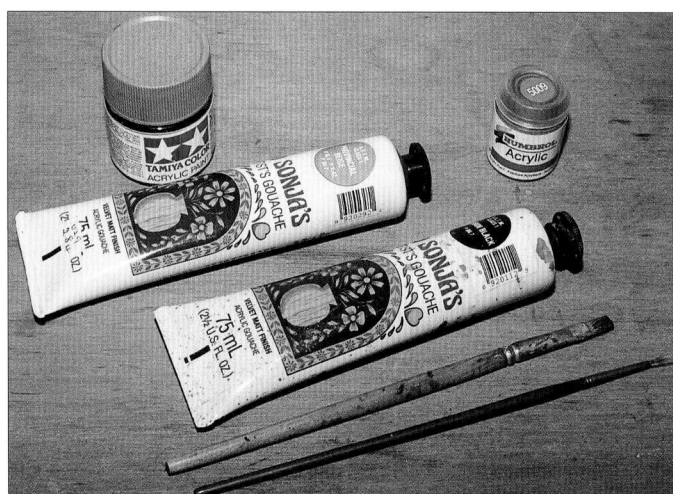

Above: **Typical extra detailing for an RTR model. This Lima BR(W) diesel railcar has the interior fully painted, passengers in the seats, a driver in the cab, screen wiper, lamp irons and lamp added, and dummy scale screw coupler and buffer beam piping. This 4mm scale model is also lightly weathered.**

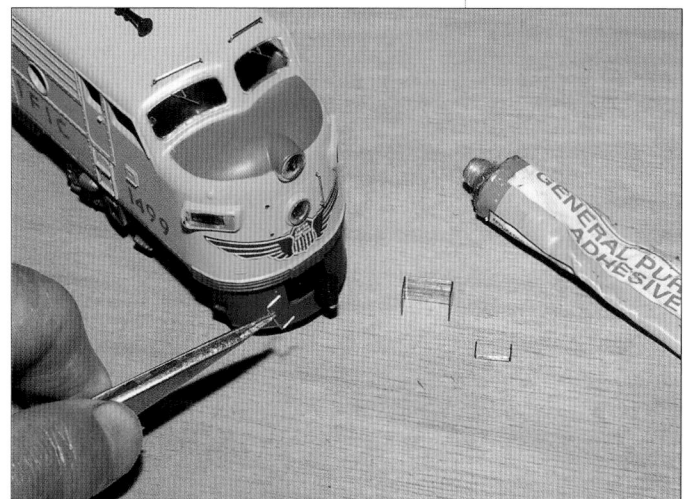

DETAILING AND ALTERING

This brings us neatly to the extra detailing that can be done on almost all models to some degree or other. Crew figures in cabs are an immediate requirement and in some models you might want to add seats or controls where the cab interior is very visible and may not be fully modelled. On a steam locomotive the fireman's shovel, pick, or fire-irons might be thrown up on the coal, propped on the footplate, or lodged on a side tank, so add these on the model too. On a guard's van or caboose platform the guard or conductor is often seen standing in real life. Add these figures on models too — most miniature guard's vans I see seem to roll by empty!

Locomotive models in HO or OO or larger scales may need extra or improved details. On models of the older type you may need to cut away (carefully) the moulded-on handrails, grips or foot rungs and substitute wire replacements. Handrail knobs and wire can be bought, along with numerous locomotive and wagon detail parts, from larger hobby shops or specialist suppliers who advertise in the hobby press. (Among these are firms like Crownline, Springside, Dart, Jackson-Evans, Taylor (N specialists) Details West and Detail Associates (USA), and Weinert (Germany) — but there are many more.)

Aside from trade produced detailed parts — which include chimneys, domes, scale couplers, grab irons, diesel exhausts, grills, etched name and number plates, etched screen wipers, brake shoes, whistles and much else — you can furnish detail parts yourself from plastic card strip (Microstrip), office staples of various sizes (especially No 56 and Bambi type), plastic cocktail sticks, fuse wire and old ball-pen refills. Every model is different; some may need little work and others will need a lot. Typically you may need to add screen wipers on diesel, electric, EMU or DMU cabs, cab access

Above left: **Typical detailing work for an RTR model. This is an S scale (1:64) EMD FP7 by American Models, and all the missing hand grips are being added from No 56 office staples and Bambi staples (depending on the required size).**

Above: **More detailing, this time on the Fleischmann Orestein & Koppel industrial diesel. All the moulded plastic handrails have been carved off and new ones from office staples are being fitted into drilled out locating holes, with a touch of glue to hold them in place.**

CONVERSION FROM KITS

Some of the small specialist companies offer conversion or detailing kits for use with RTR models. A good example is shown here. The Hornby Fowler 2-6-4T in initial LMS form (above) was altered, using a conversion kit to depict the later production form of the same class. Etched side overlays give the later cab side with smaller door opening, and other parts provide new bogie sides, steam pipes, tank vents and handrails, all shown fitted below. New LMS decals are added over a 'smoky black' weathered finish, and crushed coal is glued in the bunker (below), The same model is shown 'before and after'.

Above: **Check out references at all times. Here the Hornby LMS 'Pug' No 11232 is being compared to a photo of the real engine, revealing that the cab side sand fillers were not fitted on this locomotive. They can be cut away with the modelling knife.**

steps on truck or bogie sides, brake pipes and MU cables on buffer beams, and so on. If you model American diesels you commonly need to add arm rests and sunshades on and above cab side windows from plastic strip, and you may need to relocate air horns, number boxes or headlights, and add mini-snowploughs, depending on the locomotive or company you are modelling.

Some overseas and industrial locomotives have flashing beacons and small radio aerials on cab roofs. Roco and Herpa make red, blue and orange dummy beacons as accessories for model police cars, fire engines and ambulances, and the orange ones are ideal, too, for locomotive roofs.

Other detailing you can add includes fall plates, cab doors, radio aerials (from track pins), handrails/grab irons from office staples, lamp irons from wire or plastic strip, injector pipes from cocktail sticks, tall exhausts from ball-pen refills and so on.

Some older models might have flash, join lines, or some other moulding imperfections to make good, so you may need to touch up the paintwork after this. In fact, despite the sequence given here, where weathering is discussed first, in practice you need to do the detail and correcting work first, then touching up of the changes, and the weathering effect last of all.

On rolling stock you may also need to replace moulded handrails with wire, or add missing details like foot stirrups etc, and on some models clip-on details like ladders, brake wheels, and roof walks (on cheaper American-type freight cars) may be in shiny black plastic whereas they should be painted body colour.

CHANGES AND IMPROVEMENTS

The Hornby 4mm scale model of the famous Stroudley 'Terrier' is popular and it has a very good performance, too, ideal for shunting. However, real 'Terriers' were altered over the years and the Hornby model is produced in its early form only. Here is the sort of improvement you can do to make the model more historically correct. Here the SR version is altered to an 'Island Terrier', as on the Isle of Wight. The early front splasher is retained but the bunker is lengthened. Saw off the original bunker and tool box. Move the bunker rear to the end of the chassis and fill the gaps with plastic card (top left). Leave the glue to set, then smooth off the join lines and undercoat the bunker sides (top right). Make good the paintwork and add an IoW number, in this case W12. Crew is added in the cab and the buffers are sawn off and glued back 1mm lower down to correct height (below). Note, also, the weathered wagon here.

Right: **Felin-Dre station on the author's small EM layout is a ground-level affair, with the platform from Wills planking sheet and the buildings from old Airfix coal office and platelayer hut parts combined and slightly altered. All station parts came from the spares box.**

It is a good rule — even with model locomotives to the latest production standards — never to take them for granted. Check them out at eye level from all angles and compare to photos or drawings of the real thing. Note any missing details, or any fittings that might be improved, or need repositioning etc. Make a list of these if changes needed are extensive. There may be even more changes necessary if you want to alter the model to another locomotive of the same class or at a later or earlier period.

Sometimes you may want to change the colour scheme. This is particularly true of American locomotives where there were many companies using the same type of engine. You may only get the finish you want by repainting. This is really a subject in its own right, but for anyone who jibs at the idea of a complete locomotive repaint, it is not difficult if the colour scheme is simple and does not involve intricate lining out. For example, Southern Pacific grey/red, Conrail blue, BR blue, BR green and GWR plain green are among colour schemes easy to apply. I've repainted black BR versions of GWR locomotives back to plain GWR green on several occasions, to give just one example of what can be done.

Decal (transfer) sheets for the most important companies are widely made. Fox is a big name (among others) in Britain, Microscale and Walthers have a huge choice of American/Canadian company markings, and in their respective countries you can find decal sheets for Germany (a huge selection is available in Britain through the German Model Railway Society), France, Switzerland, Austria and so on.

THE SPARES BOX

As well as a box for tools and paints the successful modeller needs a spares box, and this is to keep all oddments left over from kits and models to form a 'bank' of pieces that can be used in later modelling projects. In fact the more of a 'magpie' you are, the better equipped you'll be for pleasing and distinctive modelling in the years

ahead. Typical spares you should collect are windows, doors, chimneys, wheels of all sorts, handrails, brake pipes, unused accessory parts, and scrap oddments like ball-pens, refills, cocktail sticks, wire, pins, balsa wood offcuts and the like.

When you start, the spares box might literally be an old kit box, but very soon — if you are an assiduous model maker — you'll gather so many spares that you'll need to sort them out into useful categories. This could mean getting more old kit boxes, but it is more efficient and convenient to invest in the small plastic drawer units sold in DIY and hardware stores, and some chain stores, intended for screws, nails or domestic accessories. Over the years I've acquired a number of these. Each drawer can be labelled, and typical categories I have sorted out in my spares collection include USA diesel fittings, UK diesel fittings, UK steam locomotive fittings, USA steam locomotive fittings, German steam locomotive fittings, wagon wheels, coach wheels, magnetic couplers, scale couplers, rolling stock parts, and so on, all for HO or OO — and some others for N, TT, O, S and 1 scales. Make up your spares collection depending on your interests, and you can sub-divide as you progress. A beginner, for instance, might need just one compartment marked 'locomotive parts', only expanding to more compartments when there is enough variety to justify it.

Additional to locomotive and rolling stock spare parts, you can also build up spares for structures, road vehicles,

track accessories and any other categories you want. Hence I have drawers labelled doors, windows, drainpipes, chimneys, telegraph posts, street lights, and so on, again for the various scales I work in. Other drawers include car parts, truck parts, point levers, buffer stops, uncoupling ramps/magnets, and yet more. Some spares left over from structure kits are too big for these little drawers, so I have shoeboxes labelled for walls, roofs, platforms/pavements and bridge parts etc.

With a good collection of spares it is actually possible to make up new structures from oddments, or combine them with raw materials, such as plastic card walls with ex-kit doors and windows. In this general 'spares box' category also come transfer (decal) and miniature adverts, which can be kept in folders or shallow card boxes. Never throw away any unused transfer signs or adverts from a kit — they can all be used later, sometimes 20 years hence as I have often discovered!

To round off this section, you also need to keep any good quality card, wire rod, thin wood, transparent sheet or plastic card sheet for future use. Some plastic card, balsa sheet, plastic strip and so forth you will buy as you go along, so we are not talking huge outlay here. I have a box for wood used in model work — balsa sheet, balsa strip, hardwood strip, thin ply, etc — plus another box for card and another for plastic card and plastic strip.

With a well-stocked spares and materials 'department' you'll be well equipped for any modelling task or

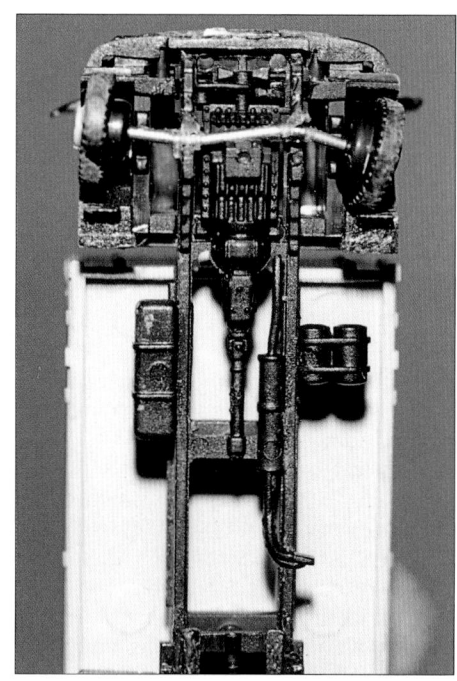

Above left: **Buses are rarely seen empty in service. This Herpa MAN 250F HO bus has been disassembled and the driver and passengers glued inside. The model was also weathered, had destination blinds added, and screen wipers and rearview mirrors added.**

Above right: **The front wheels of this HO model truck were unclipped and the axle was bent slightly with pliers to put some 'lock' on the front wheels, a neat way to add realism to parked vehicles.**

Centre left: **Do not forget loads for wagons and lorries, preferably made so that they can be removed. The log load for the wagon is made from garden twigs glued to a balsa base, and the barrel load in the Skoda truck is glued to a card base so that it can be lifted out.**

Below: **This 4mm scale AEC artic flat truck by EFE has simple added detail, including screen wipers, rearview mirrors, licence plates, a folded tarpaulin, coil of rope and wood packing chocks, the latter all on the flatbed trailer. The model is also lightly weathered, as are the wheels.**

challenge, but let me repeat that stocks of spares and materials are what you build up gradually over years of modelling. If you are a relative beginner don't get worried because you have not yet got enough spare parts to fill a small box. If you keep on modelling you'll be surprised how quickly the stock builds up.

ROAD VEHICLES, ROADSIDE AND LINESIDE

Though this chapter concentrates on locomotives and rolling stock, all the same comments apply to any road vehicles you have on the layout. Aside from being weathered, you may need to pick out tail lights, headlights, door handles and other details, then add licence plates and put driver/passenger figures inside any that are meant to be driving along. Road vehicles are often inadequately prepared even on layouts which pay good attention to the trains. How often do you see on layouts buses with no passengers or crew aboard, or cars waiting at level crossings with no drivers inside? Very glossy plastic road vehicles may need repainting matt, or matt varnishing.

Also, you can alter trucks nicely by adding tail lifts (commonly seen but rarely modelled) or putting cargo aboard. On 'parked' vehicles, bending the front axles to put 'lock' on the wheels adds some realism — all models come with wheels set straight ahead which is not as you see all real vehicles on the road.

Just like locomotives and rolling stock, such roadside items as street lights and pillar boxes need to be weathered, as do yard lights, yard cranes, water cranes and any other such fitting on the layout. Never take any scenic accessory out of its box and position it on the layout without assessing its need for weathering or toning down first.

FIGURES

It hardly needs saying, but any figures you put on a layout need checking out too. Painted ones might need some correction if the painting is less than perfect (as is the case with some cheap Chinese-made ones), and unpainted ones will need painting in any case.

Seated figures may need their lower legs chopped off to fit bus, car, lorry cab or even passenger coach seats. Obviously you need to disassemble road vehicles to glue figures inside, but this is rarely a difficult task. Opinion varies on the use and placing of figures. There are plenty of figure sets depicting vigorous activity and movement, such as runners, footballers, in-line skaters, waving passengers and so on. When placed on the layout, these all give a 'frozen in time' appearance, Some modellers think this to be unrealistic, but on the other hand a lot of youngsters and viewers of layouts find the 'frozen' activity amusing, as do some layout builders. My preference — and that of many others — is to use less 'mobile' figures such as standing or sitting people whenever possible. Since miniature figures are necessarily static while the trains move, the more inert the people appear to be, the more realistic is the scene.

FROM SHOP TO SERVICE

All too many RTR locomotives are taken straight from the box and run just as they come. The Kato HO EMD NW2 switcher is one of the nicest models on the market with a superb performance and excellent finish. But it looks almost too new and glossy, fresh from the box in the old black and orange 'tiger stripe' Southern Pacific livery of the 1940s (bottom). As the later grey/red SP livery of the 1960s was required the model was altered a little. The cab windows were opened up and crew figures were added in the fully detailed cab. Sunshades and armrests were added to the cab side windows. Some fittings were repositioned and a toolbox was added on the front verandah as per prototype. Then it was repainted, given Microscale SP decals as No 1904, and after light weathering it went into service on the layout (top), some way different from its as-purchased state. Almost all locomotives can be enhanced in small ways like this. Many models lack crew figures for a start.

CHAPTER 9

KEEPING IT SIMPLE

Even though you can still find a few adherents to clockwork propulsion, and there are a few live steam models in HO and OO — Hornby have devised a clever version of the latter — virtually all small scale models are electrically powered. True there are steam models in gauge O and gauge 1, too, but they are mostly used on garden railways which are not covered in this book.

Certainly all the models likely to be bought by beginners are electric. In *First Steps in Railway Modelling*, Cyril Freezer gave a very thorough coverage of basic electrics as applied to model railways (Chapter 4) and in Chapter 3 he also gave good details for the common 'under baseboard' electrical control of points, and mechanical control of points come to that — a method I most often use — so there is no need to repeat it all again in this book.

However, there are a few extra hints and observations about model railway electrics which are worth giving here, not least because they make life a lot simpler, and in my experience anything that does that in connection with model railway control is greatly to be desired.

NO SOLDERING

Some modellers, notably beginners or youngsters, take fright at the amount of soldering suggested for power feeds and tags etc when it comes to layout working. It is enough to put some people off at an early stage. The good news here is that you can get away for most purposes without soldering — in fact I haven't done any for years and years and I make several (admittedly compact) layouts a year.

The secret is to use the pre-soldered power feeds available through the trade. This simple idea is just a pair of rail joiners with a feed wire soldered to

Below left: **Hornby's 4mm scale live steam system uses electric power in the rails to generate the heat. Here a live steam Gresley 'A4' Pacific has its tender water tank refilled while two other trains steam past.**

Upper right: **These are the power feed rail joiners which obviate the need to solder power feeds to the rail. These rail joiners have the feed wires ready attached.**

Lower right: **'Chocolate block' connectors are cheap, widely available and make wiring up a layout easy without the need to solder. The blocks can be screwed neatly in place below the baseboard or to the framing.**

each — see the illustration here if this is new to you. In other words, the soldering is done for you. All you need to do is use a convenient join in two rail sections for the power feed position, remove the rail joiners already on the track ends, and use the power feed rail joiners in their place. Use a mini-drill to drill a hole in the baseboard adjacent to each rail joiner and take the wires through the baseboard, to run underneath to your controls.

This idea is so obvious you would think that every model shop would have these power feeds readily on sale, but the fact is that very few of them do, and some don't even seem to have heard of them.

At the time of writing one sure source in Britain is The Signal Box, 1 Albion Street, Austey, Lincs. LE7 7DD, who make them. They are available for Code 100 (OO or HO) tracks and N. Another maker is the Austrian firm of Roco. It has them as item 42265 for Code 100

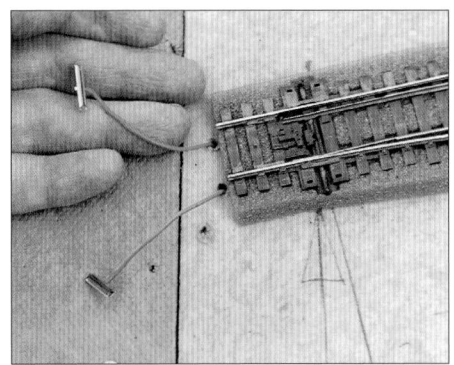

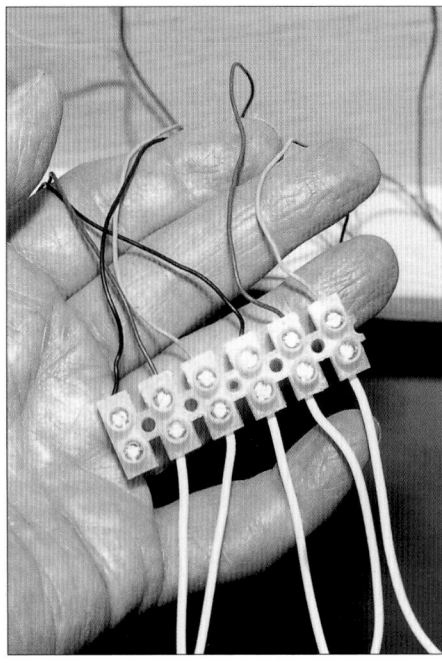

HO track (though it is discontinuing this one), 42613 for Code 83 HO track, and 22217 for N gauge track. The snag again here is that few Roco dealers keep these in stock, but you should be able to order them. Get up to ten sets at a time if you place an order, as you'll then have enough for future needs.

If you use the Peco Code 75 HO/OO Finescale track, you'll find the N gauge power feeds are the ones that fit, as those for Code 100 track will be a sloppy fit and no good at all.

Soldering wires to tags is another unwelcome chore for some, and the answer here is to use the widely available 'chocolate block' plastic connections, whereby you simply secure the bared ends of the wires into the sockets with screws. Where two or more wires come together you simply twist the bare ends together to make one single strand for insertion into the socket.

Using these alternatives you should be able to wire up a layout with no soldering. On the same theme, however, you can get quite neat sectional Code 100 power feed tracks with discreet and neat sprung terminals into which you just insert the bared ends of the power leads. Fleischmann 6008 (102mm long) is commended. Jouef and Lima used to make similar pieces, now out of production, but possibly still to be found, if only secondhand. An N gauge equivalent is Minitrix 14972 which is a curved section. More easily available, though rather more fiddly to fit, are the power connector clips in the Peco Setrack range, ST-273 for HO/OO and ST-9 for N.

REVERSE LOOPS AND TRIANGULAR JUNCTIONS

Cyril Freezer advises against using reverse loops in small layouts, where the current turns against itself, because of the complicated wiring work involved. In general I go along with this advice, too, but on real railways there are plenty of examples of triangular junctions — that is junctions with three arms — which enable a complete train to change direction by running up and back along all three legs. Or, of course, a locomotive on its own could also be turned to face the other direction. An alternative track formation is the turning circle (or reversing loop) which achieves the same effect of turning either a complete train or a locomotive - see

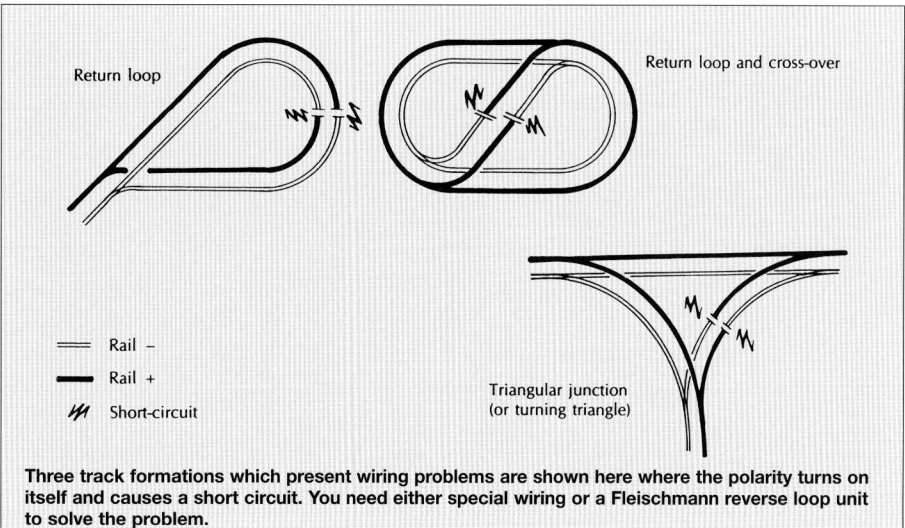

Three track formations which present wiring problems are shown here where the polarity turns on itself and causes a short circuit. You need either special wiring or a Fleischmann reverse loop unit to solve the problem.

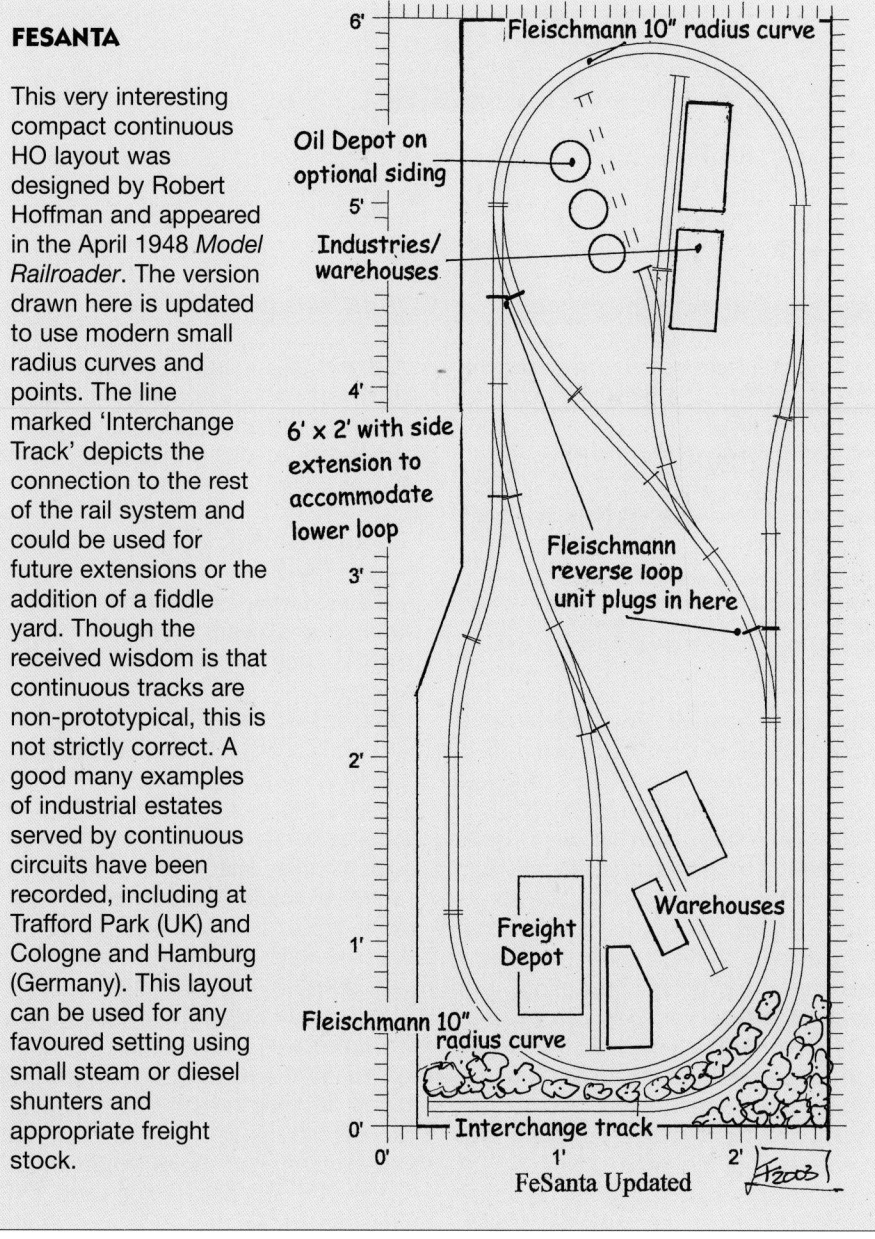

FESANTA

This very interesting compact continuous HO layout was designed by Robert Hoffman and appeared in the April 1948 *Model Railroader*. The version drawn here is updated to use modern small radius curves and points. The line marked 'Interchange Track' depicts the connection to the rest of the rail system and could be used for future extensions or the addition of a fiddle yard. Though the received wisdom is that continuous tracks are non-prototypical, this is not strictly correct. A good many examples of industrial estates served by continuous circuits have been recorded, including at Trafford Park (UK) and Cologne and Hamburg (Germany). This layout can be used for any favoured setting using small steam or diesel shunters and appropriate freight stock.

FeSanta Updated

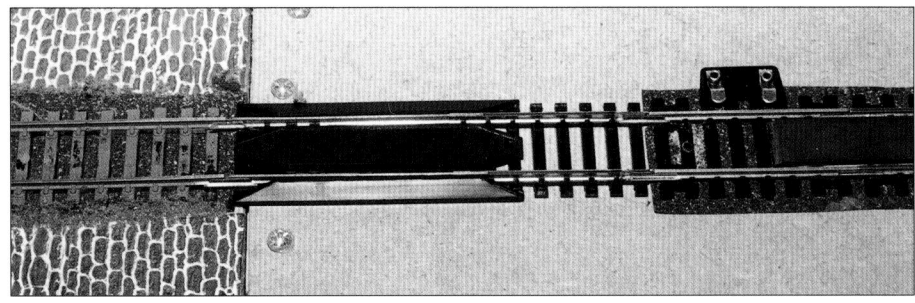

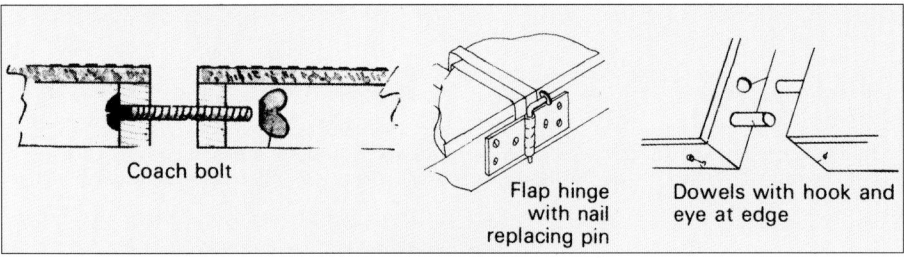

Coach bolt

Flap hinge with nail replacing pin

Dowels with hook and eye at edge

Top: **Crossing a gap between two layout sections using a Fleischmann sliding rail section 6010 which adjusts from 80mm to 120mm in HO.**

Centre: **Alternative ways of joining layout sections, drawn by Richard Gardner. Left: coach bolts secured through pre-drilled holes. Centre: hinge with pin replaced by nail. Right: dowels with hooks and eyes.**

Above: **By far the most effective way of joining adjacent layout sections is to use small hinges with the pins knocked out (or sawn away) and replaced by a nail as is being demonstrated here.**

These solve the problem for you, with no extra wiring.

Some say that reversing loops and turning triangles take up too much space anyway, but this is not always the case. A very neat small layout scheme for an industrial setting, the FeSanta Railroad, is on page 85, which uses a reversing loop to exploit fully the potential of its relatively small area. You would need two Fleischmann 6099 units to look after the polarity on the reserve loop. Note that this layout used the very tight 10in (250mm) radius 'industrial' tracks, available in Code 100 from both Fleischmann and Roco. Small steam or diesel locomotives of the 0-6-0 type have no trouble on this radius, and it enables you to make this layout in minimum width.

CROSSING LAYOUT SECTIONS

Another off-putting problem is taking track across section joins on layouts that are made up of two or more portable sections. How does the current cross the gap? The conventional answer is to saw off the track at the section crossing, solder the outer ends to screws to keep it in gauge, then use jumper wires or even contact strips on the rail ends to take the current across the join.

This all sounds very daunting to beginners or non-solderers. A quick answer is to use the sliding rail section made by some manufacturers for the purpose of crossing joins (or for adjusting rail lengths in other situations, such as run-round loops). The Fleischmann versions are most readily available. Item 6110 (adjusting from 80-120mm in length) suits Profi ballasted HO track, and 6010 suits ordinary Code 100 HO/OO track. The N gauge equivalent is 9110 (83-110mm).

With these you simply pin the track clear of the ends of the section such that a gap less than 120mm is left for HO/OO. When the two sections are joined up you place the retracted adjustable track section in line with the two ends and slide it open to close the gap. Obviously you have to remember to take the section out when the layout is dismantled again.

Joining adjacent sections of layout boards is another problem for many. As *First Steps in Railway Modelling* shows, you can drill out bolt holes in the end

diagram on page 85. They are found in Britain, but were even more common in the USA, and were used to turn complete passenger trains in the old days.

The reversing loop is also quite common at tram termini where the tram turns to face the other direction for its return journey. In model layouts both the triangular junction and the reversing loop have a great attraction. For example, a reversing loop can be used as a fiddle yard, in effect, so that a train can leave and return to a terminus station on a small layout. On a tram layout you might have a reversing loop at each end of the route.

The track is easy enough to lay in this formation but with the usual two-rail DC

system is an immediate problem in that if no measures are taken, the polarity of the track clashes as the circuit is completed, resulting in a short circuit. Special wiring is necessary to prevent this.

In essence it is necessary to change the polarity of the track (from + to - and vice versa) when the train has traversed the loop and needs to return along its original path facing the opposite direction.

As you can see, if a reversing loop is built without any alteration to the power supply it simply will not work. This is because the - rail becomes the + rail and vice versa. If power is applied to a loop in this state, the transformer/controller would immediately detect a short circuit and cut out. To remedy this, the rails must be insulated from each other.

You can do this, and you can wire up the circuit with the necessary switches to change the polarity, but it is a lot of hassle. But the good news is that you can get an instant 'plug in' unit from Fleischmann, item 9099 (N), item 6099 (Code 100 standard track) and 6199 (Fleischmann Profi ballasted track).

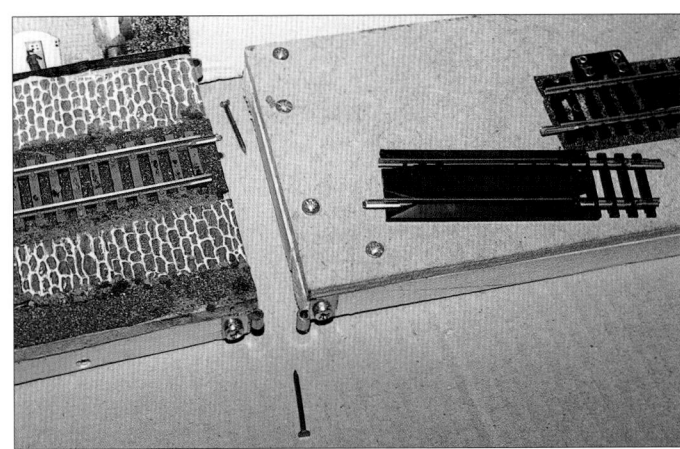

Above left: **Joining two sections of the Tuning Fork layout (scenic work is not complete on the right-hand section). The Fleischmann sliding rail section is ready for use and the hinges on the two sections are being slid together for joining.**

Above right: **With the two layout sections butted together, the nail is inserted through the hinge segments to hold them locked rigid. Because this is a shallow lightweight frame only half a hinge is used, but it still works just as well.**

members of adjacent sections and use coach bolts to do the joining. However, this can be awkward and time-consuming, often involving ducking below the baseboard, working in restricted light and having limited clearance for both the bolts and your fingers.

A quick and well-proven method of joining baseboards is to use ordinary hinges from which the pin is removed. You can cut through the pin with a hacksaw to remove it. One half of the hinge is screwed to the side framing of each adjacent baseboard section, such that they key together. A nail substitutes for the original pin. It is dropped into the hole to keep the two baseboard sections together and pulled out to free them when the layout is dismantled. Some shops sell hinges with a loose pin, which obviates the need to cut out the original pin.

For most layouts the smallest 25mm or 30mm hinges suffice as they fit the depth of the framing. But if you use a very light shallow framing less than 25mm deep (19mm planed wood is common these days), you can cut each hinge horizontally in half (put it in a vice and cut it with a hacksaw) and it will still work perfectly well. I've done that on several recent small layouts with lightweight baseboards as the pictures show.

POINT MOTORS
First Steps in Railway Modelling shows the use of conventional point motors of the sort made by Peco, Hornby and others. They are nicely out of sight below the baseboard, but you have to cut a precise locating slot, and they tend to be noisy in use.

As an alternative check out the products of firms like Fleischmann, Roco and Mehano (or American Model Power whose points are made by Mehano). These turnouts have neat low-profile point motors set alongside the tie-bar area, and very simple colour-coded wiring that needs no electrical knowledge on your part. You just take the coloured wires to the colour-coded positions on the switch unit that works

the points from your control positions.

You can disguise the low point motors easily with vegetation, and most people don't notice them. The Mehano turnouts are very cheap, for those on tight budgets. Fleischmann and Roco make non-ballasted points which are in standard Code 100 track and match up with all other makes. Roco-Line has the finer Code 83 points.

Both Fleischmann and Roco sell the turnouts separately for manual operation, and the point motors separately, so that you can motorise the points later (also possibly spreading the expense). And they sell the motorised turnouts complete. A bonus with the Fleischmann point motor is that it can be reversed, so it can be 'sunk' into a slot cut in the baseboard alongside the turnout if you prefer to have an 'invisible' point motor. Finally I find

Below left: **Because the Mehano/Model Power point switch units are very neat and low you can conceal a whole bank of them quite easily. They will screw on to the side of layout framing, but here they are ganged together and concealed behind a 'ruined' lineside hut.**

Below right: **Point motors that have to stay on the baseboard top can be concealed in various ways, most easily with bushes of 'brambles' from scenic foliage glued on top of the point motor, as being done here.**

ROD CONTROL FOR POINTS

In *First Steps in Railway Modelling* Cyril Freezer gave detailed instructions for controlling points by push-pull rods under the baseboard. See that book for more on the subject. But for those new to the idea, Peco, (and some Hornby OO/HO) points have an effective centre spring which gives a very good contact between the blade and stock rail.

Most other point designs do not have this so the idea only really works with Peco or Hornby points. A simple method is shown here with Peco Code 55 N gauge points. Seen from underneath (left), a wire rod is taken through the layout side frame via a drilled hole and bent up at 90° to be taken through a slot in the baseboard cut out before the point was laid. The vertical part of the wire rod is taken through the hole in the point's tiebar

and bent over to secure it in place (right). The knife blade points to this connection. The point can then be operated 'remotely' from the baseboard edge by pushing or pulling the rod. Some people put a knob on the end of the wire rod, but here the end is simply bent round to form a handle. The position of the point and the drilled holes must be precisely plotted before laying.

these point motors much quieter than the under-baseboard type. The Fleischmann turnouts have an added useful feature in that they are supplied all 'live' but by removing spring clips from between the rails you can convert to self-isolating.

Use of point motors is desirable for many because it means your layout can operate truly remotely with no big human hand intrusion. However, some points near baseboard edges can be directly operated by hand from the edge. If you do need to operate points by hand, I commend the excellent Caboose Industries type, sold by retailers of American models. These

have very strong built-in springs which ensure the point blades make very firm contact with the stock rails.

CONTROL PANELS

On most small layouts you hardly need a dedicated separate control panel for with only, say, two or three motorised turnouts you can just 'gang' the control switches on the corner of the baseboard near your control unit. But on larger layouts a control panel 'mimicking' the actual layout is very useful. Do not overlook the fact that Peco, Roco and Fleischmann (and some others) make neat clip-together units that allow a complete 'mimic'

control panel to be assembled. In fact there are so many useful aids to wiring and controlling layouts in the Roco and Fleischmann ranges that it is worth getting hold of their catalogues where everything is shown and described.

Below left: **On George Lowen's H0 Garfield Connecting Railroad short line there is a spacious fiddle yard area where all the controls are grouped very neatly, and a track plan guides the operator.**

Below right: **The operator at Garfield has a 'walkaround' hand controller of the conventional sort and watches and controls operation like this, with the line's GE 44-ton switcher, by looking over the backscene board.**

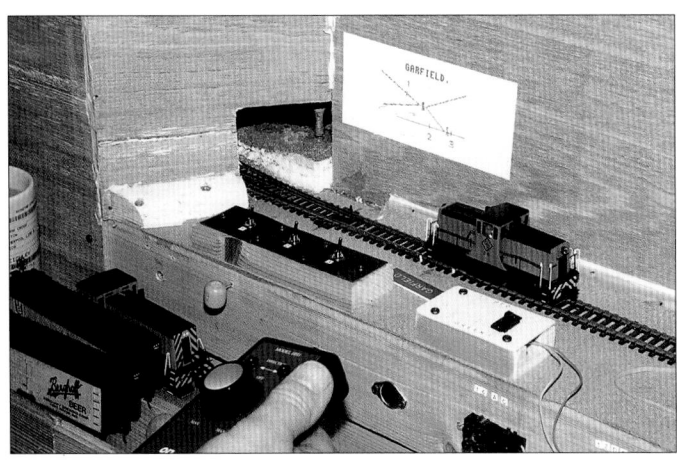

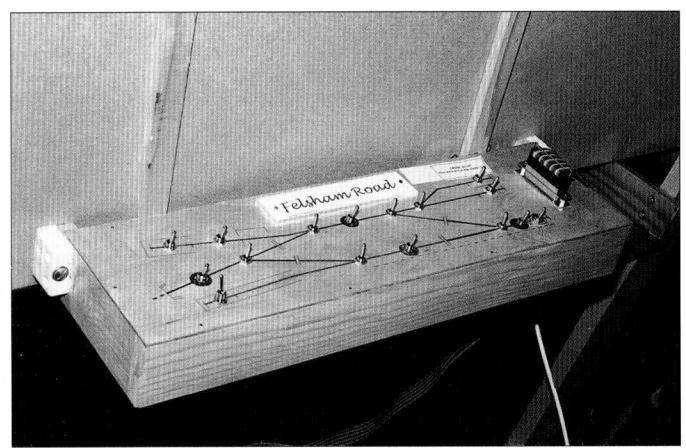

Above left: **A very neat control panel made by Greg Dodsworth to fix on the back of his On16.5 narrow gauge Felsham Road layout. As the layout is portable, the self-contained panel is disconnected when the layout is put away. This panel 'mimics' the actual layout with point switches etc in the relevant positions on the track plan.**

Above right: **A narrow gauge train arrives at the very rural Felsham Road station on Greg Dodsworth's layout. Nearly everything is scratch-built on this charming little layout.**

DCC

Digital Command Control (DCC) gets more publicity and more applications with every passing year. There are some very sophisticated systems available now, many of them using or based on Lenz designs which have been the pace-setters in effective commercial development. The NMRA in America has come up with common standards to which most makers now adhere — before that some systems were incompatible. This common standard is actually centred round the Lenz format, effectively now the world standard.

When you see modern DCC in operation it is very impressive. There is the possibility of sound effects of great realism and accuracy — even with engine noise matched to the type of locomotive — constant lighting (it doesn't go out when power is off, as with 12V DC models), operating couplers in some cases, and even operating container cranes and yard cranes, as well as integrated signalling and every other desirable sort of automation.

Virtually all new locomotive models come 'DCC ready' (with a plug to take a DCC decoder) and some come (at extra price) in actual Digital form with the decoder in place. With DCC a constant AC current (rather than DC) is fed to the tracks to provide power for the locomotive and coded pulses (picked up by the decoder in the locomotive) are laid over the track current to control individual locomotives. At the same time the decoder converts the AC to DC to drive the locomotive motor. Each locomotive has its own 'address' which you call up as required by 'punching' in the numbers on your controller. Some simpler systems suit small layouts with capacity for, say, half a dozen locomotives, but most systems allow very large numbers of locomotives and functions to be individually controlled.

DCC certainly supersedes the complex wiring needed for 'cab control' on large layouts and would be the choice for this now. For small layouts, like those in this book, you can still use DCC, but whether you consider the quite high outlay (well into three or even four figures in some cases) justified is up to individual choice. Having said that, I must stress that there are some low price 'Start' systems out now from Roco, Fleischmann and Lenz, and prices generally seem to be getting lower by the year for all the units and accessories you need. For the smaller layouts shown in this book the 'Start' systems would be sufficient, and they

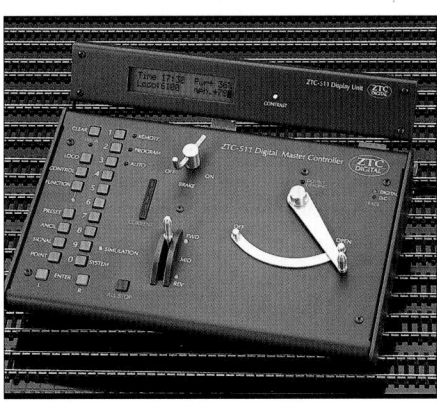

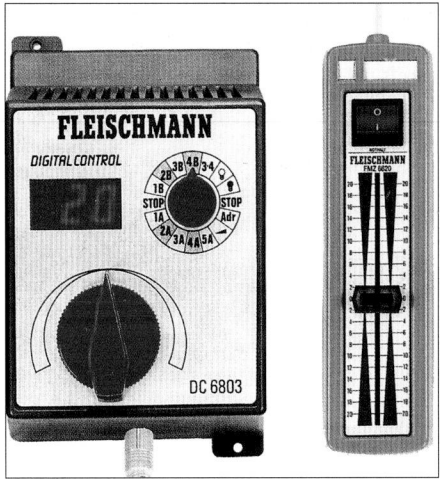

Upper right: **The British ZTC DCC system is well established and duplicates the style of real locomotive controls, complete with 'regulator handle'.**

Centre right: **The Fleischmann 6803 DCC system is easy to use and install and was supplied with the company's Digital Start Sets. Recently an improved system called Lok-Boss has replaced this but is similar in its ease of use. It can control up to four locomotives and has eight sound or special functions.**

Lower right: **The simple set up for the Digital 6803 DCC system using the special digital control transformer Trafo 6811 which is seen connected to the mains on the left of the circuit diagram.**

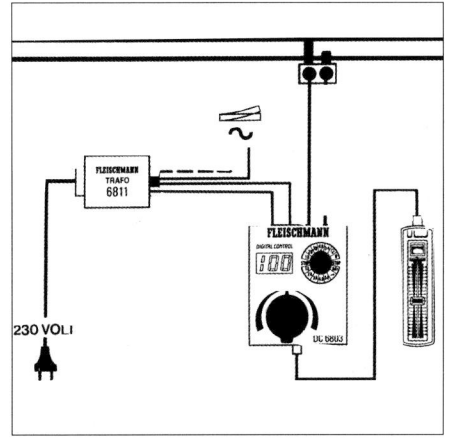

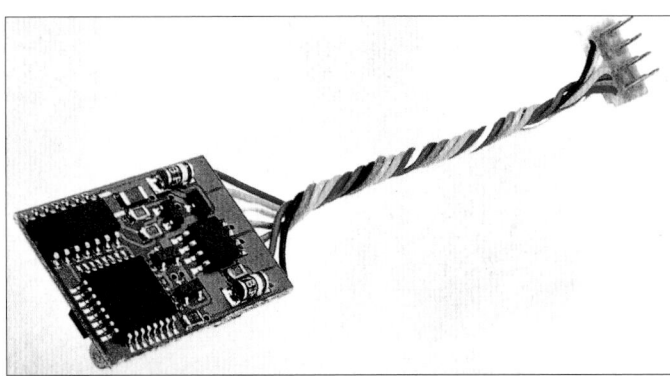

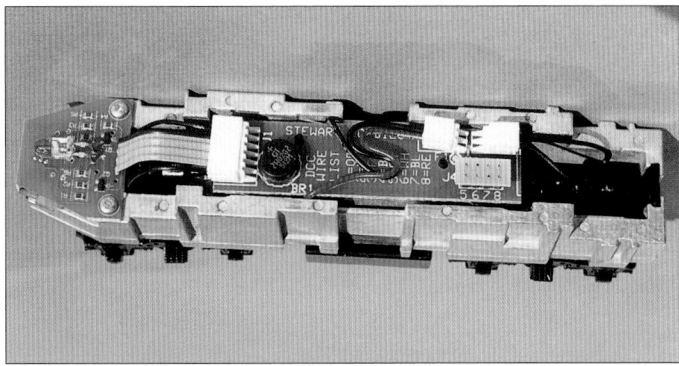

Above left: **A typical decoder to NMRA standard for installation in a 'DCC ready' locomotive. This is the standard decoder from the Roco range and has a 99 address capability.**

Above right: **A 'DCC ready' locomotive, in this case an EMD F3 diesel by Stewart in HO, with body removed to show the NMRA socket to take the decoder on a circuit board on top of the chassis and motor.**

Centre left: **In 2004 Bachmann entered the DCC market with a system called EZ Command which is competitively priced and easy to use. Here two DCC-fitted Class 37s have been brought buffer to buffer from opposite directions during a demonstration. Like other systems there is a facility to operate an ordinary DC locomotive on the layout at the same time as up to nine DCC-fitted locomotives. It can also connect to a DC controller allowing a DCC-fitted loco and a DC locomotive to be controlled simultaneously.**

Lower left: **The Lokmaus 2 is the 'walkaround' DCC controller from the Roco range, allowing up to 99 locomotives to be addressed.**

can be 'expanded' later if you build larger layouts.

Also, if you are interested in IT and computers generally, as increasing numbers are, you may well be attracted by DCC too. There is good literature, and good coverage, too, in current Roco and Fleischmann catalogues, as well as from other firms in the business like Lenz and ZTC. DCC is developing at a fast rate, so consult magazines and adverts for present availability. At the time of writing, the Lenz Compact, Roco Digital and Fleischmann Lok-Boss were the three best 'Start' systems.

So far I've kept off DCC on the small layouts I usually build, most of which are 'one engine in steam', as DCC gives no great advantage with such a small amount of motive power. But I have tried it, and it impresses. Even certain very small layouts lend themselves to DCC. Some favour small locomotive depot layouts, Here there are numerous locomotives coming and going, moving up to fuel, running on to turntables etc, and DCC is perfect for this, for conventional DC would require a lot of sectionalising to allow more than one locomotive in the same spur. With DCC you can run one locomotive buffer-to-buffer with another, most realistically. Similarly a terminus layout with lots of different locomotive movements, pilot engines removing coaches from the trains, and the like, is ideal for DCC.

STORAGE

Keeping your locomotives and stock neatly and safely when not in use is always a necessity. You can pack everything away in cupboards of course, but here are two quick and easy ideas.

Stuart Robinson came up with the notion of using conventional filing boxes for carrying rolling stock that is not boxed. You can use thick scrap card strips, held in place with parcel tape, and 'compartmentalised' to the length of each wagon or freight car. Each unit

just drops into its compartment after a running session and is safely held. The box files store neatly on any shelf but with trains inside rather the documents! It's a good idea which I now use.

If your models are kept in their original boxes, you'll find that HO/OO types fit neatly into the compartments of stout cardboard wine and beer carriers which are usually free in some supermarket drinks sections. Often the box drops in, but if necessary open the aperture a bit with scissors. For a small layout like Highfield Yard/Inglenook Sidings, you can get the locomotive and all the stock in one wine carrier — easy to carry and easy to stow on a shelf. I've got one or two of these carriers for each layout I've built in recent years.

One last point: when you add extra details to model locomotives or stock you may change its outline slightly. For example, adding a roof beacon on a diesel shunter may mean you have to cut a corresponding segment from the foam lining of the box in order to fit the locomotive in. Always check this out when converting or detailing models.

GET SOMETHING RUNNING

All too many model railway enthusiasts spend years thinking about the layout they are going to build one day. They

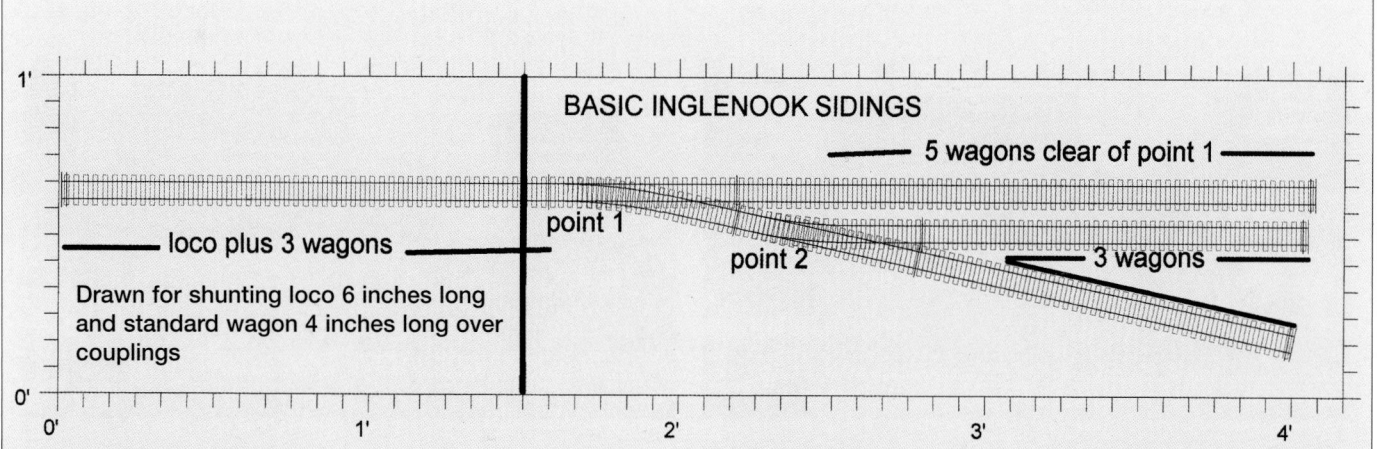

INGLENOOK SIDINGS

In *First Steps in Railway Modelling*, Highfield Yard is well drawn, described, and illustrated to demonstrate the Inglenook Sidings concept. Rather than repeat that in this book, here is an alternative version of the basic concept drawn by David Thomas to show the absolute minimum space needed for a British OO (or HO) version, with siding capacity marked. If you want to make the same layout for other settings (eg USA or modern German etc) or in other scales or gauges, you can work out the length required for the layout by measuring the lengths of the stock used. For example, for American HO a 40ft freight car and a typical diesel switcher are each 6in long. Hence three freight cars will need 18in of length in the siding. The length of points will also need to be taken into account. In other scales larger radii are often used, so point length is relatively increased.

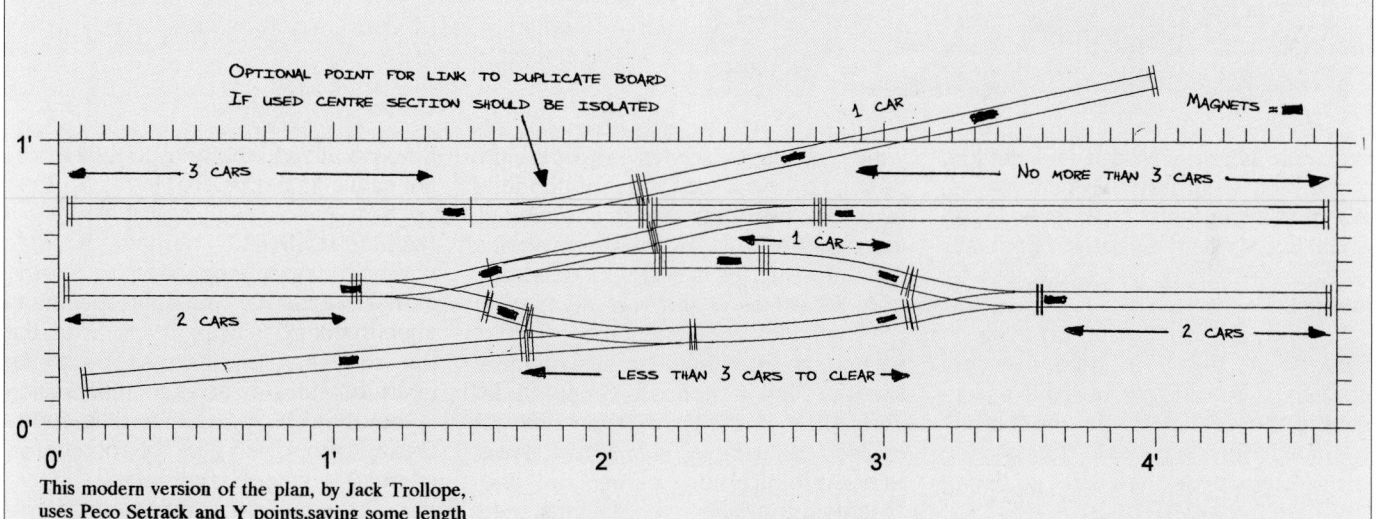

This modern version of the plan, by Jack Trollope, uses Peco Setrack and Y points, saving some length

THE TIMESAVER

Inglenook Sidings as a concept is a classic of simplicity for the modeller with limited space, time, or skill who wants a neat, compact, but prototypical layout. The other legendary classic small layout is the Timesaver, a concept first published by the late John Allen in *Model Railroader* back in 1972. Since then this classic shunting/switching layout has been built by hundreds of modellers looking for maximum operating fun in minimum space. The original layout was built on bare boards, without scenery, as a switching game for club members whereby freight car positions were changed around in the least number of locomotive moves, hence the name. However, most modellers choose to make a fully scenic version depicting a freight yard or industrial district with various trackside facilities such as factories, warehouses, or freight depots served by rail, with consequent busy shunting/switching operation.

A second option is shown at the top of the plan, a link to a parallel baseboard with a second Timesaver on it, giving even more complex operational potential. If you don't want this, omit the link arrowed. The Timesaver can be made in any scale or gauge, with width and length to suit, but the version drawn here is the shortest possible in HO/OO. It is intended for use with American 40ft freight cars and a diesel switcher as drawn, and the siding capacities are marked for these. If you make a British or European version with short four-wheel wagons the siding capacities will obviously be a little more generous.

MULTI-MODING

An example of multi-moding in action is shown here. The Chipperfield layout was built in Inglenook style with common freight station and warehouse structures, but with a different station for British, German or American modes, each station taking exactly the same area on its own free-standing platform base. Shown here are the British version, in Light Railway style, with a 'Terrier' shunting the yard; the German version with Kibri country station and Fleischmann O&K diesel shunter; and the American version with the depot made from an old box car. A Doodlebug railcar converted from a Bachmann tram provides the passenger service.

draw up plans, envisage the setting, sometimes even buy the locomotives, but no layout gets built, even if an ambitious scheme is started. Eventually enthusiasm falters, and some lose all interest.

I say more on layout planning in Chapter 4, but if all else fails get something running by building a very simple project, such as the classic Highfield Yard/Inglenook Sidings (on the previous page). You can't go wrong

Below: **The original multi-moding idea by Dave Carson was this 4ft x 9in (approx) layout in HO which was spilt scenically in the centre to form the 'Two into One' layout. Each half is developed in the style of a different railway with the appropriate backscene and structures. A longer more complex version would be possible with more track.** *Drawing by Jack Trollope*

with this, you have prototypical operation, and it won't take much time (or money) to make. You can always incorporate it in a more ambitious scheme later, for it is simply extended from the left-hand end.

If Inglenook Sidings is too complex for you, go for something even simpler like the Tuning Fork or Small Street Yard plans in this book. You can get smaller and simpler still. Small layout fan Dave Carson came up with Walmington Pier, an old-time pier railway about a metre long. It is just a length of track on a nicely modelled pier with a tram running up and down it. Too simple, you might think, but it always fascinates those who see it. Others, like Greg Dodsworth, have since built slightly bigger versions of the same simple idea.

Above all, get something running and get active as a modeller!

MULTI-MODING

Another idea of appeal to increasing numbers of those with small layouts is 'multi-moding' — using the same layout for more than one theme or era. An obvious example is the country branch layout that can be operated in 1940s steam era style. But you have an alternative set of locomotives, stock, and road vehicles that enables the same layout to jump forward, say, to the 1960s or 1970s diesel era. This certainly stops you from getting bored, by always seeing the same models in use. A third stage would be to get together locomotives, stock and road vehicles (horse-drawn) so the same layout can turn back the clock to the pre-group era, say in 1914.

You can do the same thing across country borders, My little Tuning Fork scheme can be set up for either American or German operation, similarly by switching the backscene, since the warehouses in low relief are attached to the backscene not the baseboard. You can only shunt on this

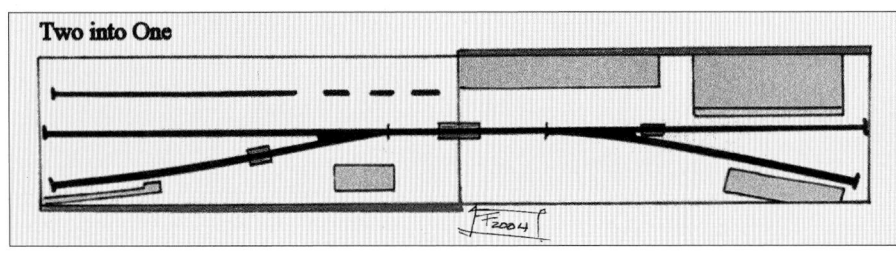

Two into One

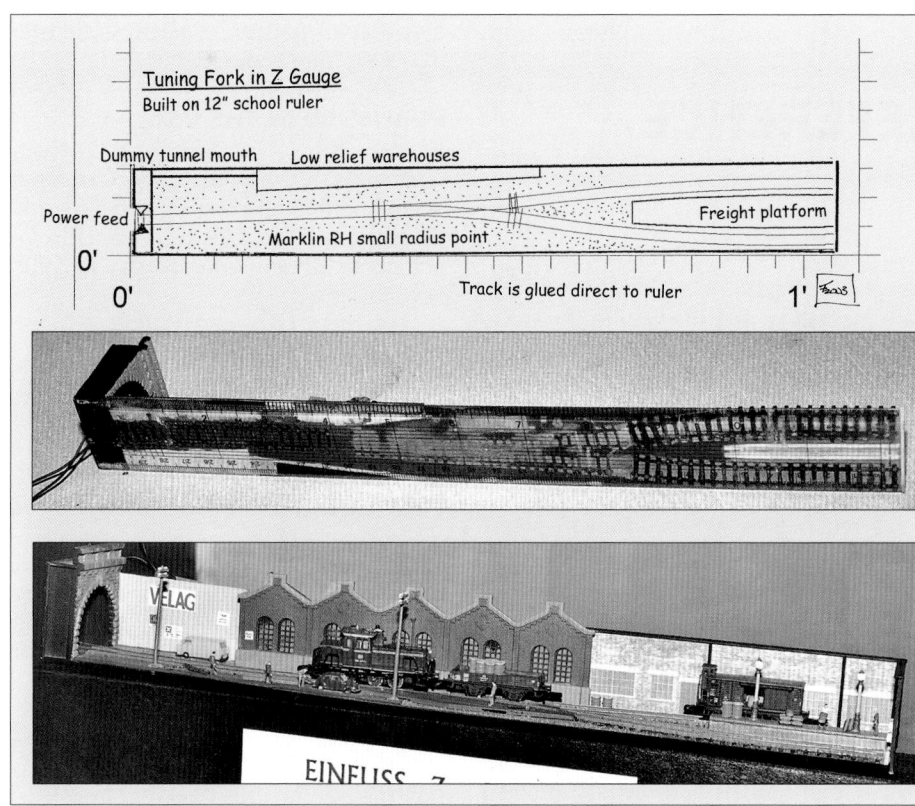

little layout, but it is nice to have a choice of locomotives, stock, and even alter the appearance of the layout.

Dave Carson designed a Micro Layout idea for multi-moding with each half developed scenically, one half for one country, the other half for another — say French one way, British the other. Depending which side you operate it from, the other half (out of sight) acts as the fiddle yard for the other. See the plan for this. Dave Carson actually modelled Philippines National Railways one way, and SNCF the other. Choose your own favourites.

For those with limited space but who may be interested in trains of more than one era or country, this is a happy way of working, and it keeps your interest going.

PROTOTYPE FOR EVERYTHING

Some schemes and operating ideas are discarded, perhaps because you may think: 'Nothing like that would exist or happen in real life.' My experience over the years is that whatever you think is outlandish has almost certainly been done somewhere, sometime, by some train operator or other.

When the Inglenook Sidings idea first grabbed attention I was one of many who said you would never find anything that simple on real railways. Ever since

then I've kept coming across real life examples, including Le Tréport (France), Dyserth (North Wales) and Export (USA). This latter, with an unusual name, is on the Pennsylvania short line Turtle Creek Railroad which sounds itself like a jokey company name made up for a model layout! There are many more examples. All these have a similar track plan to Highfield/Inglenook but all look very different scenically.

Lack of run-rounds and locomotives running along 'sandwiched' in the middle of the train, and switching (shunting) like that too? You may only rarely see this happen in Britain, but in the USA it is common on short lines and industry lines. It was done in the past, too, where a locomotive might simply push a long train along a branch line because there was no run-round provided. You can do it — and many other oddball things — in miniature too. In short never be discouraged by limitations — make the most of them!

SIMPLE OPERATING

There is no room left to cover the subject of model railway operating in detail, and there are complete books on the subject anyway.

However, when it comes to actual shunting (or switching in USA terms) there is a very simple way of doing it.

Most beginners start by shunting wagons from siding to siding quite randomly. This is not very life-like, and a neat way devised by Alan Wright of Inglenook Sidings fame, is the Tiddleywink Computer. This is described in *First Steps in Railway Modelling* too, but essentially you allocate a tiddleywink or a small card to every wagon in use. Each is numbered to correspond with a specific wagon. Tiddleywinks or cards are drawn randomly to give the sequence in which they are to be shunted into a siding or made up into a train. There are hundreds of possible combinations and it will keep you and your locomotive much busier than randomly shunting. In fact, train make-up can become a challenging exercise as you move wagons about to get them in determined order.

There are many variations on this idea, including colour coding of different 'fitted' and 'unfitted' stock, or using cards marked for actual destinations on the layout — coal merchant, freight depot, fiddle yard, etc. Articles on aspects of operating appear from time to time in the model magazines. Some are quite complex and for many modellers the Tiddleywink Computer idea is just about right.

CHAPTER 10

RESEARCH AND REFERENCE

If you go about the model railway hobby properly it will certain expand your mind. In fact, I think model railways are the ideal hobby because of this.

You can, of course, just 'play trains' with what comes in a train set and take it no further than that. Boredom soon sets in, in fact, if the models are not explored further than the process of running a train round a train set oval of track.

Fortunately most beginners — and certainly all those reading this book — are made of stronger stuff than that. An interest in trains leads to purchasing your first models in the first place. It did when I was a beginner many years ago and is still the case now, I think. Everyone has different railway interests and different levels of knowledge, so I can only generalise here. But some are experts on certain rail companies or equipment for many years before they ever start railway modelling, while at the opposite extreme some take up railway modelling when they see an irresistibly attractive miniature train, buy it, then realise they need more knowledge to make a suitable layout for it.

To make a realistic, convincing, accurate and satisfying layout you need to know the background to what you are modelling, and the way to do that is to explore all the various sources of information. You may need to be able to check out the rolling stock, locomotive, the history of the line, the terrain, the vegetation, the structures, the operating pattern, the local economy and much else. Where do you start? Well roughly in order of importance, here are some suggestions.

1. Read at least one model railway magazine covering your area of interest, but preferably more than one. The magazines carry adverts and reviews of the latest releases, have articles on all aspects of models and layouts, provide model show dates and locations, and general inspiration. The world over, there are many magazines, but some key titles are as follows at the time of writing:

PUBLISHED IN GREAT BRITAIN
Railway Modeller, *British Railway Modelling*, *Model Rail* (covering the British scene past and present); *Continental Modeller* (covering the foreign scene generally); *Model Trains International* (covering some British, but also American/Canadian, French, German, Swiss models and other countries for which models are available); *Model Railway Journal* (covering 'fine scale' British)

PUBLISHED IN THE USA
Model Railroader, *Railroad Model Craftsman* (covers the USA/Canadian scene, sometimes Mexico too); *Narrow Gauge and Short Line Gazette* (USA — and some others — narrow gauge), plus several others.

PUBLISHED IN FRANCE
Loco Revue; *RMF* (covers the French, also some Belgian and other models); *Voie Libre* (covers mainly narrow gauge or 'backwoods' type railways, both in France and elsewhere).

PUBLISHED IN GERMANY
Eisenbahn Kurier; *Modell Eisenbahner* (covers the German scene, plus some Swiss and Austrian) and a number of others.

Note there are many more model railway magazines than this covering Switzerland, Austria, Canada, Australia, South America, Scandinavia, Eastern Europe and other places. The number of magazines in German actually runs to double figures. Only the best known titles are listed above. However, in Great Britain, the Motorbooks shops stock many of these magazines from overseas.

There are also many magazines covering the modern or historical real railway scene, published in all countries. These run to dozens, and some of them are bound to cover areas of interest to you.

Some key magazines you may wish to keep (binders are useful for this), and back numbers are sold at model shows. From magazines you do not wish to keep, you could tear out key articles of interest for filing before the magazines are disposed of. Try to be far-seeing when doing this and keep articles you think might be useful later. Quite often I meet modellers who only kept, say, LNER related articles because that was what they were modelling at the time. Ten years or so on they decide to switch to GWR modelling, or German or American, and then realise they have let

Left: **Proving that you do not need a large area to capture the atmosphere of the British Rail era, here is a real life version of Inglenook Sidings at Crianlarich Lower Yard in March 1983. No 37411 is making up its train by collecting a consignment of timber from the yard on its Oban to Mossend Speedlink run.** *A. O. Wynn*

go of dozens of articles which would now be invaluable. As an actual example, I started collecting articles on American logging lines back in 1982 because they looked interesting, but it was 2003 before I started modelling logging line equipment. What I had on file was immediately useful, of course, but I missed having all the logging line articles before 1982 that I had discarded, and much effort was needed to get more information.

2. File all the useful magazine articles. All the articles you tear out of magazines can most easily be filed in cheap ring binders, as sold by stationers. I have more than 40, all titled on the spine under such categories as British Narrow Gauge, German Narrow Gauge, USA Narrow Gauge, SR, LMS, GWR, LNER, BR steam era, BR diesel era, Lineside, Small Layouts, Trains, Buses, Cars and Trucks, Industrial, German Branch Lines, German diesels, German steam, USA short lines and many more. You would build up this collection over the years and it becomes an invaluable reference source. Obviously cover your own interests. Mine are widespread, but others may only ever be interested in, say, British or American railways, so you may not collect so many binders.

3. Build up a home library. Most model rail enthusiasts are also interested in the real thing, and so they acquire plenty of railway books. For modellers the key reference books are always useful, such as those by the late Brian Haresnape, published by Ian Allan, that covered the locomotives of famous British designers like Fowler, Stanier, Churchward, etc in a big series, and another series by the same author that covered BR motive power in the diesel/electric era. These are just typical examples from many. If you model light railways you might want any books on the Colonel Stephens lines, and if you model USA short lines you might want Kalmbach's *Short Line Guide*, and so on.

4. Use your local public library. All public libraries usually have a transport section with railway books included. They can usually get others to order. From these you can take further notes to add to your files. Libraries also have books covering physical geography and regions. If you want to model, say, a line set in the German Black Forest there are tourist books that picture the area and include maps etc, even if they don't cover railways in the area. Almost everything is covered by libraries. For example, if you want to model better trees, there are plenty of tree books, and if you want to model a canal lock there are plenty of canal books.

5. Videos. There are railway videos covering just about every interest and period. If you want to see the Pennsylvanian Railroad in the 1940s and 1950s, or the early diesel era of the Santa Fe (ATSF) you can do so, just as you can view Deltics or Class 40s in action on BR lines. I have a useful video showing East Anglian branch lines in the early 1980s, where there was still local coal merchant traffic, and two videos purchased cheaply in Germany showing respectively Hungarian forestry railways and the Deutsche Reichsbahn in the 1930s. Clearly these visual references are nearly as good as being there.

Think beyond the purely railway videos, however. For example, there are travel videos showing locations you might like to model. I made a layout set in the Baltic Rügen island area, taking all the structure and terrain details from a German travel video, never having visited that area myself. Even feature films, available on video, can be useful. There are some of direct railway interest, such as *Terminus* (Waterloo station in 1962) and *Night Mail* (LMS mail trains in 1936), but as just one example from many, the feature film *Clash by Night* (1952) has invaluable views of the Southern Pacific line and fish canneries in the Monterey area of North California — perfect if you wanted to model a small American fishing port branch.

6. Photographs. Self-evidently photographs of the real thing are always useful. You can find postcards old and new, archive photos are sold in some railway bookshops, and at model shows, and you can take your own photographs on your travels, leading to the next suggestion that you should have a camera, even if of the simplest type. With this you can take reference photos, location photos, and photos of trains. Don't forget that mundane everyday trains you see today may be of no immediate interest, but in 10 or 20 years' time the photographs will have historic reference value. Albums or shoe boxes or conventional files can be used to hold prints in the categories you wish to record. I've got mine filed under such headings as SR, GWR, LMR, LNER, BR steam, USA diesels, British stations, and so on, Keep a notebook to record photo locations and relevant details.

7. Collect maps. Aside from books on the area, the study of maps is particularly useful. Old British Ordnance Survey maps (many are now available as reprints from Alan Godfrey Maps) show routes, sidings, locations, etc. With maps you can plot plausible routes for imaginary lines, and work out destinations and other factors which would influence the railway. Some books, notably the Middleton Press series, give OS maps of station and yard areas. You can also get maps of overseas locations. When I built my Nürnberg-Tragbar layout, an imaginary extension from the Ringbahn (belt line) round the city, a large scale city map (with all rails tracks on it) allowed me to plot the exact location of the supposed setting. The same use of a large scale map of Maine allowed me to plot out a very plausible, but fictional, Maine Two-Footer layout. In Britain the specialist Stanford map shops (London and Manchester) stock maps from all over the world.

8. Make location visits. Obviously visit any preserved line you can, just to absorb the railway atmosphere and take photos and notes (always take camera and notebook). Whether you

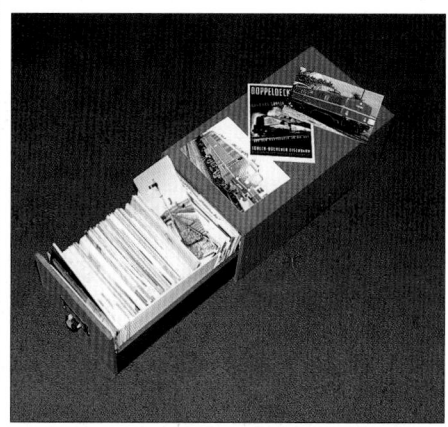

Above: **Photographs and railway postcards you collect can be kept neatly for future reference in filing boxes like this.**

holiday at home or abroad, take every chance to look at and photograph any local rail activity. You may get layout ideas. A lot of modellers take up building foreign layouts after seeing the real thing on holiday.

If you are planning a layout located in a specific spot, visiting the area can furnish you with much useful information. When veteran modeller Richard Gardner built his Stokenham layout, an imagined connecting line of the GWR across the South Hams area of Devon, he tracked and photographed the supposed route by car, and the layout backscene faithfully records actual places, including a church orientated at exactly the angle you'd see it from the train if the line actually existed!

9. Visit any local model railway exhibition. This is obviously useful. Go to as many shows as you can. You can see what others have done, what can be achieved, standards to aim for, and get generally inspired. At shows too, there are demonstrations of techniques, and traders selling models, kits, accessories and books etc. Secondhand model books and magazines are generally on sale, as are current model railway magazines.

10. Join a club or society. This is optional — some enthusiasts remain 'loners' for their whole time in the hobby. For those who want to get involved there are two sorts of clubs. First comes the local model railway club of which there are many. They usually have regular meets, organise an annual model show, and invariably have layout projects on the go, done as co-operative club ventures by the members.

Then there are the special interest societies which cover almost every subject, including overseas railways. For instance, there is the SNCF Society (French railways), German Model Railway Society, the Historical Model Railway Society, the NMRA (American) and many more covering the trains of all countries, and many individual old companies (eg, The Lancashire &

Yorkshire Railway Society). Further clubs cater for those interested in specific ranges of models, such as Fleischmann, Roco, Märklin, Hornby and more. Others cover various scales, such as the 3mm Society, the 2mm Society, the EM Gauge Society, the O Gauge Guild, the British 1:87 Scale Society, and yet others.

News, addresses, events and so on for specific clubs and societies are given in current model railway magazines throughout the year. All sorts of specialised information can be obtained from club experts.

11. Use the internet. This, again, is optional because not everyone has access to the internet or the inclination to get involved. But you probably do know someone who is a keen user.

Huge amounts of railway and model information can be gleaned from the web. Most manufacturers and big retailers have websites with adverts and product information, and many magazines have websites too. There are websites devoted to layout design, others to prototype trains, and special interest groups covering companies and all aspects of railways. To demonstrate the value, I've painted and detailed three specific American locomotives recently, all from illustrations found on a website after I had failed to find any of the actual locomotives illustrated in conventional reference books. When researching Shay geared locomotives the internet yielded a copious list of all Shays ever built, information I had never found elsewhere.

If you have a PC or other home computer you can also get helpful model railway software to cover track planning and development. These

range from the fairly basic Hornby Virtual Railway to the more sophisticated 3rd Planit which even gives the chance to simulate operation to 'prove' a layout's potential before you build it. There are many programs of this type, plus such programs as 'Track those Trains' which allow inventories of models and other records to be put on a database. Finally, you can, of course, buy products and books over the internet, including secondhand items.

The importance of IT and computers generally to the model railway hobby should not be under-estimated even if you have no personal involvement in it. Development of software proceeds at a great rate and there is still a lot to come on the layout design and simulation side. Young modellers are coming into the hobby, making acquaintance via the PC screen rather than the simple train set of old. Others are creating and operating 'virtual' layouts and proving a layout's viability and operating potential before actually building it. Others link computers to their layout's operating or control systems, or use them for timetabling or freight dispatching. The applications are almost limitless.

12. Collect catalogues. It is always useful to have up-to-date books and catalogues of model ranges that interest you. They can be kept neatly in binders or in magazine files. An adjunct to this is collecting track plan books done by firms like Hornby, Peco and Atlas. Also worth keeping are brochures sometimes done by plastic building firms such as Faller and Vollmer — they often have good large reproductions of model buildings in them which can be cut out and used in backscene work.

Right: **Location visits are a valuable aid to modelling. The colourful signposting for companies with rail-served facilities at Hasenbuck yard in Nürnberg, Germany, provided a direct reference for the HO version shown here, made for a model German freight yard.**

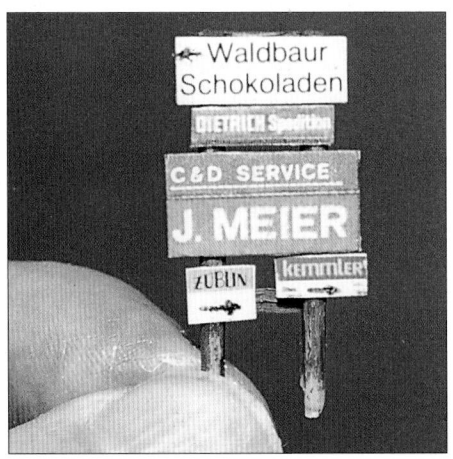